Neofunctionalism and After

Twentieth-Century Social Theory

Series Editor: Charles C. Lemert

Twentieth-Century Social Theory invites authors respected for their contributions in the prominent traditions of social theory to reflect on past and present in order to propose what comes next. Books in the series will consider critical theory, race, symbolic interactionism, functionalism, feminism, world systems theory, psychoanalysis, and Weberian social theory, among current topics. Each will be plain to read, yet provocative to ponder. Each will gather up what has come to pass in the twentieth century in order to define the terms of social theoretical imagination in the twenty-first.

Titles in the series in print:

Neofunctionalism and After

Jeffrey C. Alexander

BLACKWELL
Publishers

First published 1998

2 4 6 8 10 9 7 5 3 1

Blackwell Publishers Inc.
350 Main Street
Malden, Massachusetts 02148
USA

Blackwell Publishers Ltd
108 Cowley Road
Oxford OX4 1JF
UK

Library of Congress Cataloging in Publication Data
Neofunctionalism and after / Jeffrey C. Alexander.
    p. cm. — (Twentieth-century social theory)
    Includes bibliographical references and index.
    ISBN 1–55786–629–5. — ISBN 1–55786–630–9 (paperback)
    1. Sociology—Philosophy. 2. Functionalism (Social sciences)
    3. Parsons, Talcott, 1902– —Criticism and interpretation.
    I. Alexander, Jeffrey C.   II. Series.
    HM26.N38   1998
    301′.01–dc21   97–8621
                                            CIP

British Library Cataloguing in Publication Data

A CIP catalogue record for this book is available from the British Library.

Typeset in 10 on 12pt Sabon
by Graphicraft Typesetters Ltd, Hong Kong
Printed and bound in Great Britain by MPG Books Ltd, Bodmin, Cornwall

This book is printed on acid-free paper

For Paul Colomy
who stimulated me to begin this project

For Bernard Barber
who supported me throughout it

For Ron Eyerman
whose enlightened friendship helped me to see what lay after it

Contents

Series Editor's Preface

By coincidence, Jeffrey Alexander started work on his book *Neo-functionalism and After* in the same year that Kingsley Davis died. Though there is nothing happy in the coincidence, there is good reason to use it to recall Professor Davis's famous 1959 essay "The Myth of Functional Analysis as the Special Method in Sociology and Anthropology." Davis had plausibly argued, roughly, that at some level all social analysis is functionalist.

In this present book, Jeffrey Alexander brings to gentle closure (if not to a close) his own twenty-plus year project of criticizing in order to advance Parsons and functionalism. He takes this bold step, as he so well explains, not because he is done with Parsons and functionalism but because the work he started on in the 1970s school has now been largely completed. Though there is still plenty of controversy surrounding the audacity of any project aimed at retrieving Parsons from the dustbin to which many consign him, Alexander makes a strong case for a version of Davis's 1959 insistence on the centrality of functionalism to social science thinking.

Alexander's argument is elegantly straightforward. It is impossible to think as a sociologist without being Parsonian. Though Alexander does not put it quite this way, the idea is close enough to Foucault's similar remark upon the impossibility of being an historian without being Marxist, just as impossible as being a physicist without being Newtonian or Einsteinian. Foucault made the remark in 1975 in clever retort to those who wanted him to proclaim intellectual and political allegiance to one or another of varieties of Marxism on the Paris scene in those days. Alexander's attitude toward Parsons is more honest, and proportionately less cautious, than Foucault's toward Marx. Foucault meant to keep the Marxists and Marxism at bay. Alexander has never been embarrassed to embrace Parsons, though many have famously tried to embarrass him for it.

Anglo-American neofunctionalism, of which Alexander is surely
the chief spokesman, has done its work almost entirely against the
prevailing grain of popular opinion in the sociological community.
It would not be too far wrong to say that the post-1960s generation
in sociology marched under the banner of C. Wright Mills' famous
attack on Parsons' grand theory. The attack appeared, we might
note, in *The Sociological Imagination* in 1959 – the same year as
Kingsley Davis's affirmation of functionalism's importance. That year
was well under the high-water mark of Parsonian influence which is
what made Mills' snide rebuke of him so exhilarating to youngish
rebels who later found a similar inspiration in Alvin Gouldner's *The
Coming Crisis of Western Sociology*, which contained a much more
careful, if just as snide, attack on Parsons.

Since 1959, many in the last two generations of sociologists have
grown up in the field under the imperative that Parsons and functionalism were to be avoided at all cost. The present generation of sociologist has followed in this rather thoughtless habit. As recently as
early spring 1997 I heard the familiar plaint from a brilliant newer,
still younger, sociologist – a woman as likely to be one of the stars
of her generation as Alexander has been of his. Her purpose was to
characterize the distinctive concerns of her cohort of scholars leaving
the graduate schools in the late 1990s. What she said was along the
lines of: "We all have the vague suspicion that modern sociology
invented itself when Parsons or someone like that defined the canon.
I don't know, though . . ." Although her exact words escape me, it
was clear that she meant to announce that her generation could not
care less about the old order; that whatever teachers require them to
read is not what they read with seriousness: "Assign us Parsons if
you will; but we'll read Foucault." This is rebellion, and it is good.
What is to be regretted, however, is that it perpetuates a mindlessness
about Parsons and many others in the classic tradition which my
generation began. When my generation of sociologists who started
out in the 1970s attacked Parsons, we at least tried to understand
him; or, more accurately in many cases, we were not bold enough to
refuse our teachers' assignments of his books.

Jeffrey Alexander decided early in the 1970s not to go along with
the crowd. It was not that Alexander was ignorant of the Marxisms
that were then winning the hearts and minds of the new generation
of sociologists; nor that he was antagonistic to the critical movements of the day. On the contrary, he knew his Marx very well. This
is why, as he says in his introductory chapter to this book, he was

moved by, and felt such kinship with, radicals such as Herbert Gintis and Mark Gould who read Marx *and* Parsons. Although, as his graduate career at Berkeley evolved, Alexander came down ever so much more on the side of Parsons, he never, ever took Parsons on Parsons' own terms. The idea was to critique and revise in order to reconstruct the theoretical logic of sociology.

Alexander's long and successful labor in defining sociological neo-functionalism has been an act of courage *and* a political act. True, his first and major work, the four-volume *Theoretical Logic in Sociology*, was in form an exegetical work of pure theory. But it was also very much in the tradition of Durkheim, even Weber – an attempt to reconstruct the tradition of sociological knowledge so that sociology might better confront the social and political realities of the world. It is all too easy to forget that the final pages of the fourth volume of *Theoretical Logic* resolve in a criticism of the inherent contradictions in Parsons' thinking *and* a plea to revise the tradition in such a way that a postpositivist sociology might do what Parsons could not do: to found itself on universalistic judgments that are able to tolerate and account for the resistant particularities of social reality.

This is the point of demarcation between Alexander's neofunctionalism and Parsonian functionalism, and this is why in retrospect it was neither accurate nor fair to have spoken of the author of *Theoretical Logic* as "Parsons, Jr." Since that important book appeared in 1982–3, Alexander has devoted an increasing measure of his work to investigation of the three themes he recommends to us all in his concluding chapter to the present book: action, culture, and civil society. These should be the preoccupying themes of a postfunctionalist sociology because, among other good reasons, they are the themes with respect to which civil societies in late-modern global societies are being tested. Consider the following passage from near the end of *Neofunctionalism and After*:

> The divisive classes generated by economic life, the oligarchies generated by political and organizational power, the gender and age hierarchies of families, the demonology frequently legitimated by religious institutions, and the ethnic, regional and racial dominations so often generated by the very construction of national civil states – such intrusions fragment and split civil society even while its very existence promises participation and restoration of the social whole.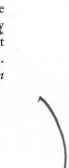

Today, anyone who attempts to think through the fragmentations of modern societies, much less live with their effects, is required to make an informed judgment on these matters. How, indeed, are we to understand, and contend with, forces that split the social whole into conflicting parts – forces that are energized by a democratic society's promise of participation to the hitherto excluded even as they simultaneously put the whole at tangible risk of collapse. In other words, Alexander's final words in the present book are in quite specific fulfillment of the promises with which *Theoretical Logic* concluded.

How, indeed, does the whole survive the conflicting particularities? How, as a practical matter, do we make universal judgments about what is common while living as members or sympathizers with one or more of the newly fragmented, yet restorative, groups that are shaking the foundations of civil society? Some political questions are perhaps more practically urgent, but even they return to these basics. The dismantling of the social securities of the postwar welfare states in Europe and America is as much a punishment visited upon those perceived to have broken the false universalism of modern states as it is a question of fiscal restraint and the like. Though, on some questions, many would come to conclusions different from those of Alexander, we who are honest about our oppositional politics must realize that somewhere out there is a limit beyond which the divisions must not go. In 1968, the year before Alexander began his graduate work at Berkeley, many thought that the Euroamerican social synthesis had come upon its final collapse. Few then would have predicted that the turmoil on the streets in that era would one day be thought of as political child's play when compared with the current, real prospect of a war of all against all. Dust off your Hobbes, for today we face fragmentations of the social whole aggravated by the seemingly permanent disappearance of decently paid jobs, in the absence of which the number of those with little or no stake in the social whole expands beyond the ameliorative capacities of the residual institutions. Such a crisis is far removed from the conditions that inspired Kingsley Davis's 1959 boast on behalf of functionalism, just as it bears little honest comparison with the no less triumphalist radicalism of C. Wright Mills in the same year.

Alexander is among those who remind us that, however we view the current crisis, there remains an overriding obligation not to ignore the hard work of reconstructing whatever social filaments might still be able to sustain a working semblance of the social pattern while allowing the many to adapt to a hostile economic environment – to adapt sufficiently well as integrated members of our aggressively goal-seeking societies. Having done what he could do to rehabilitate what is productive in the functionalist ideal, Alexander now allows himself to look to what lies beyond, and recommends the same to us.

Neofunctionalism and After is a book that will teach us all, whatever may be our generational attitudes toward past, present, and future. To the cultured despisers of theoretical work, this wonderful book demonstrates so very well just how good theory rises strong against the empirical realties of which it speaks. To those who years ago joined the march against the claims of Parsons and Davis and others, this book reminds us just what has come to be at stake in the concerns of functionalisms, new and old. And, to those just now coming into the field, those who read what they will whether or not it bears the imprimatur of the sociological canon, this book is as good a handbook as there is to what the older functionalism sought to do and how it failed; to what the newer functionalism did in saving that which might otherwise have been lost; and to why we must join Jeffrey Alexander in moving beyond, by accepting Parsons no less than Marx, and others, as among those without whom it is difficult to think as a sociologist.

CHARLES C. LEMERT

Preface

The essays that form chapters 2–8 of this work were composed over a ten-year period that stretched from the mid-1980s to the mid-1990s. They represent a collaborative project in every sense of the word. Without the urgings of Paul Colomy, my first doctoral student, I might not have created this new project, and without his later stimulation, when he became my colleague, the project would not have assumed the form that it did. David Sciulli also played an important collaborative role, in personal terms and through the exemplars he provided in his own writings.

My German colleague and friend Richard Munch was a close collaborator throughout much of this period as well, providing both intellectual inspiration and confirmation that this movement of theoretical revision was not limited to America alone. Neil Smelser, Shmuel Eisenstadt, and Bernard Barber were supportive mentors as well as creators of works that adumbrated the kind of neofunctionalism I had in mind.

As I worked through the neofunctionalist project, first elaborating its potential and, later, understanding its limitations, I benefited enormously, both intellectually and personally, from the friendship of my Swedish colleague Ron Eyerman. Finally, I must record the debt I owe to Charles Lemert. Both in spite of, and because of, the difference between our theoretical inclinations, from the beginning Charles affirmed my intellectual explorations. It is only fitting that as my editor he has played a vital role in critically shaping this book.

JEFFREY C. ALEXANDER
Mexico City

Acknowledgments

The author and publishers would like to thank the relevant copyright-holders for permission to reproduce previously published material:

"Traditions and Competition: Preface to a Postpositivist Approach to Knowledge Cumulation" (chapter 2, with Paul Colomy) first appeared in George Ritzer (ed.), *Metatheorizing* (1992), pp. 27–52, and is reprinted here by permission of Sage Publications.

"Neofunctionalism Today: Reconstructing a Theoretical Tradition" (chapter 3, with Paul Colomy) first appeared in George Ritzer (ed.), *Frontiers of Sociological Theory* (1990), pp. 33–67, and is reprinted here by permission of Columbia University Press.

"Parsons' *Structure* in American Sociology" (chapter 4) first appeared in *Sociological Theory*, vol. 6 (Spring 1988), pp. 96–102, and is reprinted here by permission.

" 'Formal Sociology' is Not Multidimensional: Breaking the Code in Parsons' Fragment on Simmel" (chapter 5) first appeared in *Teoria Sociologica*, vol. 1, no. 1 (1993), pp. 101–14, and is reprinted here by permission.

"On Choosing One's Intellectual Predecessors: Why Charles Camic is Wrong about Parsons' Early Work" (chapter 6, with Giuseppe Sciortino) first appeared in *Sociological Theory*, vol. 14, no. 2 (1996), pp. 154–72, and is reprinted here by permission.

"Structure, Value, Action: What Did the Early Parsons Mean and What Should He Have Said Instead?" (chapter 7) first appeared in

American Sociological Review, vol. 55, no. 3 (June 1990), pp. 339–45, and is reprinted here by permission.

"The New Theoretical Movement in Sociology" (chapter 8) first appeared in *Revista Brasileira de Ciencias Sociais*, vol. 4, no. 2 (1987), pp. 5–28, and later in N. J. Smelser (ed.), *Handbook of Sociology* (1988), pp. 77–101, and is reprinted here by permission.

Part I
Origins of a Theoretical Project

1

From Functionalism to Neofunctionalism: Creating a Position in the Field of Social Theory

The essays collected in this book, introduction and conclusion excepted, were written from the mid-1980s to the mid-1990s. They were not the only theoretical pieces I wrote during this period, but they include virtually all the essay-length writing I devoted to Talcott Parsons. They represent the principal articles in which I constructed and elaborated the neofunctionalist project, a project that was undertaken with a small number of like-minded colleagues in the USA and Europe and which attracted increasing attention during this time.

In terms of the discipline of sociology and social theory more broadly conceived, neofunctionalism has been understood as a movement of ideas that marked a shift in the predicted slope of knowledge/power, to mix a concept from trigonometry with a term of Foucault's. Faced with the emergence of a neofunctionalism in the 1980s, theorists whose formation occurred in the 1960s – when a radical sociology was supposed to have broken definitely with Parsons – spoke of a "surprisingly successful comeback" and of neofunctionalism's "important impact on contemporary theory." Younger, post-sixties theorists saw the emergence of a neofunctionalism as a refutation of the linear assumptions about scientific development that the preceding generation had continued to hold. "The revival of Parsonian thought is one of the distinguishing features of 1980s sociology," one such reviewer wrote. It suggested a "cyclical pattern," one which features replacement rather than displacement and suggests that "different schools of thought replace each other in commanding our attention over time" and that "leading figures in the various theoretical traditions follow this same pattern."[1] In the most recent effort yet to essay the position of neofunctionalism in contemporary sociological theory, Mouzelis (1995, p. 81) describes what he calls "the present feeling about Parsonian grand theory" in a similar way. Observing that "Parsonian functionalism, after a rashly sweeping dismissal during the 1960s and 1970s, experienced a considerable revival in the 1980s and 1990s," he concludes that "given the remarkable rigor and depth of Parsons' theoretical constructions, the present task of sociological theory should be not its overall rejection, but a thorough restructuring of its weaker, problematic dimensions."

As a development that shifts intradisciplinary divisions, and as a movement in theoretical ideas more generally, neofunctionalism has had an effect that is increasingly broad and widespread. Indeed, conceived of as an effort to alter not only disciplinary structures but the discourse and self-consciousness of contemporary social theory, neofunctionalism has accomplished what it originally set out to achieve. It is virtually impossible, at this point, to theorize about contemporary society without reference to some of the major themes in Parsons' work: to his notions about structural differentiation, which continued Durkheim's and Spencer's earlier ideas in a more sophisticated form;[2] to his ideas about inclusion, which built upon Weber's ideas about rationalization and fraternization and Durkheim's thinking about solidarity;[3] to his thinking about culture, which translated Weber's focus on the economic ethics of world religions into a much more general theory of moral institutionalization;[4] to his ideas about the necessary interplay of personality and social structure, which built upon Freud and Mead.[5]

In the 1950s and early 1960s there were many important sociologists who believed that these and other issues could be understood only in "Parsonian" terms. Today, almost nobody would think in this way. On the other hand, in the early 1980s, before the neofunctionalist movement appeared, many of the most influential thinkers believed that it had finally become possible to think about issues such as these without any reference to Parsons at all. Today, only a few persons continue to argue in this way. "Parsons" has moved from being a dominant intellectual force, to a figure upon whose very significance many important social theorists cast serious doubt, to a "classical" figure in contemporary intellectual life.[6]

Parsons' contributions are now accepted as unquestionably important, even while his theories are no longer acceptable as such. This paradox is only an apparent one. Thus, there are very few, if any, contemporary social scientists whose work follows Weber's detailed plan for the study of society. Neither are there any "Durkheimians" or "Simmelians" in this sense. Yet the enormous influence of these earlier classical figures remains. They are regarded as exemplars of certain ways of thinking, as providing particular paradigms for particular kinds of delimited studies, as supplying polemical resources for criticisms that allow broader intellectual links to be established and denied. Parsons' position in the social sciences is now much the same. As a theoretical figure in contemporary life his star will undoubtedly rise and fall. But as a figure in history, and in the living history of the social sciences and social theory, his position now seems secure. His writings and career are increasingly treated as data for the history of sociology as such.[7]

Neofunctionalism has been a major project for me, in a personal as well as in a theoretical and professional sense. Insofar as I have succeeded in helping to (re)establish the legitimacy of some of Parsons' central conerns, I regard this project as completed. It is this very completion that has allowed me increasingly to separate my own understanding of social theory from Parsons' own, to look beyond Parsons, to think about what comes "after Parsons," to build not only upon "Parsons," but upon other strands of classical and contemporary work, to create a different kind of social theory. Still, whatever comes after neofunctionalism will be deeply indebted to it. This is true, I would argue, not only for my own intellectual development, and for the increasing number of other contemporary thinkers whose ideas have passed directly through the filter of Parsons' work, but for sociological theory in most, but not all, of its contemporary manifestations.[8]

During the time I composed the essays collected here I wrote also about other things. Rereading Weber, I focused particularly on the antipathies in his theorizing about modern society (Alexander 1987a) and on the relationship between his rationalization theory and Durkheim's later work on the symbolic basis of society (Alexander 1992a). I immersed myself in microsociologies of action (Alexander et al. 1987) and semiotic and poststructural analyses of meaning (Alexander 1990). I deepened and made more systematic my earlier objections to Parsons' theories of action and value (Alexander 1987b), and I began critically to examine problems of contemporary democracy (Alexander 1991a) and to develop a sociological model of civil society (Alexander 1992b). From these investigations there percolated a series of theoretical and empirical publications that, it must be said, cannot very well be understood in a precisely neofunctionalist way. They must, rather, be seen more broadly, as part of that wider stream of contemporary thinking which I have called "the new theoretical movement" (see chapter 8). I write about these developments in my thinking, and their relation to neofunctionalism, in the concluding chapter of this book, chapter 9, which I have entitled "After Neofunctionalism: Action, Culture, and Civil Society."

The new theoretical movement can be seen as a third phase in postwar sociological theory. Parsons' ideas had a certain hegemony in the late 1940s through the mid-1960s, a hegemony which was relative, to be sure, less a form of domination than an influence that displaced but in no way prevented the elaboration of other traditions. When this hegemony ended, there followed an intense and productive period of one-sided polemical theories that were built upon criticisms of Parsons and aimed to substitute one particular element of action or order for the synthesis that Parsons had tried to build.[9] Sometime during the 1970s, however, there emerged the beginnings of a different kind of theoretical emphasis, one that sought to integrate different lines of thought and move beyond the one-sided polemics of earlier years. The theorists who have formed the main lines of this movement employ concepts that reflect different emphases and interests, and I have at one time or another offered pointed criticisms of most of their work. Some of these critical remarks are reproduced in the essays included here; other have appeared in some earlier collections of my essays (Alexander 1988a, 1989). It is upon the basis of these disagreements that I offer the suggestions for new directions in social theory in my concluding chapter. Nonetheless, despite these deep disagreements, I believe that my own ideas and the theories I criticize together form part of the same broad yet nonetheless distinctive theoretical movement of contemporary sociological thought. Each of the central theoretical currents in this stream forms variations on common themes.

One may understand what was, and remains, distinctive about this new theoretical movement in sociology by employing some of the terms that Paul Colomy and I develop in our investigations of knowledge accumulation and competition in science (chapter 2), a general model that can be taken as framing the other contributions in this book. Initially, the figures who are now considered to be representatives of this new theoretical movement – among them Giddens, Habermas, Luhmann, Munch, Bourdieu, Boltanski and Thevenot, Collins, and myself – were intent on revising the perspectives we had inherited from Parsons and his critics. Our intention was to move beyond the most destructive and debilitating divisions of post-Parsonian thought. I am thinking here of works like Giddens' *Capitalism and Modern Social Theory* (1971), Habermas's *Toward a Rational Society* (1971), Collins' *Conflict Sociology* (1975), Bourdieu's (1970) early writings on Algeria and his middle period work on educational reproduction (e.g., Bourdieu 1973), and my own *Theoretical Logic in Sociology* (1982–3).

These earnest early efforts soon gave way, however, to more forceful challenges to the inherited perspectives of the two early theoretical phases, to a deepening sense of their inadequacy that led, not to revisionism, but to full-blown reconstructions of earlier lines of thought, for example, Giddens' *New Rules of Sociological Method* (1976) and *Central Problems in Social Theory* (1979), the essays collected in Habermas' *Communication and the Evolution of Societies* (1979), Collins' work in the early 1980s on interaction ritual chains, and my collective volume *Neofunctionalism* (1985).[10] For some of the participants in this new theoretical movement, even these reconstructive ambitions eventually seemed too limiting. They began to devote themselves not to revision or even to reconstruction, but to developing entirely new and original positions of their own, e.g., Giddens' *The Constitution of Societies* (1984), Bourdieu's *Outline of a Theory of Practice* (1977), Habermas' *Theory of Communicative Action* (1984), and Boltanski and Thevenot's *De la justification* (1991).[11] I can now see in some of my own efforts of the late 1980s a subtle but distinctive shift in theoretical emphasis and tone. In addition to the pieces noted above, I think particularly of my surprisingly sharp criticisms of Parsons' approaches to differentiation (Alexander 1988b) and culture (Alexander 1987b, 1990).

At the same time, it must be acknowledged that other theorists who were involved in efforts at reconstruction resisted the temptation to develop new theories or dramatic shifts in emphasis. Weberian sociologists, for example, sought to reconstitute the originating paradigm by incorporating new theoretical developments in a "Weberian" way (e.g., Schluchter 1981, 1989). Conversation analysts claimed that they were only doing ethnomethodology in a different key. Efforts like these to maintain the continuity of traditions have sometimes taken the form of antagonism to more radical efforts at reconstruction; arguments have been made that the purity of second-phase theories must be maintained (e.g., Pollner 1991).[12] There is, nonetheless, an undeniable and growing recognition that the theoretical terrain is shifting beneath our feet, that we are in the midst of what might be called a postclassical phase of sociological theory.[13] For the first time in a generation, new and very different kinds of sociological theories are being produced.

From the very beginning, in fact, neofunctionalism was an effort to relate Parsons to different forms of classical and contemporary work. In telling this story, it seems relevant to introduce some auto-biographical information, particularly since neofunctionalism, at least in its Anglophone form, has often been associated with my name.[14] In chapter 3, Paul Colomy and I specifically take up the movement from functionalism to neofunctionalism, and most of the other chapters in this book can be understood as expressions of this movement and theme. As Parsons has achieved "classic" status, however, this story is coming to an end. The narrative shifts to the future and away from the past, to the movement beyond neofunctionalism, from within the movement and outside of it as well. I take up this second story in my concluding chapter.

I became interested in the thought of Talcott Parsons just at the point, during my last years at Harvard in 1968 and 1969, when I began to see myself as a politically engaged Marxist theorist. It was this interest that separated my own intellectual development from others in my intellectual generation of "young radicals" in the United States. In this separation I was stimulated particularly by Parsons' last brilliant student, Mark Gould, who insisted that, just as Marx had built his theory upon Hegel and the classical political economists, so contemporary radical theory would have to build upon Parsons as well. During my first year in graduate school at Berkeley, in 1969–70, as I became more involved in the sophisticated intricacies of contemporary Marxian thought, I kept this advice in mind, following closely the lectures of Neil Smelser, for example, who was Parsons' most original structurally oriented student. I recall that when I returned to Cambridge, Massachusetts, at the end of that first year, Gould reiterated his "warning" to me (cf., Gould 1981), as did the radical political economist Herbert Gintis, who had put Parsons' ideas to such highly original use in his PhD thesis on welfare economics, which Gintis formally dedicated to Parsons and Marx.

I followed my young counselors' advice, agreeing with them that Parsons was a "great" thinker, not just another influential one. From the very beginning of my interest in Parsons, then, I intended to combine his ideas with those of thinkers in other frames, at first with those of Marx, later with those of Durkheim and Weber, whom I began to read more systematically after that first year. My ambition was to create a more synthetic social theory, and I regarded Parsons not as an end point but as a place to begin. I found Parsons' theory something I could think with, but never with it alone. Parsons himself persistently claimed to be building directly upon the ideas of Marx, Weber, and Durkheim, although as he matured he became more interested in using these other ideas to develop his own. However, neither I nor my German neofunctionalist colleague Richard Munch thought of Parsons' own ideas in this kind of linear, evolutionary way. We viewed them, rather, as providing a pathway back to the classics, and eventually to contemporaries as well. In the end, the most bracing thing about Parsons' ideas was, in fact, their synthetic ambition and scope. Because he aimed at creating a total theory – a method, a philosophy, a macrosociological model, even a new morality – he inspired me and my neofunctionalist colleagues to think broadly and inclusively as well.

This ecumenical ambition has taken in my work both analytical and substantive forms. It is clear, for example, that the chapters in this book aim to incorporate and interrelate various, often antagonistic strands of contemporary and classical thought. In this effort, I employ, sometimes explicitly but more often implicitly, the "theoretical logic" I developed in my initial books as a criterion for criticizing the one-sided nature of many individualistic and collectivist theories. Yet, especially in light of the highly "analytic" nature of these early works, it is important to emphasize that, from the beginning, I also explicitly employed Parsons' ecumenical ambition in a political and moral way. My early graduate student years in Berkeley coincided with a Leninist turn in the politics of the New Left. Secrecy and political authoritarianism were increasingly displacing the openness and emphasis on participatory democracy that had characterized radical student politics in the sixties. In its conflicts with Maoist and Stalinist splinters and sects, some campus movements associated with Students for a Democratic Society (SDS) began to advocate revolutionary violence in turn. I looked to Parsons and to Weber in order to find a theory of democratic social change that took violence as an exception rather than a rule. In their writings I found theorizing that recognized and encouraged the capacities for criticism and anti-authoritarian action within democratic societies themselves. This ideologically democratic and pluralist dimension of Parsons' work is in a formal sense independent of the analytical thrust toward theoretical integration and multidimensionality, and was never recognized as an ideology by Parsons himself. Nevertheless, it has an elective affinity with this analytic orientation that seemed to me very important at the time, and still does today (cf., Holton and Turner 1986).

Such a combined commitment to a critical pluralist ideology and a synthetic analytic theory informed my first published article on Parsons, "Formal and substantive voluntarism in the work of Talcott Parsons: a theoretical and ideological reinterpretation" (Alexander 1978).[15] The spirit of this early piece, which mirrored that of my PhD dissertation at Berkeley, was that with some substantial but not fundamental adjustments Parsons' theoretical model could provide an appropriate scheme for reincorporating classical ideas and producing a new, truly synthetic vision. After I left graduate school in 1976 and assumed my first faculty position at UCLA, however, this line of thinking began to change. I realized that the Parsons I had written about should be understood more as "Parsons," that my reading was interpretive and not just descriptive.

Between 1976 and 1980, as I revised my dissertation, I came face to face with the strong currents of microsociology at UCLA and also with the new movements of culturalism that were emerging in the social sciences at large. I realized that, in order to construct "Parsons," rather than Parsons, there would need to be a larger reconstruction of his thought. As a result, during these years I came to feel increasingly distant from Parsons himself, from many of the established, more senior Parsonians, and from most – although by no means all – of his later students. When I published *Theoretical Logic in Sociology*, I devoted the initial volume to developing a discursive model of social science that challenged, among other things, the scientistic self-understanding that Parsons had of his own theory.[16] In the fourth volume (Alexander 1983), devoted entirely to Parsonian ideas, I spent fully half of my discussion criticizing Parsons' originating work, and I carefully culled the writings of his "revisionist" students to identify new lines of development from his brilliant but deeply flawed original position.

When some of the initial reviews of *Theoretical Logic* appeared, I realized that I had not been clear enough about the distance that now separated me from the original tradition, a distance that, at the same time, did not imply a critical break. It was in response to being misunderstood that I introduced the term "neofunctionalism" (Alexander 1985). While admitting that "functionalism" in itself communicated relatively little, I intended with this usage to draw a parallel between the kind of revisionism – Colomy and I later called it reconstruction – that had created neo-Marxism.

The neofunctionalist label succeeded in providing for me and my like-minded colleagues a theoretical space. It allowed us to maintain our links to some of Parsons' key ideas while criticizing his theories in fundamental ways. It was precisely the failure publically to register complaints, we suggested, that had inhibited and eventually undermined earlier, more traditionally Parsonian work. Without making claims for comparable importance, we explicitly argued that our theorizing would be as different from Parsons' originating theory, and as similar to it, as the work of Lukács or Gramsci had differed from, and resembled, that of Marx. Just this kind of reconstructionist ambition has informed the very wide range of neofunctionalist writing that Colomy and I describe in chapter 3: historical and comparative discussions of structural and cultural fusion rather than differentiation; feminist analyses of patriarchal socialization rather than rational ego formation; socialist and radical investigations of the exploitation and domination that continues to permeate democratic life.[17]

During this period of the middle and late 1980s I began systematically to revisit theoretical traditions that I had previously understood to be antithetical to the project of synthetic, Parsonian, and even neofunctionalist work. I read much more sympathetically than I once had the writings of microsociological thinkers like Goffman, Homans, and Garfinkel; of conflict theorists like Rex; and of critical social theorists like Habermas and Walzer. While I remained convinced that these alternative traditions were not satisfactory in themselves, I came to believe that "Parsons" would have to be altered as fundamentally as they. In *Twenty Lectures: Sociological Theory since World War II* (1987d), I argued that only a new kind of synthetic model – one which built upon some of Parsons' basic ideas but differed from it both in specific and general ways – could get beyond the problems these challengers had discovered in Parsons' work. The growing sense that there were fundamental and intrinsic difficulties in Parsons' theorizing also informed my contributions to the collective work on the microlink that I helped organize during the same period of time (Alexander et al. 1987), and it also underlay, as I have suggested above, my criticisms of the endemic optimism of Parsons' differentiation theories (Alexander 1988b) and the reductionism that debilitated his "value" theory of culture.

During these years I felt increasingly impatient, not only with Parsons' original ideas, but with "Parsonian" thinking on these and a wide range of other issues.[18] At an international meeting in the late

1980s, a theorist in the older Parsonian generation asked me if I ever had anything positive to say any more about Parsons. It was a question well taken, although by no means entirely fair. I began to realize that, for me, the neofunctionalist reconstruction of Parsons' legacy was not going to be enough, despite my commitment to defending the integrity and brilliance of Parsons' founding theory and despite my admiration and support for the impressive new lines of neofunctionalist work. When I defend "Parsons" from his critics in chapters 3–7, below, my aim is to preserve the integrity of his ideas, but not to preserve them as such. I wish to prevent basic misunderstandings of his thought.[19] If such distortions prevail, they would encourage the mistaken belief that contemporary theorizing can avoid the necessity to systematically work through Parsons' ideas. As Habermas warned in *Theory of Communicative Action*, such a "detour around Parsons" would undermine the possibility of creating truly sophisticated forms of critical theorizing about the contemporary world.

Neofunctionalism has succeeded in helping to establish Parsons as a classical figure. One illustration of this new status is that theorists pick and choose from among Parsons' many, often contradictory, ideas without apologizing for leaving the rest behind. David Lockwood, one of the first and most acute radical critics of Parsons' middle period work, has recently (Lockwood 1992) employed the presuppositional framework of Parsons' first book, *The Structure of Social Action* (1937), not only to criticize the determinism of neo-Marxist class analysis but to attack the very Durkheimian ideas about solidarity that Parsons himself thought *Structure* had advanced.[20] Eschewing Parsons' developmental history and his cultural and psychological theories alike, Mouzelis (1995) builds upon Parsons' differentiation of analytic from substantive theorizing, and his AGIL model of functional requisites, to advance his own more institutional approach to the micro–macro link.[21] Jean Cohen and Andrew Arato (1992; cf. Alexander 1994), two of the most important contemporary political theorists in the Habermas tradition, draw deeply and originally from Parsons' ideas about social differentiation and the societal community to reconstruct Habermas's ideas about communication and the contemporary public sphere, ideas that Habermas himself believed to have fundamentally displaced Parsons' own. Another illustration of Parsons' new status can be seen in the fact that, while various segments of his writing provide exemplars for contemporary research and theorizing in a range of specialized fields (see, e.g., the contributions to Colomy

1992a and also Robertson and Turner 1991), these writers rarely feel compelled to place their treatment within the broader Parsonian frame, much less to identify themselves with neofunctionalism.

Finally, and most paradoxically, Parsons' work is once again being used, this time in a relatively unpolemical manner that suggests a kind of perverse respect, to exemplify theoretical and empirical paths that contemporary authors wish to argue against. When Holmwood and Stewart (1991), for example, take issue with the synthesizing tendencies I have discussed above, not only with my own work but also with that of Bourdieu, Giddens, Collins, and Habermas, they condemn them not only as "just like" Parsonianism but as having been inspired by it. At the same time, they suggest with apparent nonchalance that a truer reading of Parsons might actually show a way out of the cul-de-sac they believe to have been created by this new synthetic wave. Likewise, when Dimaggio and Powell (1991) construct an intellectual pedigree for the "neo-institutional" approach to organizations, they highlight the distinctiveness of this contemporary tradition by contrasting it with Parsons' and Selznick's original understandings of values and legitimation in institutional life. That it was Parsons himself who first identified institutionalization with the capacity for legitimation, and that Selznick conceived of his own work as a critical response to Parsons' own, are points that Dimaggio and Powell do not feel compelled to make. When Joas (1996) wants to make the case for placing creativity and expressivity in the center of general sociological theory, he legitimates his position by engaging in a polemic against, not only Parsonian, but neofunctionalist thought.

This melange is the fate of those who have achieved a classical position in social science. It indicates a position of historical eminence rather than contemporary domination. Such a status is not, of course, exactly what Parsons and his followers had in mind. Contemporary importance is the ambition of every great and ambitious systematic thinker; in the end, however, historical eminence is all that any thinker in the social sciences can ever attain. Neofunctionalism today is a vital current in contemporary work. As one strong strand in the fabric of the new theoretical movement, there is every reason to expect that creative and important sociological studies will continue to be written in its name. At the same time, there is a dialectic in the movement of creative thought that cannot be ignored. The very success of neofunctionalism points beyond it as well.

Notes

1 For these and other remarks about the context of neofunctionalism, see the first section of chapter 3.

2 See, for example, the very wide range of the articles devoted to social differentiation in Alexander and Colomy (1990). The general thrust of Niklas Luhmann's work remains closely informed by Parsons' approach to differentiation (e.g., Luhmann 1990), this despite the movement toward communication and autopoesis in his later work. One should also mention the series of articles and books on "interpenetration" by Richard Munch (e.g., 1983), a concept explicitly derived from Parsons' particular approach to differentiation.

3 See, for example, work by the British and Australian sociologist, Bryan Turner (e.g., 1986, 1992) and the writings of Mayhew (1990, 1997).

4 See, for example, Eisenstadt's writings on civilization (e.g., 1988), Robertson's (1990) on globalization, Lipset's (1990) comparison of the USA and Canada.

5 See, for example, Chodorow's (1978) discussion of feminism, which was deeply affected by Parsons' early work on sex and gender and his later work on the assymmetries of socialization. Johnson's (1988) contributions to this debate can be read as a radical-feminist reconstruction of Parsons' approach to these topics. See also Parsons' continuing prominence in recent collections of psychoanalytically related sociological writings (e.g., Prager and Rustin 1996).

6 In his plenary address to the World Congress XIII of the International Sociological Association, Alain Touraine spoke of "the classical founders of sociology, Marx, Weber, Durkheim, Simmel, and Parsons." I mean "classical" in the constructivist sense I elaborated in Alexander (1987c), according to which the name of an intellectual figure comes to function communicatively as a kind of condensed, shorthand symbol for a complex set of ideas. In referring to Parsons in quotation marks, as "Parsons," I mean to refer to this constructed figure rather than to the works of the man himself.

7 See the work of writers like Camic (e.g., 1991 and chapter 6, below), Wearne (1989), Buxton (1985), Wenzel (1990), Neilson (1991), Joutsenoja (1996), Sciortino (1993), and Gerhardt (1993) for examples of the serious historiography that is now ongoing about Parsons' relationship to sociology, society, and other disciplines. At the present moment, there may be more historical investigation on Parsons than on any other figure in the history of social science.

8 Giddens' shifting position in relationship to the neofunctionalist tradition is revealing in this regard. In the Preface to his systematic statement of structuration theory, Giddens (1984) acknowledged that, while his

theorizing intended to integrate various hitherto separated strands of theoretical work, he had avoided any reference to the revival of functionalist thinking that could be seen in the work of writers such as Luhmann, Munch, and myself. Yet in his prolific writings on "late modernity" in the 1990s, Giddens has based much of his empirical thinking upon the idea of the risk society introduced by Ulrich Beck, whose ideas clearly represent a reformulation of Luhmann's notions about systems differentiation and action as the reduction of uncertainty. He has also incorporated many of the dichotomous ideas about modern and traditional societies associated with Parsonian work on modernization. For a critique of this overreliance on these earlier Parsonian simplicities, see Alexander (1996).

9   For a discussion of these historical developments, see Alexander (1987d).

10 It will be noted that these theorists are all macro in their orientation, despite the fact that the work of each is distinguished precisely by efforts to bridge the micro–macro link. I am not aware of any contemporary effort to create a general social theory that has a distinctly micro-orientation. It is difficult, moreover, to find the same kind of revisionist and reconstructionist impulses within the microtraditions that emerged in the postwar theory's second phase, despite the fact there have clearly been major changes, for example, in Chicago school theories, changes that Colomy and Brown (1992) have clearly linked to the rise of functionalism. Conversation analysis can certainly be seen as a revision of ethnomethodology, but it is not a revision that points toward a more synthetic, micro–macro aim. Although there has developed a more institutionally related strand of conversation analysis (e.g., Boden and Zimmerman 1990), this strand does not, by and large, make an effort to establish systematic links with cultural or institutional analysis (for a recent exception, see Roth 1995); to the contrary, it continues to insist on maintaining its distinctiveness vis-à-vis them. Contemporary exchange theory, most formidably represented by Coleman's *Foundations of Social Theory* (1990), is the only microtradition that has participated in some of the synthesizing effects of the third phase. Two reservations are in order here. It has done so by moving toward a macro level of theorizing, and with few exceptions (Elster 1992) it has sought to remain a one-sided theory and not to participate in the kind of "outreach" that so characterizes the dominant general theories of our day. For an extended critique of Coleman's work in this regard, see Alexander (1992c).

11 In terms of the last reference, I am suggesting that, although the timing and national context is different, one finds in France a similar movement from revision and reconstruction to theory-creation in the "second generation" of theorizing that has developed recently vis-à-vis the legacies of Bourdieu and Touraine. Boltanski was more pragmatic and constructivist than his teacher in his still Bourdieuian work, *Les cadres* (1982),

but he went beyond recontruction when he created, with Thevenot, *De la justification* (1991), which forcefully broke with Bourdieu and incorporated discourse theories, pragmatism, and pluralism. The same kind of break, this time vis-à-vis Touraine, can be seen in Dubet's important *Sociologie de l'expérience* (1994).

The national variations of the "new theoretical movement" are obviously highly significant. In France, for example, there never was any Parsonian hegemony. Instead there was a clear domination of Marxian and structuralist thought, despite Gurvitch's institutional influence. In this context, the ideas of Bourdieu, Touraine, Boudon, and Crozier can be seen as creating a "second phase" which was decisively influenced by the second phase of American theorizing as well as by the European traditions which gave some of these American traditions their roots. While none of these French theorists were microsociologists, each represents a much more decisively agency-centered idea. There are elements in Touraine's thought, and particularly in Bourdieu's, which can be seen as representing "third" phase movements to create more synthetic models. The highly original recent efforts of Boltanski and Thevenot (1991) and Dubet, however, represent this synthetic effort in more distinctive, more ecumenical, and I think ultimately more effective ways.

12 Collins' (1986) collection of probing historical and comparative essays, entitled *Weberian Sociological Theory*, represents another variation. Rather than identifying this collection in terms of the rubric "conflict theory," the second-phase term he did so much to elaborate, he chose to identify in terms of a classical figure. In other words, Collins' movement into a more synthetic position – his third-phase, micro–macro link – has clearly displaced the terminology of phase two, Collins' (1990) own protests to the contrary.

13 This new theoretical freedom in relation to the polarizing dichotomies of postwar debate in sociology has, not surprisingly, corresponded with a much more permeable boundary between sociological theory in a disciplinary sense and social theory more broadly conceived in a post- or non-disciplinary way. To move beyond the second phase of postwar theoretical development is, in fact, to move beyond any necessary relation, not only to Parsons but to his theoretical antagonists, virtually all of whom were theorists in a specifically sociological sense. Whereas reconstructive efforts in the second phase tried to create new syntheses by breaking down boundaries within sociological theory – between Parsons and his antagonists, and among the antagonists themselves – third-phase efforts have tried to reconstruct sociological traditions by breaking down boundaries between sociology and theorizing that has emerged in other disciplines, not only in social science but in literary theory and philosophy. Third-phase efforts to create genuinely new theories in sociology have moved even further in this regard, systematically

incorporating ideas from semiotics, poststructuralism, postmodernism, deconstruction, geography, hermeneutics, pragmatism, symbolic anthropology, rhetoric, game theory, and speech act theory, among others.

While the discussion of sociological theory in this chapter is entirely an internalist one, these developments were certainly deeply affected by movements in the intellectual world more generally and by broader societal change (see, e.g., Alexander 1995a). Thus, third-phase movements toward reconstruction and theory-creation were, and are, stimulated by the emergence of new politically generated theories such as feminism, multiculturalism, civil society, and postcolonialism. Because these other kinds of "new theoretical movements" do not have a disciplinary emphasis *per se* – although they have, in fact, often been influenced by many of the disciplinary developments I have discussed here – they have further contributed to the boundary blurring qualities of contemporary efforts at theory construction and creation in sociology. Joas's *The Creativity of Action* (1996) is the most recent case in point. In his third-phase effort at theory creation, Joas draws his inspiration primarily from American (pragmatic) and German (idealist) philosophy to mount an argument against what he claims to be the normative, antiexpressive biases of Luhmann and Habermas, on the one hand, and Parsons and American neofunctionalists, on the other. For a broader discussion of historical shifts in the relation between sociological theory and social theory more generally, especially theoretical developments in philosophy and literary studies, see Alexander (forthcoming).

14 The question about the quite different yet related trajectory of German neofunctionalism is an issue that Colomy (1990a) has taken up explicitly but which deserves to be more widely discussed. The question is made more complex by the apparently growing reluctance of some German neofunctionalist theories to acknowledge the linkages between their theoretical reconstructions and Parsons' earlier ideas. In addition to Luhman's own persistent efforts to deny his indebtedness to classical thinking as such, see Munch's recent attempts (e.g., 1991, 1993) to distance himself and his German colleagues from "American sociology." I critically respond to the distortions of this claim, and to what I regard as Munch's gratuitously geopolitical emphasis, in Alexander (1995b). See Munch (1995) for a reply to this criticism, and the extended debate in the subsequent issues of *Revue suisse de sociologie*, which reprinted the dialogue that first appeared in *Theory*, the Newsletter of the Research Committee on Sociological Theory of the International Sociological Association. While issues of national ideology are clearly relevant here – as the most recent and most historical contribution to this debate (Hess 1997) attests – in theoretical terms the main differences between Anglo-American and German neofunctionalism relate to the fact that the latter were not compelled to make their way vis-à-vis

the wide swath of micro and macro critiques of traditional Parsonian
ideas. One finds, as a result, much more continuity in German thought
with such core Parsonian ideas as evolutionism and systems theory, and
much less emphasis than American neofunctionalism on contingency
and power, conflict and group interest, and institution building.

15 These emphases – analytic and substantive revision, and critical pluralism
– have forcefully and productively informed the neofunctionalist writings of Sciulli (1992), who aims explicitly at creating a "non-Marxist
critical theory," and Leon Mayhew (1990, 1997), who has drawn upon
Parsons' theory of the societal community to develop a critical alternative to Habermas' approach to the public sphere.

16 This discursive position is elaborated and specified in chapter 2.

17 The most systematic and sophisticated collections of neofunctionalist
work along these lines are Colomy 1990b and 1992a. Colomy's introductions to these volumes (1990c, 1992b) and to his companion volume
on the functionalist tradition (Colomy 1990b) stand out as the most
mature and nuanced presentations of the relation between the functionalist and neofunctionalist traditions. They also represent original "case
studies" of the theoretical model of scientific development that Colomy
and I discuss in chapter 2, as does Colomy and Brown (1992).

18 The two *festschrift* articles I wrote during these latter years – upon the
retirements of Bernard Barber (Alexander 1991b) and S. N. Eisenstadt
(Alexander 1992d) – are revealing examples of the shift vis-à-vis Parsons
that my thinking was undergoing during this time. When I spoke about
Barber and Eisenstadt in my earlier discussions of revisionism (1979
and 1983, pp. 277–8), I had emphasized their continuity with Parsons'
ideas even while they critically responded to its problems. In the later
treatments, I emphasized, instead, the distance between their work and
his, and I tried to highlight the manner in which their recent thinking
had contributed to the solution of problems shared by a wide range of
classical and contemporary work.

19 While all of the essays in Part II are written with reference to "Traditions and Competition" – the general model of the cumulation and
disaccumulation of scientific knowledge that Colomy and I develop in
chapter 2 – they elaborate this argument in very different ways. Chapter
3, "Neofunctionalism Today: Reconstructing a Theoretical Tradition,"
represents a kind of broad case study for the model, presenting an
analysis and overview of neofunctionalist developments in relation both
to Parsons' founding theory and developments in contemporary theory.
By contrast, chapters 4–7 are directed very specifically to debates about
Parsons' early writings. In "Parsons' *Structure* in American Sociology,"
I relate the changing interpretations of *Structure*'s argument to ongoing
historical shifts in what was considered the cutting edge of contemporary theoretical debates, and to sociological theory today. Certainly the

discussions in chapters 5 and 6 are similarly insistent in their efforts to relate *Structure* and other early works to contemporary concerns, but they do so much more in relation to disputes about the historical setting of Parsons' work and its theoretical intent. The chapters are closely interrelated, since both are responses to arguments – made by Donald L. Levine and Charles Camic (who was his student) – that the one-sided, polemical intent of Parsons' supposedly synthetic early writings is disturbingly revealed by the theories he failed to incorporate into his synthesis. While trying to address these claims in their own textual and historical terms, the intent of these essays is, once again, decidedly theoretical and contemporary. (See Levine 1989 for his response to chapter 5 and Camic 1996 for his response to chapter 6.) "Structure, Value, Action" (chapter 7) is written in response to the publication of a previously unpublished but extremely interesting early manuscript Parsons devoted to institutions and organizations. The three sections of this chapter – "Historicist Claims," "Interpretive Disputes," and "Theory Today" – graphically reflect the different concerns I am trying to balance in the essays throughout Part II.

20 See Smith's (1994) penetrating review of Lockwood's book, which, in addition to criticizing Lockwood for his failure to understand the complexity of the late Durkheimian frame, notes the striking paradox that Lockwood fails to acknowledge how heavily the very framework he constructs for criticizing normative functionalism is indebted to Parsons' early work.

21 Mouzelis' rationale (1995, p. 7) reflects rather precisely the new, pragmatic eclecticism I am suggesting here: "Without being a Parsonian, my own theoretical strategy . . . aims more at restructuring rather than transcending functionalism. . . . Following Habermas, we must relate what is happening in theoretical sociology today to the Parsonian 'constitutive' contribution."

References

Alexander, J. C.   1978, Formal and substantive voluntarism in the work of Talcott Parsons: a theoretical and ideological reinterpretation. *American Sociological Review*, 43, pp. 177–98.

—— 1979, Paradigm revision and "Parsonianism." *Canadian Journal of Sociology*, 4, pp. 343–57.

—— 1982–3, *Theoretical Logic in Sociology*, 4 vols. Berkeley and Los Angeles: University of California Press.

—— 1985 (ed.), *Neofunctionalism*. Beverly Hills: Sage.

—— 1987a, The dialectic of individuation and rationalization: Weber's rationalization theory and beyond. In S. Whimster and S. Lash (eds), *Max Weber and Rationality*, London: Allen and Unwin, pp. 185–206.

—— 1987b, Action and its environments. In J. C. Alexander et al. (eds), *The Micro–Macro Link*, Berkeley and Los Angeles: University of California Press, pp. 289–318.

—— 1987c, On the centrality of the classics. In A. Giddens and J. Turner (eds), *Sociological Theory Today*, London: Macmillan, pp. 11–57.

—— 1987d, *Twenty Lectures: Sociological Theory since World War II*. New York: Columbia University Press.

—— 1988a, *Action and Its Environments: Towards a New Synthesis*. New York: Columbia University Press.

—— 1988b, Durkheim's problem and differentiation theory today. In J. C. Alexander, *Action and its Environments*. New York: Columbia University Press, pp. 49–77.

—— 1989, *Structure and Meaning: Relinking Classical Sociology*. New York: Columbia University Press.

—— 1990, Introduction: understanding the "relative autonomy of culture." In J. C. Alexander and S. Seidman (eds), *Culture and Society: Contemporary Debates*. Cambridge: Cambridge University Press, pp. 15–39.

—— 1991a, Bringing democracy back in: universalistic solidarity and the civil sphere. In C. Lemert (ed.), *Intellectuals and Politics: Social Theory in a Changing World*, Beverly Hills: Sage, pp. 157–76.

—— 1991b, Must we choose between criticism and faith? Reflections on the later work of Bernard Barber. *Sociological Theory*, 9(1), pp. 124–30.

—— 1992a, Durkheimian sociology and cultural studies today. In J. C. Alexander (ed.), *Durkheimian Sociology: Cultural Studies*, Cambridge: Cambridge University Press, pp. 1–21.

—— 1992b, Citizen and enemy as symbolic classification: on the polarizing discourse of civil society. In M. Fournier and M. Lamont (eds), *Where Culture Talks: Exclusion and the Making of Society*, Chicago: University of Chicago Press, pp. 289–308.

—— 1992c, Shaky foundations: the presuppositions and internal contradictions of James Coleman's "Foundations of Social Theory." *Theory and Society*, 21, pp. 203–17.

—— 1992d, The fragility of progress: an interpretation of the turn toward meaning in Eisenstadt's later work. *Acta Sociologica*, 35, pp. 85–94.

—— 1994, The return of civil society. *Contemporary Sociology*, 27, pp. 797–803.

—— 1995a, Modern, ante, post and neo: how intellectuals have tried to understand the "Crisis of our time." *New Left Review*, 210, pp. 63–102.

—— 1995b, How "national" is social theory? Critical notes on some worrying trends in the recent theorizing of Richard Munch. *Revue suisse de sociologie*, 21 (3), pp. 541–6. (Expanded version in *Sociologia*, 24 (2–3), pp. 120–38.)

—— 1996, review of Giddens et al., Critical reflections on "Reflexive Modernization," *Theory, Culture and Society*, 13, no. 4, pp. 133–8.

—— forthcoming, Sociology, theories of. *Routledge Encyclopedia of Philosophy*. London: Routledge.

Alexander, J. C., and Colomy, P. (eds) 1990, *Differentiation Theory and Social Change: Historical and Comparative Perspectives*. New York: Columbia University Press.

Alexander, J. C., Giesen, B., Munch, R., and Smelser, N. (eds) 1987, *The Micro–Macro Link*. Berkeley and Los Angeles: University of California Press.

Boden, D., and Zimmerman, D. (eds) 1990, *Talk and Social Structure: Studies in Ethnomethodology and Conversation Analysis*. Cambridge: Polity.

Boltanski, L. 1982, *Les cadres: la formation d'un groupe social*. Paris: Minuit.

Boltanski, L., and Thevenot L. 1991, *De la justification*. Paris: Gallimard.

Bourdieu, P. 1970, La Maison Kabyle ou le monde renversé. In J. Pouillon and P. Maranda (eds), *Echanges et Communications: Melanges offertes à Claude Lévi-Strauss*. Paris and Hague: Mouton, pp. 739–58.

—— 1973, Cultural reproduction and social reproduction. In R. Brown (ed.), *Knowledge, Education, and Cultural Change*. London: Tavistock, pp. 71–112.

—— 1977, *Outline of a Theory of Practice*. Cambridge: Cambridge University Press.

Buxton, W. 1985, *Talcott Parsons and the Capitalist Nation-State: Political Sociology as a Strategic Vocation*. Toronto: University of Toronto Press.

Camic, C. 1991, Talcott Parsons before *The Structure of Social Action*. In C. Camic (ed.), *Talcott Parsons: The Early Essays*, Chicago: University of Chicago Press, pp. ix–lxiix.

—— 1996, Alexander's antisociology. *Sociological Theory*, 14 (2), pp. 172–86.

Chodorow, N. 1978, *The Reproduction of Mothering*. Berkeley and Los Angeles: University of California Press.

Cohen, J., and Arato, A. 1992, *Civil Society and Political Theory*. Boston: MIT Press.

Coleman, J. 1990, *Foundations of Social Theory*. Cambridge, MA: Harvard University Press.

Collins, R. 1975, *Conflict Sociology*. New York: Academic Press.

—— 1986, *Weberian Sociological Theory*. Cambridge: Cambridge University Press.

—— 1990, Conflict theory and the advance of macro-historical sociology. In G. Ritzer (ed.), *Frontiers of Social Theory: The New Syntheses*, New York: Columbia University Press, pp. 68–87.

Colomy, P. 1990a, Revisions and progress in differentiation theory. In J. C. Alexander and P. Colomy (eds), *Differentiation Theory and Social Change*, New York: Columbia University Press, pp. 465–95.

—— 1990b, (ed.), *Neofunctionalist Sociology*. Brookfield, VT: Edward Elgar Publishing.

—— 1990c, Introduction: the neofunctionalist movement. In P. Colomy (ed.), *Neofunctionalist Sociology*, Brookfield, VT: Edward Elgar Publishing, pp. xi–xlii.

—— 1990d, Introduction: the functionalist tradition. In P. Colomy (ed.), *Functionalist Sociology*, Brookfield, VT: Edward Elgar Publishing, pp. xiii–lxii.

—— 1992a, (ed.), *The Dynamics of Social Systems*. London: Sage.

—— 1992b, Introduction. In P. Colomy (ed.), *The Dynamics of Social Systems*, London: Sage, pp. 1–35.

Colomy, P., and Brown, J. D. 1992, Elaboration, revision, polemic, and progress in the Second Chicago School. In G. A. Fine (ed.), *The Second Chicago School*, Chicago: University of Chicago Press.

Dimaggio, P. J., and Powell, W. W. 1991, Introduction. In P. J. Dimaggio and W. W. Powell (eds), *The New Institutionalism in Organizational Analysis*, Ithaca: Cornell University Press, pp. 1–40.

Dubet, F. 1994, *Sociologie de l'expérience*. Paris: Seuil.

Eisenstadt, S. N. 1988, Transcendental vision, center formation, and the role of intellectuals. In L. Greenfeld and M. Martin (eds), *Center: Ideas and Institutions*, Chicago: University of Chicago Press, pp. 96–109.

Elster, J. 1992, *The Cement of Society: A Study of Social Order*. Cambridge: Cambridge University Press.

Gerhardt, U. 1993, *Talcott Parsons on National Socialism*. New York: Adline de Gruyter.

Giddens, A. 1971, *Capitalism and Modern Social Theory*. Cambridge: Cambridge University Press.

—— 1976, *New Rules of Sociological Method*. New York: Basic Books.

—— 1979, *Central Problems in Social Theory*. Berkeley and Los Angeles: University of California Press.

—— 1984, *The Constitution of Societies*. London: Polity.

Gould, M. 1981, Parsons versus Marx: an earnest warning. *Sociological Inquiry*, 51 (3–4), pp. 197–218.

Habermas, J. 1973, *Theory and Practice*. Boston, MA: Beacon Press.

—— 1979, *Communication and the Evolution of Society*, Boston, MA: Beacon Press.

—— 1984, *Theory of Communicative Action*, vol. 1. Boston, MA: Beacon Press.

Hess, A. 1997, Future's past revisited: a critique of Richard Munch's attempt to nationalise social theory, *German Politics and Society*, 15 (1).

Holmwood, J., and Stewart, A. 1991, *Explanation and Social Theory*. New York: St Martin's Press.

Holton, R. J., and Turner, B. S. 1986, Against nostalgia: Talcott Parsons and sociology for the modern world. In R. J. Holton and B. S. Turner

Talcott Parsons on Economy and Society, London: Routledge and Kegan Paul, pp. 207–34.

Joas, H.   1996, *The Creativity of Action.* London: Polity.

Johnson, M. M.   1988, *Strong Mothers, Weak Wives: The Search for Gender Equality.* Berkeley and Los Angeles: University of California Press.

Joutsenoja, M.   1996, *The Calling of Sociology: Early Talcott Parsons and the Construction of a Disciplinary Ship.* Finland: University of Lapland Press.

Levine, D. N.   1989, Parsons' *Structure* (and Simmel) revisited. *Sociological Theory*, 7 (1), pp. 110–17.

Lipset, S. M.   1990, *Continental Divide: The Values and Institutions of the United States and Canada.* New York: Routledge.

Lockwood, D.   1992, *Solidarity and Schism: The "Problem of Disorder" in Durkheimian and Marxist Sociology.* Oxford: Oxford University Press.

Luhmann, N.   1990, The paradox of system differentiation and the evolution of society. In J. C. Alexander and P. Colomy (eds), *Differentiation Theory and Social Change*, New York: Columbia University Press, pp. 409–40.

Mayhew, L.   1990, The differentiation of the solidary public. In J. C. Alexander and P. Colomy (eds), *Differentiation Theory and Social Change*, New York: Columbia University Press, pp. 294–322.

—— 1997, *The New Public.* New York: Cambridge University Press.

Mouzelis, N.   1995, *Sociological Theory: What Went Wrong? Diagnoses and Remedies.* London: Routledge.

Munch, R.   1983, Modern science and technology: differentiation or interpenetration? *International Journal of Comparative Sociology*, 24, pp. 157–75.

—— 1991, American and European social theory: cultural identities and social forms of theory production. *Sociological Perspectives*, 34 (1), pp. 313–35.

—— 1993, The contribution of German social theory to European sociology. In B. Nedelmann and P. Sztompka (eds), *Sociology in Europe: In Search of Identity*, Berlin and New York: Walter de Gruyter, pp. 45–66.

—— 1995, Geopolitics in the guise of universalistic rhetoric. *Revue suisse de sociologie*, 21 (3), pp. 547–55.

Neilson, J. K.   1991, The political orientation of Talcott Parsons: the Second World War and its aftermath. In R. Robertson and B. S. Turner (eds), *Talcott Parsons: Theorist of Modernity*, London: Sage.

Prager, J., and Rustin, M. (eds)   1996, *Psychoanalytic Sociology*, vols 1 and 2. London: Edward Elgar Press.

Pollner, M.   1991, Left of ethnomethodology: the rise and decline of radical reflexivity. *American sociological Review*, 56, pp. 370–80.

Robertson, R.   1990, Globality, global culture, and images of world order. In H. Haferkamp and N. J. Smelser (eds), *Social Change and Modernity*, Berkeley and Los Angeles: University of California Press, pp. 395–411.

Robertson, R., and Turner, B. (eds) 1991, *Talcott Parsons: Theorist of Modernity*. London: Sage.

Roth, A. L. 1995, "Men wearing masks": issues of description in the analysis of ritual. *Sociological Theory*, 13 (3), pp. 301–27.

Schluchter, W. 1981, *The Rise of Western Rationalism: Max Weber's Developmental Theory*. Berkeley and Los Angeles: University of California Press.

—— 1989, *Rationalism, Religion, and Domination: A Weberian Perspective*. Berkeley and Los Angeles: University of California Press.

Sciortino, G. 1993, Un capitolo inedito de La Struttura dell'azione sociale. *Teoria Sociologica*, 1, pp. 13–41.

Sciulli, D. 1992, *Theory of Societal Constitutionalism*. Cambridge: Cambridge University Press.

Smith, P. 1994, Review of David Lockwood, *Solidarity and Schism*. *Contemporary Sociology*, 23 (5), pp. 758–60.

Turner, B. 1986, *Citizenship and Capitalism*. London: Allen and Unwin.

—— 1992, Citizenship, social change, and the neofunctionalist paradigm. In P. Colomy (ed.), *The Dynamics of Social Systems*. London: Sage, pp. 214–37.

Wearne, B. C. 1989, *The Theory and Scholarship of Talcott Parsons to 1951*. Cambridge: Cambridge University Press.

Wenzel, H. 1990, *Die ordnung des Handelns: Talcott Parsons' Theorie des allgemeinen Handlungssystems*. Frankfurt: Suhrkamp.

2

Traditions and Competition: Preface to a Postpositivist Approach to Knowledge Cumulation

Co-written with Paul Colomy

Sociology once aspired to be a cumulative science. Its practitioners once sought to develop and continuously expand verified knowledge about social patterns, social processes, and their underlying causal dynamics. A generation ago, sociologists shared a fervent belief that such cumulation of scientific knowledge required only that scholars "work like hell" testing hypotheses and theories (Cressey, quoted in Laub 1983, Zetterberg 1955). The result of these labor-intensive efforts was a plethora of paradigms, models, concepts, and empirical investigations concerning virtually every imaginable facet of the social world. Like the natural sciences it emulated, sociology seemed to be making indisputable progress (Stinchcombe 1968).

Today, for a large and growing number of sociologists (e.g., S. Turner 1988), this vision of progress seems to have been a mirage. The contrast between the earlier generation's ardent faith in the possibility of scientific growth and the current cohort's profound uncertainty about the ultimate product of their social science labors is stark and dramatic. Skepticism has supplanted faith, and words like malaise, pessimism, disintegration, and disillusionment increasingly color discourse about contemporary sociology (J. Turner 1989a, B. Turner 1989, Collins 1986).

To account for this change is certainly important, and we hope that one by-product of this discussion is the outline of an explanation that adds something to those already offered (e.g., Wiley 1979, 1985, Collins 1986, J. Turner 1989a, S. Turner and J. Turner 1990). This is not, however, our primary concern. This chapter is not an explanation but a response to the demoralization of sociology's orthodox scientific creed. An effective response, we argue, requires an alternative framework for understanding the nature of social science. The growth and decline of social scientific knowledge must be assessed in terms of new and more nuanced criteria than the earlier orthodoxy allowed.

Toward this end, we present the rudiments of a postpositivist model that identifies and explains advances and declines in sociological knowledge. Resting upon an alternative conception of the relationship between theory and fact, the model develops a counterintuitive assumption: it hypothesizes that sociological traditions are the critical units of analysis for assessing the cumulation of social scientific knowledge. Building upon this tradition-bound framework, we outline several distinct patterns of social scientific growth, using important classical and contemporary cases of theoretical and empirical shifts to illustrate the viability of our approach.

Existing Theories of Knowledge Cumulation in the Social Sciences

At present, sociology is being pulled in opposite directions by two competing theories of knowledge cumulation and decline: one a continuing version of the "hard," quasi-natural science orthodoxy, the other a reformulation of the "soft" approach to sociology as a literary and humanistic enterprise. In an important sense this debate revolves around the issue of boundaries between social science and other disciplines.

In an intriguing set of papers, Gieryn (1983) and Gieryn et al. (1985) argue that scientists engage in "boundary-work" to establish and reaffirm a positive public image for science. They do so by invidiously contrasting science with "nonscientific" intellectual activities. Gieryn shows that boundary-work is used strategically to legitimate a scientific discipline's professional claims to authority and its requests for tangible resources. The line demarcating science from nonscience, his studies demonstrate, is highly contingent and markedly responsive to changing historical circumstances.

Gieryn's imagery of a moving line between science and nonscience speaks directly to our concerns about the current condition of sociology. It should be emphasized, however, that these shifting boundaries have cognitive as well as ideological consequences, and we accord the former more attention. Furthermore, the pertinent boundaries are often multiple rather than singular, and proponents frequently frame their arguments in terms of social science's boundaries with two or more disciplines. Finally, intergenre boundary work may be positive as well as negative. Gieryn is primarily concerned with the negative boundary work involved in distinguishing science from nonscience. But it is also instructive, and this is particularly true in the case of the social sciences, to consider the positive boundary work manifest in attempts to forge powerful links between one set of intellectual activities and another.

Positivism (Toulmin 1953, J. Turner 1992) is the philosophical basis for the quasi-natural science view of sociology. Until very recently, positivism not only supplied the dominant theory of how knowledge cumulates and declines in sociology, but it also directly informed virtually all social science practice. Attempting to forge a strong identification with the natural sciences, its proponents asserted that if a boundary between the social and the hard sciences existed at all, it was minuscule. Sociologists were urged to embrace the methodological apparatus and procedures of the more mature sciences and to investigate "social facts" (Durkheim [1894] 1938) with the same dispassionate objectivity that hard scientists purportedly brought to their study of physical ones.

The Frenchman who invented the term *sociology*, August Comte, argued forcefully for the construction of a negative boundary between the science of society and speculative philosophy. Sociology was to be as devoid of metaphysical commitments as were the sciences of nature. This "positive science," as Comte called it, would consist entirely of propositions, laws, and causal statements; interpretations and value judgments would not intrude. As many have noted (e.g., Fuchs and Turner 1986) these efforts to wed the fledgling discipline of sociology to the more prestigious natural sciences represented, in part, a readily transparent maneuver to wrestle legitimacy, status, and material resources from both the established scientific community and the wider public. But "ideal" interests were at stake as well, and in the long run these proved (contra Mullins 1973) even more consequential.

In the century-long development of sociology (Eisenstadt and Curelaru 1976, Shils 1970, S. Turner and J. Turner 1990), this perspective was refined in various ways, and contrasting versions were elaborated. Nonetheless, a broad "positivist persuasion" (Alexander

1982a) continued to provide for sociology a unifying, if rarely articulated creed. That persuasion rested upon a series of postulates that continue to form the basis for its adherents today. First, it presumes that a radical break exists between empirical observations and non-empirical statements. Thus theory is a qualitatively different entity than fact. Second, positivism argues that more highly generalized intellectual issues have no fundamental significance for the practice of an empirically oriented discipline. In its most contemporary rendition, this argument holds that "metatheoretical" discussions and debates dissipate intellectual energies that could be employed more productively in "real" scientific work (see J. Turner 1985, 1989b,[1] in contrast with Ritzer 1988, 1990a, 1990b, Fuhrman and Snizek 1990). Third, the positivist persuasion holds that the elimination of nonempirical referents is a distinguishing feature of the natural sciences and, therefore, that a truly scientific sociology must follow suit if it is to assume an equally scientific stature (Stinchcombe 1968). Fourth, questions of a general theoretical nature, it is argued, can be adequately addressed only in relation to empirical observation. Several additional points follow. With regard to the formulation of social theories, the positivist persuasion argues that the process should be one of induction and generalization from observation, or specification through hypothetico-deduction. Critical empirical tests and falsification are enshrined as the final arbiter in theoretical disputes. Finally, it is held that there is no logical basis for generalized, ongoing, and structured types of scientific disagreement.

The revolutionary development of the natural sciences gave tremendous impetus to the positivist persuasion in social science. At an earlier period in the history of human thought, explanations of nature were deeply embedded in metaphysical and speculative themes. Before physics, there was natural philosophy; before astronomy, there was cosmology. If, as Barnes and Becker (1952) once asked, thinking about nature could make the transition to rationality and positive empiricism, why not thinking about society? Indeed, Durkheim's ([1894] 1938) influential methodological program was premised on the belief that this transition had already been made. In the 20th century, the growing power, prestige, and self-confidence of the natural sciences pushed social science even further in this direction. With the development in the postwar period of sophisticated methodological techniques borrowed directly from the natural sciences, this positivist dream seemed as if it were becoming a reality (e.g., Blalock 1976).

In recent years, however, developments in the history and philosophy of natural science (e.g., Toulmin 1953, 1972; Kuhn 1970) have thrown increasing doubt on the positivist persuasion. These broad intellectual developments have made positive ties between the sciences of nature and the human studies more difficult to sustain in consistent and unambiguous ways. Although there are important differences of emphasis within this antipositivist movement, there is a widely shared understanding that the match between scientific theories and external reality is much more problematic than the positivist persuasion envisioned; indeed, antipositivists hold that theories necessarily involve conjecture and highly contestable interpretations. These investigations have underscored the independent contributions that nonempirical and generalized elements make to the most respected scientific work. Not surprisingly, these trenchant criticisms of positivism have had tremendous ramifications for disciplinary communities (like sociology) that had used the hard sciences as a cognitive and legitimating exemplar (cf. Gouldner 1970). If positivism does not fully explain how knowledge grows in the sciences of nature, then how can it account for the growth of knowledge in sciences that hardly approximate their rigor, precision, and impersonal controls? If positivism does not adequately explain the cumulation of knowledge in the natural sciences, how can its precepts continue to be dutifully accepted as dictums for social science practice?

In sociology, positivism still has articulate and passionate defenders (e.g., J. Turner 1985, 1990, 1992; Collins 1975, 1988, 1992), and it continues to function as an orienting strategy for contemporary sociological work. Even its defenders, however, are well aware that the discipline's stance toward orthodox positivism has changed fundamentally, that what once could be readily assumed about the nature of sociological inquiry has become an object of skepticism, if not downright derision (J. Turner 1989a; Giddens and Turner 1988).

It is within this context of growing skepticism about positivism that reflections about the current "malaise" of sociology should be understood. The discipline's apparent transition from a single to a multiple paradigm science (Ritzer 1975) exacerbated the relativism and self-doubt that accompanied the loss of positivist self-confidence. The proliferation of apparently disconnected subfields (J. Turner 1989a; Dogan and Pahre 1989; Collins 1986) and the ostensible split between theoretical work and a multifarious array of substantive areas (J. Turner 1989b, 1990; B. Turner 1989) contrast sharply with the positivist alliance, shaky though it was, of functionalist theory and quantitative methods that characterized an earlier day.

In contrast with positivism, the other leading perspective about knowledge cumulation in the social science assumes a negative stance toward natural sciences and a positive relation to what it refers to as the "human sciences." Although this position has been available throughout the twentieth century, outside of the exceptional German case it never posed a serious intellectual threat to the proponents of a positivist sociology. That in recent years it has acquired increasing stature and a wider audience must be understood in the context of positivism's decline and sociology's fragmentation.

Against Comte, the German philosopher Wilhelm Dilthey (1976) argued that between the human studies and natural science there stands an unbridgeable gulf. In a more constructive vein, Dilthey sought to build strong links between the social sciences and the arts and literary interpretation. According to what he called the hermeneutic position, social science consists of interpretations and descriptive models; if and when causal statements are attempted, they can emerge only from within the subjective world of the social scientist's own experience.

In this view, social science is a fundamentally different kind of activity from its counterpart in natural science. Its objects of investigation – "social facts" – are either states of mind or conditions that are interpenetrated with them. In order to construct the very objects of a social science, therefore, investigators must draw on their own life experience and on their personal understandings of other human beings. This places a premium not only on observation and measurement but on imagination and speculative thought experiments. Once the objects of social science are conceptually constructed, moreover, it is not easy to verify or falsify in a definitive way the social science theories that generalize from them. Because the personal experiences and evaluative standards of investigators are bound to differ, the embeddedness of social science in value judgments, different personal sensibilities, and political ideology is impossible to avoid.

The human studies position raises serious and unavoidable questions about the possibility of cumulating knowledge about the social world (Friedrichs 1970). Advocates of a hermeneutics approach argue that *understanding* rather than *explanation* should be the major goal of social inquiry. In its weak form (Giddens 1984), hermeneutics allows generalizations, although cautioning that they will be of a fundamentally more tentative character than those in the natural sciences.

In its strong version, hermeneutics declares that the possibility of a universal, objective, and generalizing science is completely illusory and that the human studies should be restricted either to critical analysis from a moral perspective (Gouldner 1970, Haan et al. 1983) or to descriptive accounts of unique or "idiographic" events (Winch 1958).

This alternative to mainstream positivism throws the cumulation of social scientific knowledge into doubt. Because research and theorizing are heavily dependent on the interpretive skills of the individual investigator, the dynamics of social studies are viewed as largely idiosyncratic and essentially unstructured. One logical conclusion is to celebrate subjectivity and relativism (Hollinger 1985) and to abandon the search for general principles that are applicable to a wide range of phenomena in favor of the pursuit of thick description (Geertz 1973) and moral interpretation (Friedrichs 1970, Haan et al. 1983). We will argue against this course.

A Postpositivist Approach to Knowledge Cumulation

Although the hermeneutic, human studies approach supplies a fundamental corrective to positivist orthodoxy, it embraces a framework about which we believe the social sciences must be extremely wary. Philosophically (Alexander 1990a, 1992, Toulmin 1972), this path leads to an extremely vulnerable form of relativism; socially (Alexander 1990b), it can lead to a dangerous and enervating distrust of reason itself.[2] An alternative paradigm that moves beyond both positivism and its antipositivist extreme is necessary if sociology is to avoid the difficulties associated with either of these positions.

In contrast to both of the approaches outlined above, we propose a substantially different model to examine both progressive and regressive developments in sociological knowledge. This perspective is a reaction to both the powerful critique leveled at orthodox positivism by philosophers and historians of science (e.g., Kuhn 1970, Lakatos 1968, 1970, Toulmin 1953) and to the severe limitations the human studies approach would impose on efforts to generate cumulative social knowledge. Unlike human studies, it suggests that social scientific knowledge can grow and, over the long run, certainly has grown. At the same time, its characterization of how knowledge advances and declines is quite different from conventional positivism. Our postpositivist alternative rests on four basic assumptions.

The first holds that sociological work is profitably analyzed as falling along a scientific continuum ranging from abstract, general, and metaphysical elements on the one end to the concrete, empirical, and factual on the other (Toulmin 1953, Alexander 1982a). Other elements of scientific discourse, including ideologies, models, concepts, laws, propositions, methodological assumptions, and observational statements, fall between these endpoints. Even though its overall form may be characterized more by one element than another, every social scientific statement contains implicit or explicit commitments about the nature of every other element on the scientific continuum. The nature and types of social scientific debate are limited by the distinctive character of these elements. The discussion and controversies that mobilize the profession focus on particular elements and emphasize certain kinds of discourses over others.

Second, these basic elements with which sociology is built cannot be formulated in an infinite variety of ways. Although social scientists usually accept one formulation or another without hard and definitive evidence in a natural scientific sense, they do not accept a position without argument and vigorous efforts at intellectual persuasion. Such efforts are rational in the sense that they refer to generalized criteria that themselves must ultimately be justified through open and uncoerced debate (Habermas 1984). Indeed, it is our contention that important social scientific debates largely consist of arguments over the criteria for evaluation that are immanent in different levels of discourse (e.g., criteria about presuppositions, ideologies, models, and methods).

Third – and here we draw from pragmatist thinking about the importance of practical experience (e.g., Dewey 1996 [1916]: pp. 139–51) – in the history of sociological thought the options available at each discursive level have been sharply limited. In terms of what they presuppose about human nature, for example, students of society have usually been preoccupied with the degree to which persons act in either an instrumentally rational fashion or with reference to moral rules or emotional need (Parsons 1937, Ekeh 1974, Alexander 1987a, Stinchcombe 1986). The options for ideological discourse are more historically bounded (Gouldner 1970), but in the modern era at least a continuous argument between relatively coherent conservative, liberal, and radical arguments can be observed. As for models of society (cf. Eisenstadt and Curelaru 1976), the axes of dispute have concerned the relative randomness or coherence of systems, on the one hand, and the relative dynamic versus equilibriating tendencies of systems, on the other. The conflict between interpretive and causal approaches has preoccupied general methodological disputes.

Fourth, although in principle there is no intrinsic relationship between the different elements arrayed across the scientific continuum, there is a clear tendency for certain kinds of commitments to hang together. Thus there are no empirical or logically compelling theoretical reasons for an interpretive methodology to be combined with the commitment to a nonrational or normative understanding of action. Yet, *structural* considerations of theoretical logic must not be confused with the *contingent* issue of historical and empirical probability. In the history of social thought, the commitments made at different scientific levels have not been randomly interrelated. To use a Weberian phrase, there has often appeared to be an "elective affinity" between some theoretical commitments and others (Eisenstadt and Curelaru 1976, Gouldner 1970). Conflict models of society, for example, tend to be more attractive to radical than conservative thinkers, and rationalistic presuppositions are more characteristic of liberals than conservatives. But an even more powerful contingent factor must be considered. Whatever the purely logical possibilities for intrinsic (as compared with elective) affinity between options at different levels, practicing social scientists usually *believe* that certain imperative linkages do exist. The reason is that social science practice unfolds within powerfully stated theoretical traditions, and every tradition stipulates the relationship between theoretical elements in a sharply defined way (Tiryakian 1979, 1986, Shils 1970, Wiley 1979, Seidman 1983).

In our view, the various forms of sociology are carried forward by traditions, which are typically called "schools."[3] We would define sociology, indeed, as a multilevel rational- pragmatic discourse about society and its constituent units, with the patterns and directions of that discourse being conditioned by the discipline's leading traditions. The elements of this definition form a paradox but not a contradiction. Traditions, of course, are patterns of perception and behavior that are followed not, in the first instance, because of their intrinsic rationality, not because they have "proven their worth," but because they are inherited from the past. The traditional status of social scientific schools confers upon them prestige and authority, which is reinforced because they are typically upheld by organizational power and supported with material resources (Mullins 1973, Fuchs and Turner 1986). These considerations do not, however, mitigate the rational aspirations of social science, its sharply delimited structure of debate, and its often extraordinary practical ability to approximate and understand social reality.

Like other traditions, the rational movements of social science are founded by intellectually charismatic figures, whose followers believe that their powerful attraction stems from their awe-inspiring scientific prowess. At the beginning of a discipline, such great intellectual figures are regarded as classical founders (Alexander 1987b); at later points, they are accorded quasi-classical status and are treated simply as the founders of powerful disciplinary traditions. This organizational fact shows in yet another way why social science practice cannot be understood simply as the confrontation between scientist and social reality. Social reality is never confronted in itself. Because perception is mediated by the discursive commitments of traditions, social scientific formulations are channelled within relatively standardized, paradigmatic forms. The matrix social scientists inhabit need not be drawn from a single tradition or be wholly of a piece, but inhabit it they must, aware of it or not.

Although traditionalism implies habitual behavior, it need not imply stasis or lack of change. In social science, this openness to change is intensified by the universalism of institutionalized standards that mandate impersonal rationality and push against the particularism of a traditionalist response (Merton [1942] 1973). Social science traditions define themselves by staking out theoretical cores that are highly resistant to change, but there are substantial areas surrounding these nuclei that are subject to continuous variation (Lakatos 1968, 1970, Kuhn 1970). In ideal-typical terms, changes in the peripheral areas of traditions can be conceived as proceeding along three lines: *elaboration, proliferation*, and *revision* (Wagner 1984, Wagner and Berger 1985, Berger et al. 1989, Alexander 1979, Colomy 1986, 1990). Although these lines of development present themselves as loyally carrying out traditional commitments, they differ in the creativeness with which they pursue this task. Because elaborative and proliferative sociological work proceeds from the assumption that the original tradition is internally consistent and relatively complete, they aim primarily at refinement and expansion of scope. In revisionist work, by contrast, there is a greater sense of the vulnerabilities of the established tradition; in the guise of loyal specification, an often implicit effort is made to address these strains and to offer formulations that can resolve them (Alexander 1979, Colomy 1986, 1990).

Elaboration, proliferation, and revision are lines of specification that recur periodically in a tradition's history, not only in the period of routinization that immediately follows the charismatic founding but in the wake of the powerful reformulations that must emerge if a tradition is to remain intact. The latter possibility points to a fourth ideal-typical form of theoretical change. Insofar as cores themselves undergo substantial shifts – without abandoning their association with the overarching tradition – there occurs a theoretical activity that can be called *reconstruction* (Alexander and Colomy 1990b). Reconstruction differs from elaboration, proliferation, and revision in that differences with the founder of the tradition are clearly acknowledged and openings to other traditions are explicitly made. Reconstruction can revive a theoretical tradition, even while it creates the opportunity for the kind of development out of which new traditions are born (e.g., Habermas 1979).

The most far-reaching form of scientific change carries the reconstructive impulse farther still and brings us back full circle to the intellectually charismatic founders of sociological traditions. *Tradition-creation* involves generating new schools organized around historically distinctive cores. The essence of tradition-creation is the synthesis of elements drawn from several existing and often competing intellectual paradigms, with the aim of generating the theoretical core of a new school. Marx's reconfiguration of elements from Hegelianism, the Enlightenment, French socialism, and British political economy represents the best documented (Alexander 1982b) instance of this form of scientific change.

One should be careful not to see these ideas – elaboration, proliferation, revision, reconstruction, and tradition-creation – as presenting either a necessary historical sequence or a scale of theoretical significance. As for sequence, with one important exception to be noted below, different types of change weave in and out of both the history of sociology and the historical course of each particular tradition. As for significance, most of the greatest minds in social science never made the transition from reconstruction to tradition-creation. Many who attempted to make the transition, moreover, were much the worse for it. The works of Von Wiese are long forgotten; the writings of Gramsci, Lukács, Mannheim, and Mauss continue to be intently pursued.

Traditions can also be destroyed (*tradition-deconstruction*). This does not happen because core and peripheral commitments are falsified in the narrow sense. It occurs because these commitments have become delegitimated in the eyes of the scientific community. Delegitimation leads to the withdrawal of trust from core commitments. Only after core commitments are abandoned can fundamental falsification be understood as having occurred. Even in this situation, however, traditions do not so much disappear as become latent; the possibility always remains (cf. Eisenstadt and Curelaru 1976) that they may be picked up again.

Elaboration, proliferation, revision, reconstruction, tradition-creation, and tradition-deconstruction describe the closeness of fit between subsequent theoretical and empirical work and an original tradition. It is important to emphasize that they do not describe the degree of real scientific advance. Elaboration, for example, may be thin or thick, to redeploy Geertz's (1973) ethnographic standard. Traditions may be enriched and elevated by the processes of theoretical change we have identified, but they may also be impoverished and simplified, robbed of their sophistication, and denuded of some of their most powerful intellectual sustenance. If social science change can be progressive, therefore, it can be regressive as well.

Over the long run, the dynamics of traditions within a disciplinary community (cf. Shils 1970) – the shifting fortunes of its theoretical positions – are not determined by the theoretical effectiveness and sophistication of the respective positions, nor by their objective empirical scope. Shifts in a discipline's "scientific sensibility" (Alexander 1986), usually precipitated by significant social and global developments (e.g., the anti-Vietnam War movement, the Civil Rights struggle, and the push for democracy in Eastern Europe), put different questions on the floor; they place a premium on the creation of different modes of discourse. Indeed, it is often only after highly generalized and discursive commitments (e.g., Gouldner 1970) are made to a new approach that increased theoretical sophistication and empirical scope emerge. It is in this sense that one can speak less of social scientific "development" than of social scientific "movements." Disciplines (contra Merton 1968) should not be understood as being organized primarily by specialties defined by their empirical objects of investigation (i.e., into middle-range subfields like deviance, political sociology, and stratification). The deep structure of a discipline (Toulmin 1972) consists of the networks and literatures that are produced by the contact between empirical objects, ongoing traditions, and new disciplinary movements.

Traditions and Competition

Competition plays a critically significant role in the cumulation and decline of social scientific knowledge. Indeed, according to our model, social science does not grow simply because of the compulsion to understand empirical reality, nor can its growth be measured merely in relation to the expansion of empirical knowledge or conceptual scope. The primary motor of social scientific change is a pragmatic one – conflict and competition between and within traditions. The primary reference points for measuring scientific growth are established by the relations between traditions and by signposts internal to a given tradition itself. Instead of speaking about theoretical or empirical progress per se, one must speak of relative explanatory and theoretical success, vis-à-vis one's own tradition or competing ones (B. Turner 1989).

Every ideal-typical pattern of knowledge cumulation and decline is driven by competition. Implicitly or explicitly, every scientific statement claims to be more incisive or compelling on some point(s) than previous work. Accordingly, potential contributions are always partially assessed by comparison to earlier efforts.

Competition occurs in both discursive genres, and it occurs between and within traditions. At the level of generalized discourse, competition proceeds through disputes centered about a tradition's residual categories, its analytic and empirical breadth, its theoretical acumen in interpreting the classics, its avowed or implied ideological stance, its resonance with the epoch's reigning issues and social movements, its logical coherence (or lack thereof) as expressed through its conceptual schemes, and its utility for empirical investigation. At the level of research programs, competition is organized around rival attempts to explain empirical structures and processes regarded as significant by the discipline. In either case, a tradition advances when it issues statements deemed superior relative to comparable work produced by other schools.

At any given time, the field on which traditions compete is organized hierarchically.[4] Traditions are invidiously compared, and a small subset are accorded high levels of prestige. Such recognition is contingent on intermittent displays of scholarly virtuosity. Advantages accruing to those affiliated with prestigious traditions (e.g., greater publishing opportunities and a larger audience for those publications) unquestionably can facilitate the production of first-rate work. At the same time, however, the more renowned a school, the more likely its products will be subject to rigorous scrutiny. This disciplinary judgment that a tradition is especially illustrious encourages competing schools to frame their discussions as critical alternatives to the reigning approach. Proponents of less esteemed paradigms are

constrained to demonstrate their tradition's relative merit by highlighting its theoretical and empirical strengths vis-à-vis more hegemonic
paradigms. Thus a recent discussion of the Chicago school's "second
generation" (i.e., the contributions of many of the sociologists who
received their PhDs from the University of Chicago's Department of
Sociology between 1945 and 1960) indicates that Chicago sociology's
generalized discourse as well as its research programs in role theory,
deviance, social problems, the professions, formal organizations, and
collective behavior and social movements were presented as critical
responses to the then prominent functionalist tradition (Colomy and
Brown 1992).

When a tradition is challenged, and especially when the challenge
is regarded as legitimate and meritorious, its proponents are obliged
to respond. For a variety of reasons, however, an insular strategy may
be embraced with advocates presenting only occasional, perfunctory
rebuttals or dismissing virtually all outside criticism as uninformed
and unwarranted. In the short run, an insular strategy can sustain
stability and some intellectual progress, primarily through elaboration
and proliferation. In the long term, however, isolationism tends to
delegitimate a tradition in the eyes of the disciplinary community and
leads to its eventual eclipse.

Competition spurs incomplete or incipient traditions to devise
more comprehensive formulations. Research programs that have not
yet devised a complementary body of generalized discourse are highly
vulnerable to metatheoretical critiques explicating the implicit and
often restrictive assumptions upon which the research is premised.
Thus despite the impressive empirical advances generated by the status
attainment program, its failure to develop an explicit metatheoretical
rationale led some to discredit it as atheoretical (e.g., Buroway 1977,
Coser 1975) and others to suggest that the generalized discursive questions raised about the program have precipitated a crisis in status
attainment research (Colclough and Horan 1983).[5] The most effective response to such charges, of course, is to articulate and defend
the analytic grounds of the research program. Likewise, critics frequently assail incipient traditions that emphasize generalized discourse
to the apparent neglect of empirical research. In this context, Giddens's
analytically innovative and sophisticated structuration theory has been
indicted for its failure to devise a compelling research program
(Gregson 1989, Muller 1990). Again, the most viable rejoinder is to
demonstrate the tradition's empirical fruitfulness by launching research
programs in several specialty areas. This retort is most persuasive,

moreover, if the new research proves superior to extant programs affiliated with long-standing traditions. For instance, Saks (1983) rebukes neo-Marxists and neo-Weberians for their continuing dependence on the patrimony of discursive attacks leveled against earlier functionalist and interactionist treatments of the professions rather than devising a viable research program of their own. For more established traditions, competitors' critiques and alternative explanatory models constitute a conceptual and research agenda that the focal school can address through elaboration, proliferation, revision, and/or reconstruction of both its genres. Recent revisions of the functionalist research program on social change, for example, are self-consciously presented as rejoinders to the charges leveled by the theory's critics (Colomy 1986, Alexander and Colomy 1990a).

Because established traditions constantly change and new schools frequently emerge, the boundaries linking and separating paradigms are regularly subject to reassessment. Typically cast as discussions of the similarities and differences between competing schools and usually pitched at the level of generalized discourse,[6] this intertradition boundary work – whether between symbolic interaction and ethnomethodology (Zimmerman and Wieder 1970, Gallant and Kleinman 1983), neofunctionalism and structuration theory (Muller 1990), feminism and Parsonian theory (Johnson 1988, 1989), Marxist and Weberian theory (Antonio and Glassman 1985, Wiley 1987), or postmodernist and critical theory (Habermas 1981, 1987, Kellner 1989, 1990) – can clarify and reaffirm existing divisions, introduce alterations in the intellectual core of one or more traditions, and/or, by highlighting previously unrecognized commonalities, lay the groundwork for syntheses of variable scope between approaches once regarded as largely irreconcilable.

As the preceding remarks imply, traditions are not hermetically sealed and competition between them can produce some convergence in both generalized discourse and research programs. When members of antagonistic schools address a similar problem and draw on some of the same intellectual resources to resolve it, their theorizing and research frequently reveal agreements alongside continuing differences. Highlighting common themes in the work of scholars affiliated with several rival approaches, Ritzer (1990c), for example, detects a diffuse, cross-tradition movement toward a synthetic position on the micro–macro issue. Commonalities can also emerge through expropriation, which occurs when proponents of a given approach openly appropriate an idea developed by competitors and employ it, usually with significant modifications, to extend their home traditions. Collins (1985, 1988), for instance, adopts the neofunctionalist notion of multidimensionality to advance a more inclusive version of conflict theory.

Over time, competition engenders significant changes on the disciplinary field. Established and highly regarded traditions are discredited and sometimes disappear, lowly ranked schools gain prominence, and new paradigms flourish. The alterations reflect schools' varying abilities to fashion persuasive responses to both the critiques issued by rival traditions and shifts in disciplinary sensibility stemming from encompassing global and societal transformations. The difficulties in responding satisfactorily to these recurring challenges are enormous, and it is not surprising that most traditions experience periods of crisis or that many expire shortly after they are initiated. To persist, traditions must change and those that last for more than a generation are almost always substantially revised and reconstructed. Antonio (1990) suggests that Marxism has been periodically declared intellectually bankrupt only to renew and reconstitute itself and reappear phoenix-like on the disciplinary scene. We would add only that Antonio's characterization is applicable to every enduring social scientific tradition.

The discussion thus far has proceeded as if each tradition was an intellectually consensual community. By definition there is considerable consensus among a school's adherents, but this does not prevent serious disagreements from arising. Indeed, most schools contain two or more tradition segments[7] that although affiliated with the same encompassing framework and pledging scientific fealty to the same classic progenitor(s) nevertheless make disparate commitments at one or more levels of the scientific continuum. Although personal considerations undoubtedly play an important role and the availability of resources such as stable employment, students, funding, and publishing outlets exert a powerfully pragmatic conditioning effect, the fault lines along which tradition segments arise and the intellectual grounds used to support them are most readily understood as fundamental disagreements about the school's generalized discourse and research programs. For example, Meltzer and Petras (1970, see also Meltzer et al. 1975, Buban 1986, Reynolds 1990) maintain that though the (old) Iowa and Chicago schools of symbolic interactionism shared many assumptions about social action and order and acknowledged Mead as the founding figure of their school, their conflicting assumptions about methodology, determinism, and the nature of the self prompted the formation of distinct tradition segments.

Virtually every enduring tradition generates competing tradition segments; the longer a school persists the more segments it will create. Perhaps no social scientific tradition can stake a more rightful claim to longevity than Marxism and few if any have produced a larger number of segments, with distinctive renditions branching off at nearly every point along the scientific continuum (e.g., Alexander 1982b, pp. 328–70; Bottomore 1975, 1978, 1988, Bottomore and Goode 1978, Anderson 1976, 1983, Antonio 1990, Aronson 1985).

Relations among tradition segments are always competitive, but the competition ranges from the friendly and mutually enriching type to more divisive forms that precipitate rancorous, public breaks and the formation of extremely hostile moieties. Even in the latter case, however, competition between segments can be among the most productive modes of scholarly exchange, resulting in significant contributions to every type of knowledge cumulation. Because all parties are well versed in the tradition's generalized discourse and research programs and are cognizant of the school's analytic and empirical shortcomings, disputants can prepare astute critiques and equally informed replies. In some instances, a segment's proponents may adopt an insular strategy in reaction to another's challenges, but such isolation is even more difficult to sustain among competing segments than it is between rival traditions.

The tendency to structure the disciplinary field hierarchically recurs among tradition segments. Depending on the number of competing segments within a school, there is a tendency to cast one or two segments in starring roles, while relegating others to much smaller parts. This invidious division places the intellectual burden of proof on the latter camp and in order to demonstrate their relative scientific prowess, insurgent segments can be expected to emphasize how their contributions account for anomalies that more established segments purportedly cannot explain.

Founders of traditions that subsequently splinter into competing strands are usually associated with the school's most preeminent segment. So long as the founder continues to produce, it is unlikely that challengers will supplant his or her segment's privileged position.[8] Successful challenging segments more typically appear either after the founder's death or during dramatic shifts in disciplinary sensibility.

The disciplinary community as a whole tends to minimize differences between competing segments, treating a particular approach as a single and more or less coherent whole. Maynard and Clayman

(1991) note that despite the very sharp conflicts within ethnomethodology, commentators usually treat it as a unitary perspective. Apart from the intellectual commonalities and personal relations that may bind adherents of rival segments, this disciplinary perception engenders an externally imposed sense of shared fate that encourages various forms of what might be called tradition teamwork (Goffman 1959) vis-à-vis the larger discipline. That teamwork is manifest in founding scholarly associations, securing official recognition for specialty areas deemed crucial to the tradition, engaging in collaborative publishing ventures, and defending the work of competing segments from criticism by adherents of rival traditions.

Finally, it is important to recognize that although competition generates winners and losers,[9] it is hardly an infallible mechanism for advancing knowledge. Competition between and within schools is as much a sociological process as an epistemological one, and the pragmatic dynamics that propel it can impede genuine knowledge cumulation. Plainly put, the traditions or tradition segments that win in the social sciences do not always have the best arguments. The dynamics of fashion sometimes figure prominently in the rapid ascent of new traditions. Fashionable schools are not exempt from criticism – if nothing else scholarly communities are flush with critics – but the questions raised about the new approach may have little impact, at least in the short term, on the disciplinary community's assessment. On the other hand, the traditions or tradition segments that lose do not always advance the least defensible arguments. The critical effect of competition between perspectives is vastly underestimated, as is the role that general discourse plays in stimulating and framing the ongoing work within research programs.

If social science is once again to become a legitimate public activity, this crisis of confidence, which at its roots is no less than a crisis of confidence in reason itself (Alexander 1992), must be resolved. Our perspective offers the possibility that there are secure epistemological and, indeed, moral foundations for advances in the social sciences. For such a substantial conception of progress to be maintained, however, positivism must be fundamentally reconstructed and a new model of social scientific growth erected in its place.

Notes

1 J. Turner (1990) has tempered his antipathy to metatheory and suggested that it is useful "when the goal is to produce scientific sociology"

(p. 50). However, he remains highly critical of other forms of metatheory that in his view do not advance sociology as a science.

2 These broader ramifications are briefly discussed in the concluding section of this chapter and in greater detail in Colomy and Brown (1992).

3 This section elaborates an argument we have developed elsewhere (Alexander and Colomy 1990b).

4 Furthermore, competition is affected by the unequal distribution of material and symbolic resources across traditions that condition the production and reception of sociological discourse. These issues are examined in Colomy and Brown (1992).

5 Horan (1978) disputes the contention that status attainment research is atheoretical. He contends that the program is premised on a functionalist conception of social structure – one he regards as analytically restrictive and, therefore, vulnerable to criticism on discursive grounds.

6 Intertradition boundary work also occurs at the level of research programs. Handel (1979), for instance, outlines a synthesis of functionalist and interactionist treatments of the structure and dynamics of social roles. However, in this case, as in many other efforts to integrate rival research programs, the proposed synthesis proceeds by specifying complementarities in the generalized theoretical logic of each program. Similarly, attempts to highlight differences between competing research programs – e.g., Collins's (1971) contrast between functionalists, and conflict theorists' studies of education – point to disparities in each program's underlying assumptions. The central point is that generalized discourse figures prominently in most intertradition boundary work, even when the connections or discrepancies between particular research programs are the primary concern.

7 The notion of tradition segments is adapted from Bucher and Strauss's (1961) discussion of professional segments. Their analysis highlights the diversity and conflict within professions and suggests that competition between segments is an important source of change in professional communities.

8 When a splinter group competes on equal (or nearly equal) terms with the founder, it is often because the insurgent segment is itself organized around an intellectually charismatic challenger.

9 Competition can also produce stalemates. Focusing on rival research programs, Wagner (1984) argues that because competitors disagree about (a) the criteria appropriate for evaluating competing theories, (b) how to apply criteria they agree are appropriate, (c) the relevance of existing data, and (d) the interpretation of the data they agree is relevant, and because comparisons of competing theories tend to degenerate into irresolvable metatheoretical disputes, "competition is not a very efficient form of theory growth" (p. 75). It should be noted that in subsequent work Wagner has formulated a more comprehensive statement, arguing that in the context of contesting theoretical research programs competition can

advance social scientific knowledge (Wagner and Berger 1985, Wagner 1984, pp. 104–5).

References

Alexander, J. C. 1979, Paradigm revision and "Parsonianism." *Canadian Journal of Sociology,* 4, pp. 343–57.

—— 1982a, *Positivism, Presuppositions, and Current Controversies.* Berkeley: University of California Press.

—— 1982b, *The Antinomies of Classical Thought: Marx and Durkheim.* Berkeley: University of California Press.

—— 1986, Science, sense, and sensibility. *Theory and Society,* 15, pp. 443–63.

—— 1987a, Action and its environments. In J. C. Alexander, B. Giesen, R. Munch, and N. J. Smelser (eds), *The Micro–Macro Link,* Berkeley: University of California Press, pp. 239–318.

—— 1987b, On the centrality of the classics. In A. Giddens and J. Turner (eds), *Social Theory Today,* London: Polity Press, pp. 11–57.

—— 1990a, Beyond the epistemological dilemma: general theory in a postpositivist mode. *Sociological Forum,* 5(4), pp. 531–44.

—— 1990b, Between progress and apocalypse: social theory and the dream of reason in the twentieth century. In J. Alexander and P. Sztompka (eds), *Rethinking Progress,* London: Unwin Hyman, pp. 15–38.

—— 1992, General theory in the postpositivist mode: the "epistemological dilemma" and the search for present reason." In S. Seidman and D. Wagner (eds), *Postmodernism and General Social Theory,* New York: Basil Blackwell, pp. 322–67.

Alexander, J. C., and Colomy, P. (eds) 1990a, *Differentiation Theory and Social Change.* New York: Columbia University Press.

—— 1990b, Neofunctionalism today: reconstructing a theoretical tradition. In G. Ritzer (ed), *Frontiers of Social Theory: The New Syntheses,* New York: Columbia University Press, pp. 33–67.

Anderson, P. 1976, *Considerations on Western Marxism.* London: NLB.

—— 1983, *In the Tracks of Historical Materialism.* London: Verso.

Antonio, R. J. 1990, The decline of the grand narrative of emancipatory modernity: crisis or renewal in neo-Marxian theory. In G. Ritzer (ed.), *Frontiers of Social Theory: The New Syntheses,* New York: Columbia University Press, pp. 86–116.

Antonio, R. J., and Glassman, R. M. (eds) 1985, *A Weber–Marx Dialogue.* Lawrence: University Press of Kansas.

Aronson, R. 1985, Historical materialism, answer to Marxism's crisis. *New Left Review* 152, pp. 74–94.

Barnes, H. E., and Becker, H. 1952, *Social Thought from Lore to Science,* 2nd edn. Washington, DC: Harran Press.

Berger, J., Wagner, D. G., and Zelditch, M. Jr. 1989, Theory growth, social processes and metatheory. In J. Turner (ed.), *Theory Building in Sociology*, Newbury Park, CA: Sage, pp. 19–42.

Blalock, H. 1976, Implicit theories underlying macro-level data analysis: Measurement errors and omitted variables. In T. Bottomore and R. Nisbet (eds), *New Directions in Sociology*, Newton Abbot: David & Charles, pp. 76–100.

Bottomore, T. 1975, *Marxist Sociology*, New York: Holmes & Meier.

—— 1978, Marxism and sociology. In T. Bottomore and R. Nisbet (eds), *A History of Sociological Analysis*, New York: Basic Books, pp. 118–48.

—— (ed.) 1988, *Interpretations of Marx*. Oxford: Basil Blackwell.

Bottomore, T., and Goode, P. (eds) 1978, *Austro-Marxism*. Oxford: Clarendon.

Buban, S. L. 1986, Studying social process: the Chicago and Iowa schools revisited. *Studies in Symbolic Interaction*, 2(Suppl.), pp. 25–38.

Bucher, R. and Strauss, A. 1961, Professions in process. *American Journal of Sociology*, 66, pp. 325–34.

Buroway, M. 1977, Social structure, homogenization, and the process of status attainment in the United States and Great Britain. *American Journal of Sociology*, 86, pp. 618–29.

Colclough, G., and Horan, P. M. 1983, The status attainment paradigm: an application of a Kuhnian perspective. *The Sociological Quarterly*, 24, pp. 25–42.

Collins, R. 1971, Functional and conflict theories of educational stratification. *American Sociological Review*, 36, pp. 1002–19.

—— 1975, *Conflict Sociology*. New York: Academic Press.

—— 1985, Jeffrey Alexander and the search for multi dimensional theory. *Theory and Society*, 14, pp. 877–92.

—— 1986, Is 1980s sociology in the doldrums? *American Journal of Sociology* 91, pp. 1336–55.

—— 1988, *Theoretical Sociology*. New York: Harcourt Brace Jovanovich.

—— 1992, The confusion of the modes of sociology. In S. Seidman and D. Wagner (eds), *Postmodern and General Social Theory*, New York: Basil Blackwell, pp. 179–98.

Colomy, P. 1986, Recent developments in the functionalist approach to change. *Sociological Focus*, 19, pp. 139–58.

—— 1990, Revisions and progress in differentiation theory. In J. C. Alexander and P. Colomy (eds) *Differentiation Theory and Social Change*, New York: Columbia University Press, pp. 465–95.

Colomy, P., and Brown, J. D. 1992, Elaboration, revision, polemic, and progress in the Second Chicago School. In G. A. Fine (ed.), *The Second Chicago School of Sociology*, Chicago: University of Chicago Press, pp. 17–81.

Coser, L. A. 1975, Presidential address: two methods in search of a substance. *American Sociological Review*, 40, pp. 691–700.

Dewey, J.   1996, [1916] *Democracy and Education*. New York: Free Press.

Dilthey, W.   1976, An introduction to the human studies. In H. P. Richman (ed.), *Dilthey: Selected Writings*, Cambridge: Cambridge University Press, pp. 159–67.

Dogan, M. and Pahre, R.   1989, Fragmentation and recombination of the social sciences. *Studies in Comparative International Development*, 24, pp. 1–18.

Durkheim, E. [1894] 1938, *The Rules of Sociological Method*. New York: Free Press.

Eisenstadt, S. N. and Curelaru, M.   1976, *The Forms of Sociology: Paradigms and Crises*. New York: John Wiley.

Ekeh, P. K.   1974, *Social Exchange Theory: The Two Traditions*. Cambridge, MA: Harvard University Press.

Friedrichs, R. W.   1970, *A Sociology of Sociology*. New York: Free Press.

Fuchs, S. and Turner, J. H.   1986, What makes a science mature? Organization control in scientific production. *Sociological Theory*, 4, pp. 143–50.

Fuhrman, E. and Snizek, W.   1990, Neither proscience nor antiscience: metasociology as dialogue, *Sociological Forum*, 5, pp. 17–31.

Gallant, M. J. and Kleinman, S.   1983, Symbolic interactionism versus ethnomethodology. *Symbolic Interaction*, 6, pp. 1–18.

Geertz, C.   1973, Thick description: toward an interpretive theory of culture. In C. Geertz, *The Interpretation of Cultures*, New York: Basic Books, pp. 3–30.

Giddens, A.   1984, *The Constitution of Societies*. Oxford: Polity Press.

Giddens, A. and J. Turner,   1988, Introduction. In A. Giddens and J. Turner (eds), *Social Theory Today*, Oxford: Polity Press, pp. 1–10.

Gieryn, T. F.   1983, Boundary-work and the demarcation of science from nonscience: strains and interests in professional ideologies of scientists. *American Sociological Review*, 48, pp. 781–95.

Gieryn, T. F., Bevins, G. M., and Zehr, S. C.   1985, Professionalization of American scientists: public science in the creation/evolution trials. *American Sociological Review*, 50, pp. 392–409.

Goffman, E.   1959, *The Presentation of Self*. New York: Doubleday.

Gouldner, A.   1970, *The Coming Crisis of Western Sociology*. New York: Basic Books.

Gregson, N.   1989, On the (ir)relevance of structuration theory to empirical research. In D. Held and J. B. Thompson (eds), *Social Theory of Modern Societies: Anthony Giddens and His Critics*, Cambridge: Cambridge University Press, pp. 235–48.

Haan, N., Bellah, R. N., Rabinow, P., and Sullivan, W. N.   1983, *Social Science as Moral Inquiry*. New York: Columbia University Press.

Habermas, J.   1979, Toward the reconstruction of historical materialism. In J. Habermas (ed.), *Communication and the Evolution of Society*, Boston: Beacon Press, pp. 130–77.

—— 1981, Modernity versus postmodernity. *New German Critique*, 22, pp. 3–14.

—— 1984, *Theory of Communicative Action*, vol. 1. Boston: Beacon Press.

—— 1987, *Lectures on the Philosophical Discourse of Modernity*. Cambridge, MA: MIT Press.

Handel, W.   1979, Normative expectations and the emergence of meaning as solutions to problems: convergence of structural and interactionist views. *American Journal of Sociology*, 84, pp. 855–81.

Hollinger, R. (ed.)   1985, *Hermeneutics and Practice*. South Bend, IN: Notre Dame University Press.

Horan, P. M.   1978, Is status attainment research atheoretical? *American Sociological Review*, 43, pp. 534–41.

Johnson, M. M.   1988, *Strong Mothers, Weak Wives*. Berkeley: University of California Press.

—— 1989, Feminism and the theories of Talcott Parsons. In R. Wallace (ed.), *Feminism and Sociological Theory*, Newbury Park, CA: Sage, pp. 101–18.

Kellner, D.   1989, *Critical Theory, Marxism, and Modernity*. Cambridge and Baltimore: Polity Press and John Hopkins University Press.

—— 1990, The postmodern turn. In G. Ritzer (ed.), *Frontiers of Social Theory: The New Syntheses*, New York: Columbia University Press, pp. 255–86.

Kuhn, T.   1970, *The Structure of Scientific Revolutions*, 2nd edn. Chicago: University of Chicago Press.

Lakatos, I.   1968, Criticism and the methodology of scientific research programmes. *Proceedings of the Aristotelian Society*, 69, pp. 149–86.

—— 1970, Falsification and the methodology of scientific research programmes. In I. Lakatos and A. Musgrave (eds), *Criticism and the Growth of Knowledge*, New York: Cambridge University Press, pp. 91–196.

Laub, J. L.   1983, Interview with Donald R. Cressey. In J. L. Laub, *Criminology in the Making*, Boston: Northwestern University Press, pp. 131–65.

Maynard, D. W., and Clayman, S. E.   1991, The diversity of ethnomethodology. *Annual Review of Sociology*, 17, pp. 385–419.

Meltzer, B. N. and Petras, J. W.   1970, The Chicago and Iowa schools of symbolic interactionism. In T. Shibutani (ed.), *Human Nature and Collective Behavior*, New Brunswick, NJ: Transaction, pp. 3–17.

Meltzer, B. N., Petras, J. W., and Reynolds, L. T.   1975, *Symbolic Interactionism: Genesis, Varieties, and Criticism*. London: Routledge & Kegan Paul.

Merton, R. K.   1968. On sociological theories of the middle range. In R. K. Mertan (ed.), *Social Theory and Social Structure* (enlarged edn.). New York: Free Press, pp. 39–72.

—— [1942] 1973, The normative structure of science. In N. W. Storer (ed.), *The Sociology of Science*, Chicago: University of Chicago Press, pp. 267–78.

Muller, H.   1990, Neofunctionalism or structuration theory. Paper presented at the annual meeting of the International Sociological Association, Madrid, Spain, July 11.

Mullins, N.   1973, *Theories and Theory Groups in Contemporary American Sociology*. New York: Harper & Row.

——   1983, Theories and theory groups revisited. *Sociological Theory*, 1, pp. 319–37.

Parsons, T.   1937, *The Structure of Social Action*. New York: Free Press.

Reynolds, L. T.   1990, *Interactionism: Exposition and Critique*. Dix Hills, NY: General Hall.

Ritzer, G.   1975, *Sociology: A Multiple Paradigm Science*. Boston: Allyn & Bacon.

——   1988, Sociological metatheory: a defense of a subfield by a delineation of its parameters. *Sociological Theory*, 6, pp. 187–200.

——   1990a, (ed.), *Frontiers of Social Theory: The New Syntheses*. New York: Columbia University Press.

——   1990b, Metatheorizing in sociology. *Sociological Forum*, 5, pp. 3–15.

——   1990c, Micro–macro linkage in sociological theory: applying a metatheoretical tool. In G. Ritzer (ed.), *Frontiers of Social Theory: The New Syntheses*, New York: Columbia University Press, pp. 347–70.

Saks, M.   1983, Removing the blinkers? A critique of recent contributions to the sociology of professions. *Sociological Review*, 31, pp. 1–21.

Seidman, S.   1983, *Liberalism and the Origins of European Social Theory*. Berkeley: University of California Press.

Shils, E.   1970, Tradition, ecology, and institutions in the history of sociology. *Daedalus*, 99, pp. 760–825.

Stinchcombe, A. L.   1968, *Constructing Social Theories*. New York: Harcourt Brace Jovanovich.

——   1986, Reason and rationality. *Sociological Theory*, 4, pp. 151–66.

Tiryakian, E. A.   1979, The significance of schools in the development of sociology. In W. E. Snizek, E. R. Fuhrman, and M. K. Miller (eds), *Contemporary Issues in Theory and Research*, Westport, CT: Greenwood, pp. 211–23.

——   1986, Hegemonic schools and the development of sociology: rethinking the history of the discipline. In R. Monk (ed.), *Structures of Knowing*, Lanham, MD: University Press of America, pp. 417–41.

Toulmin, S.   1953, *The Philosophy of Science*. New York: Harper & Row.

——   1972, *Human Understanding*, vol. 1: *The Collective Use and Evolution of Concepts*. Princeton, NJ: Princeton University Press.

Turner, B.   1989, Some reflections on cumulative theorizing in sociology. In J. H. Turner (ed.), *Theory Building in Sociology*, Newbury Park, CA: Sage, pp. 131–47.

Turner, J. H.   1985, In defense of positivism. *Sociological Theory*, 3, pp. 24–30.

—— 1989a, The disintegration of American sociology. *Sociological Perspectives*, 32, pp. 419–33.

—— 1989b, Can sociology be a cumulative science? In J. H. Turner (ed.), *Theory Building in Sociology*, Newbury Park, CA: Sage, pp. 8–18.

—— 1990, The misuse and use of metatheory. *Sociological Forum*, 5, pp. 37–53.

—— 1991, *The Structure of Sociological Theory*, 5th edn. Belmont, CA: Wadsworth.

—— 1992, The promise of positivism. In S. Seidman and D. Wagner (eds), *Postmodernism and General Social Theory*, New York: Basil Blackwell, pp. 101–53.

Turner, S. P. 1988, The strange life and hard times of the concept of general theory in sociology: a short history of hope. Paper presented at the Albany Conference on General Social Theory and its Critics: Contemporary Debates. Albany, NY, April 15 and 16.

Turner, S. P., and Turner, J. H. 1990, *The Impossible Science: An Institutional Analysis of American Sociology*. Newbury Park, CA: Sage.

Wagner, D. G. 1984, *The Growth of Sociological Theories*. Beverly Hills, CA: Sage.

Wagner, D. G., and Berger, J. 1985, Do sociological theories grow? *American Journal of Sociology*, 90, pp. 697–728.

Wiley, N. 1979, The rise and fall of dominating theories in American sociology. In W. E. Snizek, E. R. Fuhrman, and M. K. Miller (eds), *Contemporary Issues in Theory and Research*, Westport, CT: Greenwood, pp. 47–79.

—— 1985, The current interregnum in American sociology. *Social Research*, 51, pp. 179–207.

—— (ed.) 1987, *The Marx–Weber Debate*. Newbury Park, CA: Sage.

Winch, P. 1958, *The Idea of Social Science and Its Relation to Philosophy*. London: Routledge & Kegan Paul.

Zetterberg, H. 1955, *On Theory and Verification in Sociology*. New York: Free Press.

Zimmerman, D. H., and L. Wieder. 1970, Ethnomethodology and the problem of order. Comment on Denzin. In J. Douglas (ed.), *Understanding Everyday Life*, Chicago: Aldine, pp. 287–95.

Part II

Reinventing Parsons:
Reconstructing his Tradition

3
Neofunctionalism Today: Reconstructing a Theoretical Tradition

Co-written with Paul Colomy

In 1979, Alexander acknowledged that "despite Parsons' enduring impression on the sociological tradition, it is too early to determine the ultimate fate of his theoretical legacy." There seemed a real possibility that "the Parsonian synthesis will break down completely." It was also possible, however, that in time a "more loosely-defined, less sectarian version of functionalist theory" might appear (Alexander 1979a, p. 355). In this chapter we will try to demonstrate that it is the latter, not the former, of these possibilities that actually has come to pass.

When the initial volumes of *Theoretical Logic in Sociology* began to appear in 1982 (Alexander 1982a, 1982b, 1983a, 1983b), they were not greeted with unanimous approval. Incredulity, dismay, even indignation were prominently displayed. Marxist, humanist, constructivist, and positivist theorists, and even one older Parsonian, wrote negative reviews, warning the profession away from what they considered a retrograde development. The one thing about which these critics agreed was that the Parsonian foundation of *Theoretical Logic* represented a holdover from the past, rather than a new development in contemporary sociological thought.

These initial responses emerged from self-understandings of theoretical orientations that had been formed in a struggle against structural-functional thought. Positivism, conflict theory, Marxism, exchange theory, symbolic interactionism, phenomenology – all had once been obstreperous challengers to the Parsonian edifice. By 1980, it might be said, with only some exaggeration, that they were triumphant, not challengers but the dominant theories in a new, if internally divided, establishment. Surely, if sociological progress was to have any meaning at all, the Parsonian approach could not be revived. The very *raisons d'être* of these positions demanded that such an alternative not be raised.

In the January 1988 issue of *Contemporary Sociology*, Marco Orru describes the works he has under review as sharing an "enthusiastic reappraisal of Parsonian sociology." He develops a perspective within which to view them by pointing precisely to the doubt their existence casts on linear conceptions of social scientific development.

> As social scientists, we wish for theories about the social world to build on each other in some linear fashion but more often than not we observe, instead, a cyclical pattern by which different schools of thought replace each other in commanding our attention over time. Leading figures in the various theoretical traditions follow this same pattern. (Orru 1988, p. 115)

Only after suggesting the validity of a more cyclical pattern can Orru conclude by suggesting that "the revival of Parsonian thought is one of the distinguishing features of 1980s sociology."

If Orru is right about the conspicuous importance of the Parsonian revival, and we think he is, there has been a sea change in sociology in the last half dozen years. In retrospect, at least, it seems clear that *Theoretical Logic* was not the final aftershock in response to the anti-Parsonian quake. As we will suggest later in this chapter, it was not, in fact, an effort to revive earlier, orthodox Parsonian theory at all. It was, rather, a challenge to central tenets of the Parsonian orientation, an effort to revise it in a radical, post-Parsonian way. As such, it might better be seen as a preshock, a premonition of things to come. It has become evident in retrospect that *Theoretical Logic* was not anomalous. The previous year, indeed, Habermas had pointedly demanded the relegitimation of Parsonian theory in a not dissimilar way, as had Richard Munch in a powerful double set of articles in the *American Journal of Sociology*.[1]

When Alexander (1985a) subsequently introduced the term "neofunctionalism," it was in order to emphasize the double element of continuity and internal critique. This emphasis is revealed in his analogy to neo-Marxism. Current sociology *à la* Parsonian is to the earlier orthodoxy as neo-Marxism is to its orthodox earlier variant. Neo-Marxism has tried to overcome the mechanistic rigidities of Marx by incorporating the most important advances of twentieth century social thought. The relation of neofunctionalism to the traditions that challenged early Parsonian theory, it was suggested, is much the same.

This public assertion of the continuing vitality of the Parsonian tradition drew, once again, a decidedly mixed response. In *Footnotes*, an elder statesman (Page 1985) wrote an open letter to warn his colleagues about the dangers of revivifying functionalism. A younger theorist, Charles Camic (1986), in his review of *Neofunctionalism*, reassured his readers that the revivalists had learned nothing from the criticisms of Parsons and that in their theorizing one could find nothing new. Another contemporary, George Ritzer (1985), reinforced this skepticism, while offering that he was willing to wait and see.

Today, while fundamental doubts about the validity and desirability of neofunctionalism have not disappeared, the disciplinary community is gradually coming to terms with the fact that something new has appeared on the sociological scene. Orru's observation attests to this recognition. So does Giddens and Turner's (1987, p. 3) reference to the recent "considerable revival" of Parsonian thought in their introduction to *Social Theory Today*. Contemporary textbooks in sociological theory (e.g., Ritzer 1988, Collins 1988a) are being revised to reflect this shift in the theoretical map.[2]

In the course of the twentieth century, critics and sympathizers of neo-Marxism have often asked, "What is Marxist about it?" In so doing, they have indicated the extent of the critical departure from the original form. In Jonathan Turner and Alexandra Maryanski's (1988) "Is 'Neofunctionalism really functional'?", the same doubt is raised about recent neofunctionalist work. There is no doubting that in certain respects Turner and Maryanski have grounds for complaint. Neofunctionalism differs from orthodox Parsonian thought in decisive and often radical ways. Even while it disputes the discipline's evaluation of earlier functionalism, it does not itself accept some of the central tendencies of that earlier thought. Even while it sustains fundamental links with Parsons' earlier work, therefore, it does not conceive of itself as an attempt to resuscitate an older orthodoxy. Whether its originality is undermined by its continuing roots in Parsonian thought is, of course, a matter of debate. The claim can be made, however, that neofunctionalism is the only new theoretical movement to have emerged in Western sociology in the 1980s.[3]

One of our ambitions in this chapter is to indicate the substance of this new theoretical movement in sociology – its general discursive structure, its interpretations of the classics, the scope of its research programs, and its relation to other theoretical discourse and research programs in the field. This will involve a critical look at the wide variety of work that is currently underway. We would like to begin, however, by exploring some of the reasons why this unexpected revival has come about. In this regard, to point to the intrinsic interest of current neofunctionalist works is besides the point. Their very appearance has been a response to underlying developments in sociology. Neofunctionalism, we will argue, is only one indication of a deep groundshift in the entire sociological field. To understand its relevance on the contemporary scene one must understand the new and different theoretical situation that is emerging today.

The Emerging Third Phase of Postwar Sociology

Since World War II, Western sociology has passed through two periods, and it is entering a third. In the first phase, which lasted into the 1960s, structural-functionalism, in its Parsonian and Mertonian form, could be said to be the dominant force. Whatever its ideological weaknesses, its antiempirical stance, its naive confidence in equilibrium – and we will talk about all these below – that functionalism was committed to the synthesis of what Parsons called the "warring schools" of sociological thought seems impossible to deny. This orientation toward theoretical integration and synthesis was one casualty of the rebellion against functionalism that began in the 1960s and continued triumphantly into the early 1980s.

Two major battle lines were drawn. On the one side, microsociology set contingent action against social structure in the name of creativity and individual freedom. On the other side, conflict sociology argued that social change could be explained only by emphasizing material rather than ideal forces. These propositions denied the central tenets of Parsons' work. Thus, as Goffman, Homans, and Garfinkel gained increasing authority, interest in socialization and personality structure correspondingly declined. As Rex, Lockwood, and Dahrendorf became central figures, with Collins, Giddens, Wright, and Skocpol following in their stead, macrosociological interest in culture and symbolic legitimacy dramatically declined.

Yet even as these brilliant challengers became the new establishment, even as the "multiparadigmatic" character of sociology passed from daring prophecy (e.g., Friedrichs 1970) to conventional wisdom (e.g., Ritzer 1975), the vital and creative phase of these theoretical movements was coming to an end. Stimulated by the premature theoretical closure of the micro and macro traditions, a new phase is beginning. It is marked by an effort to relink theorizing about action and order, conflict and stability, structure and culture. Such efforts have been made from within each of the newly dominant theoretical traditions, from both sides of the great micro–macro divide. They are also the most clearly distinguishing characteristics of the new directions in general theory. The old lines of confrontation are being discredited. There is a movement back to synthesis once again. We believe that it is this development that marks the third phase of postwar sociology.

In symbolic interaction, a whole spate of work has challenged the emphasis on individualistic contingency that, under Blumer's leadership, marked this tradition's earlier development. Goffman's writing (1974) on frame analysis and Becker's (1982) on the social organization of art can be seen as marked departures from earlier, much more negotiation-oriented work. Stryker (1980) has called for a reintegration of interactionism with systems theory, Lewis and Smith (1980) have argued that Mead was a collectivist, and Fine (1984, 1988) has moved forcefully into the area of cultural and organizational studies.

In the exchange tradition, leading theorists (e.g., Coleman 1986a, 1986b, 1987, Wippler and Lindenberg 1987) increasingly reject the notion that the individual/structure relation can be seen as a causal relation between discrete empirical events. Because there is empirical simultaneity, the linkage between micro and macro must be seen as an analytical one sustained by larger systemic processes. This analytical linkage is achieved by the application of what are called "transformation rules," such as voting procedures, to individual actions. In the work of theorists like Goode, Blau, and Coleman, structural explanations – about the rules of constitutions (e.g., Coleman 1987), the dynamics of organizations and intergroup relations (Blau 1977), and the system of prestige allocation (Goode 1978) – have begun to replace utility arguments.

Within ethnomethodology, one can point to similar developments in the work of Cicourel, who has recently pushed for a linkage with macrosociological work (Knorr-Cetina and Cicourel 1981). Recent work by Molotch (Molotch and Boden 1985) and Schegloff (1987) demonstrates how discursive practices are structured by organizational context and the distribution of power, even while their analytical autonomy is maintained. Heritage and Greatbatch's (1986) research on political conventions makes a similar effort to establish micro–macro links.

When one examines the structural or conflict position, one finds similar efforts to overcome the splits of the second phase. Moore (1978) has turned from objective to subjective injustice; Skocpol and Finegold (1982) have raised the possibility that religion may be an independent cause of social policy and political change. Sewell (1980, 1985), once a devoted Tilly student, and Darnton (1982), once a leading *Annaliste*, are now developing cultural approaches to social change and history. Calhoun (1982) and Prager (1986) have published polemically antistructural works of historical sociology. Meyer and Scott (1983) link organizations to cultural structures rather than technical ones. This cultural turn in macrosociology is responsible, we believe, for the emergence of a new disciplinary specialty, cultural sociology, which has just become the newest American Sociological Association section. It is instructive that theorists who associate themselves with this specialty argue that culture cannot be understood in terms of what we have called the dichotomies of the second phase. Wuthnow (1988) argues that culture need not be understood individualistically or even subjectively, Swidler (1986) argues for culture's opening to contingency, Archer (1988) for its sensitivity to change, Eisenstadt (1986) for its link to material force and institutional life.

Within general theory there is an equally strong movement away from the one-sided polemics of earlier theoretical work. Where Giddens' earlier work (1971) was part of conflict and neo-Marxist theorizing, in the last decade he (1984) has sought to interweave contingency, material structure, and normative rules. Collins' (1975) earlier work was paradigmatic of conflict sociology; in recent years, by contrast, he has embraced microsociology (1981), the later Durkheimian emphasis on rituals (1987, 1988b), and even the framing concept of multidimensionality (1988a). Habermas, too, began his career with a typical Frankfurt school emphasis on the destructively capitalist features of modern life; more recently, he (1984) has theorized about the normative and micro processes that underline and often oppose the macrostructure of capitalist societies, making these cultural forces "equal but separate" subsystems.[4]

We earlier pointed to premature theoretical closure as the intellectual reason for the denouement of phase two. One-sided theories are effective polemical means; they are decidedly less successful when they must function as sources of theoretical cohesion, if not disciplinary integration, in their own right. Social and institutional factors, however, are also involved. One certain factor is the changing political climate in the United States and Europe. Revolutionary social movements have faded away; because of developments like Solidarity and revelations about the Chinese Cultural Revolution, in the eyes of many critical intellectuals Marxism itself has been morally delegitimated.

The ideological thrust that fueled post-Parsonian discourse in its micro and macro form and that justified Marxist structuralism on the Continent is largely spent. There is a new realism, even pessimism, about the possibilities for social change, which has manifest itself in two very different ways. On the one hand, there is the resignation, even fatalism, of so much postmodern thought, with its nostalgic return to localism (Lyotard 1984) and its abandonment of the possibility of a more rational social life (Foucault 1984). On the other hand, there is the search for less apocalyptic ways of institutionalizing rationality, approaches which concentrate on the difficulties of preserving political democracy rather than on the unlikely, and perhaps undesirable, possibility of some socialist transformation (Lefort 1986, Alexander 1988a).

Parsons' New Relevance in the Contemporary Phase

Is it any wonder that neofunctionalism has flourished in this changing social and disciplinary environment? Parsons' original work contained within it a wide and contradictory range of theoretical ideas. There are central areas in his corpus, however, that complement this third phase. Developing in a period of reaction against the limits of the second phase, neofunctionalists have interpreted the "natural concerns" of Parsons' thought in just this way. They have argued that it provides critical theoretical resources for addressing the concerns of this new period in postwar sociological work.

More than anything else, perhaps, neofunctionalism has presented itself as a prototypically synthetic form of theorizing. After all, it was Parsons' original and flawed effort at theoretical integration – and what were seen as its attendant weaknesses – that provoked micro and macro theorists to launch the one-sided theories that themselves have recently come under increasing doubt. It is not surprising, therefore, that as contemporary theorists have returned to the project of synthesis, they have often returned to some core element in

Parsons' earlier thought. It is striking that this return is manifest in the work of theorists who have never had any previous association with Parsonian thought. The motive is theoretical logic, not personal desire.

No more clear example of this theoretical pressure can be found than Habermas' *Legitimation Crisis* (1975). Departing from the safe harbor of critical theory, Habermas wanted to incorporate into his model of economic contradictions factors like personality strain, the universalist potential of value commitments, and the latently anti-capitalist pressure that emanate from the formal equality of political and legal institutions. What he ends up employing, *de facto* if not *de jure*, is Parsons' AGIL model and also his division between culture, personality, and social system. Similar examples can be found in a wide range of recent theoretical work. When Schluchter (1979, 1981) wants to present a newly integrated view of Weber's civilizational work, he makes use of the evolutionary and developmental language of Parsons' differentiation theory. When Collins (1988b) pushes to expand his "conflict-Durkheimian" theory of social rituals into the realm of democratic politics, he is forced to acknowledge the importance of Parsons' multidimensional theory of political support. In Holton's (1986) effort to transcend both market and Marxist approaches to political economy, he turns with relief to the rich conceptual legacy of Parsons and Smelser's model of the economy–society relation. To reaffirm the delicate but distinctive pluralism of Western social systems, B. Turner (1986a, 1986b, 1987) extends the concepts of inclusion, citizenship, and value generalization from Parsons' theory of social change. In our own efforts (Alexander and Giesen 1987, Alexander 1987a, Colomy and Rhoades 1988) to construct a model of the micro–macro link – efforts that challenge orthodox functionalism in fundamental ways – we have found that Parsons' analytic model provides the only viable foundation for a new synthesis.

This new relevance of Parsonian thought can also be seen in the renewed theorizing about culture and society. It is not accidental, in this regard, that it has been the former students and coworkers of Parsons who have assumed a central role in the revival of macro-cultural studies. Geertz (1973) initiated this "cultural revolution" with his essays in the 1960s, which stood firmly upon Parsons' insistence on the analytical autonomy of the cultural realm. Bellah's (1970, 1973) argument for the relationship between symbolic realism and democratic social integration can also be traced back to key themes in Parsons' normative work. When Eisenstadt criticizes contemporary structuralist approaches to historical and contemporary sociology for their "ontological' rather than analytical approach to culture and society relations (1986), he is drawing from Parsons' theory of the institutionalization of values. Archer's (1985, 1988) ambitious meta-theory of culture begins from the Parsonian distinction between culture, action, and social system. Robertson's (1987) work on global culture issues in critical respects (Robertson 1982, cf. Robertson 1988) from Parsons' concepts of value generalization and societal community. In Alexander's (1982b, pp. 211–96; 1984, 1988b) own effort to construct a model of cultural structures and processes, he, too, begins with the analytic differentiation of symbolic patterns from the exigencies of social and personality systems.

We have indicated here the convergence between the interests that mark the current, third phase of sociological thought and some of the earlier concerns of Parsonian work. We have demonstrated this co-incidence in terms of the desire for theoretical synthesis and the new attempt to theorize culture. The third element of this third phase – the clearly changing ideological environment of sociology – will be taken up below, in the context of a more systematic discussion of neofunctionalist work. Up until this point, we have noted the convergence between developments in neofunctionalism and more general movements in the theoretical field, but we have not looked at specific arguments or tried to construct the details of a new disciplinary map. Before taking up these tasks, we need a framework within which to consider issues of disciplinary conflict and change.

Social Science as Discourse and Research Program[5]

To understand correctly the issues involved in the emergence and decline of theoretical orientations, we must see that social science is neither the fact-bound nor middle-level enterprise that empiricists describe. Social science is organized by traditions, and traditions, whatever their aspirations for rationality, are founded by charismatic figures. At the beginnings of a discipline, powerful intellectual figures are regarded as classical founders (Alexander 1987b); at later points, they are accorded quasi-classical status and treated as founders of powerful schools. Social reality, then, is never confronted in and of itself. Because perception is mediated by the discursive commitments of traditions, social scientific formulations are channeled within relatively standardized, paradigmatic forms. The matrix social scientists inhabit need not be drawn from a single tradition or be wholly of a piece, but inhabit it they must, aware of it or not.

While traditionalism implies habitual behavior, it need not imply stasis or lack of change. In social science, this openness to change is intensified by the universalism of institutionalized standards that mandate impersonal rationality and push against the particularism of a traditional first response. Social science traditions define themselves by staking out theoretical cores that are highly resistant to change. The substantial areas surrounding these nuclei, however, are subject to continuous variation. In ideal-typical terms, changes in the peripheral areas of traditions can be conceived as proceeding along two lines, "elaboration" and "revision." While both lines of development present themselves as loyally carrying out traditional commitments, they differ in the creativeness with which they pursue this task. Because elaborative sociological work proceeds from the assumption that the original tradition is internally consistent and relatively complete, it aims primarily at refinement and expansion of scope. In revisionist work, by contrast, there is a greater sense of the vulnerabilities of the established tradition; in the guise of loyal specification, an often implicit effort is made to address these strains and offer formulations that can resolve them (see, e.g., Alexander 1979a, Colomy 1986).

Elaboration and revision are lines of specification that recur periodically in a tradition's history, not only in the period of routinization that immediately follows the charismatic founding but in the wake of the powerful reformulations that must emerge if a tradition is to remain intact.[6] It is this latter possibility that points to a third ideal-typical form of theoretical change. Insofar as cores themselves undergo substantial shifts – without abandoning their association with the overarching tradition – there occurs the theoretical activity we will call "reconstruction." Reconstruction differs from elaboration and revision in that differences with the founder of the tradition are clearly acknowledged and openings to other traditions are explicitly made. Reconstruction can revive a theoretical tradition, even while it creates the opportunity for the kind of development out of which new traditions are born.[7] Finally, of course, traditions can be destroyed. This does not happen because core and peripheral commitments are falsified, but because they have become delegitimated in the eyes of the scientific community. Even in this situation, however, traditions do not so much disappear as become latent; the possibility always remains that they may be picked up once again.[8]

According to this model, then, social science does not grow simply because of the compulsion to understand empirical reality; nor can its growth be measured merely in relation to the expansion of empirical knowledge or conceptual scope. The primary motor of social scientific growth is conflict and competition between traditions. The primary reference points for measuring scientific growth are established by the relations between traditions and by signposts internal to a given tradition itself. Instead of speaking about theoretical or empirical progress per se, one must speak of relative explanatory and theoretical success vis-à-vis one's own tradition or competing ones.[9]

Elaboration, revision, and reconstruction are concepts that describe the closeness of fit between subsequent theoretical work and original tradition. They do not describe the degree of real advance. Elaboration, for example, may be thin or thick, to redeploy Geertz's ethnographic standards. Traditions may be enriched and elevated by these processes of theoretical change; they may also be impoverished and simplified, robbed of their sophistication and denuded of some of their most powerful intellectual sustenance.[10] If social science change can be progressive, therefore, it can be reactionary as well. It is rare, moreover, for these modes of theoretical development to proceed in either an entirely progressive or reactionary way.

A disciplinary community's switch from one theoretical position to another is determined neither by the theoretical effectiveness and sophistication of the respective positions nor by their objective empirical scope. It is usually motivated, rather, by broad shifts in what might be called the disciplinary community's "scientific sensibility."[11] Shifts in disciplinary sensibility put different questions on the floor. They place a premium on the development of different modes of discourse. Indeed, it is often only after new discursive commitments are made to an approach, that increased theoretical sophistication and empirical scope emerge. It is in this sense that one can speak less of social scientific "development" than of social scientific "movements." Disciplines should not be understood as being organized primarily by specialties defined by their empirical objects of investigation, into Mertonian middle-range subfields like deviance, stratification, or political sociology. The deep structure of a discipline consists of the networks and literatures that are produced by the contact between empirical objects, ongoing traditions, and new disciplinary movements.

By this route we can return to the topic of neofunctionalism. In the phase of routinization that followed the emergence of Parsons' founding work, functionalism was presented as a consistent and increasingly completed theory, and elaboration and revision were the order of the day. In the second phase of postwar sociology, shifts in the disciplinary sensibility delegitimated these efforts and functionalism as a vital tradition came near to extinction. In the emerging third phase, scientific sensibility has shifted once again. In an altered theoretical and historical climate, new questions are being asked. These questions represent opportunities for dramatic disciplinary shift. In response, the functionalist tradition has entered a phase of reconstruction. Neofunctionalism is the result.

To fully elaborate the changes that have occurred within the functionalist tradition would be a complex and detailed task, for one would have to examine developments at every level of the scientific continuum. The discussion can be simplified by examining the process in terms of two basic genres, generalized discourse and research programs. By generalized discourse, we refer to discussions that argue about presuppositions, about ontology and epistemology, about the ideological and metaphysical implications of sociological argument, and about its broad historical grounding. Within the context of research programs, by contrast, such generalized issues are assumed to be relatively unproblematic. What becomes problematic, what propels this mode of scientific activity, is the need to provide interpretations or explanations of specific empirical structures and processes.

The discourse/research program distinction must not be confused with the distinctions introduced above. It is not isomorphic, for example, with core and peripheral concerns. The specific commitments that are pursued by research programs may be considered vital to the core of a tradition. Generalized discourse, for its part, is often directed to peripheral elements. Thus, in twentieth century Marxism, in contrast to that of the nineteenth century, presuppositions about materialism and idealism have been considered part of the core; shifts toward idealism are not conceived of as threatening the "Marxist" character of theorizing. As for our model of scientific development, the processes we have identified as elaboration, revision, and reconstruction can occur through both discourse and research programs alike. In practice, it is usually discourse about more general issues that announces and introduces a reconstructive phase, for it is generalized issues that provide a framework within which more specific explanatory concerns can be conceived.[12] Indeed, in our consideration of neofunctionalism, we will focus primarily on the new kind of generalized discourse that has challenged the core. Following that discussion, we will present a brief overview of the research programs that have followed in its wake.

The Generalized Discourse of Neofunctionalism

Generalized discourse occurs in both interpretive and expository modes. Via interpretation, theorists treat the work of the founder and other major figures in the tradition as difficult and problematic texts. Interpretive challenges are also mounted against the primary and secondary texts of other classical traditions and against the secondary literature that has developed within the home tradition as well. In the expository mode, by contrast, discourse is conducted on its own terms, general principles are set out and comparative frameworks established. While these modes of generalized discourse can be carried out by different theorists or at different points in the same discussion by a single person, they are connected to one another in an intimate way. No matter how apparently scholastic an interpretive discussion, the broader context of disciplinary struggle ensures that texts will never be considered simply for their own sake. Arguments about the meaning and validity of various texts represent one alternative, and sometimes the most effective one (Alexander 1987b) for engaging in substantive theoretical debate.

Generalized discourse makes arguments within the framework of, and in reference to, presuppositions, models, metamethodological commitments, and *Weltanschauung*, or world views. While it is possible to argue that Parsons took definite positions on each of these elements, we would argue, as neofunctionalists, that on each of these levels Parsons' orientation was ambiguous (Alexander 1983b). In terms of the problem of action, Parsons committed himself to a synthesis of material and idealist presuppositions; yet he consistently deviated from this professed aim in an idealist way. In terms of order, he aimed at linking individual actions and social structures, but from within his collectivist position he never theorized contingent effort. In terms of Parsons' theoretical model, functional and systems terminology are employed to describe a society of interrelated yet relatively independent parts. None of these are conceptualized as dominant, and equilibrium is considered an analytic reference point for evaluating social systems, not an empirical description of them. When Parsons' converted this model into a cybernetic system, however, he tilted toward one set of social system parts, the normative, raising it to a vertical position over another set, the material. He had great difficulty, moreover, in maintaining the analytic status of his model, often conflating the conceptualized ideal of equilibrium with the condition of an empirical society. Finally, there are extremely significant ambiguities in Parsons' ideology or *Weltanschauung*. Over the course of his long career, his ideological outlook shifted from critical to quiescent liberalism. What was a hopeful pessimism in the 1930s and 1940s became full-throated optimism in the 1950s and 1960; as a dedicated social scientist who aimed at constructing general covering laws, Parsons denied the connection of facts and values. Yet his growing confidence in modern, and particularly American, society made his work significantly less sensitive to the darker sides of modernity, to a wide range of depressing but undeniable facts about contemporary life.

What is perhaps most distinctive about the initial phases in the elaboration and revision of a sociological tradition is that they typically do not occur in a discursive mode. If we examine the three or four decades of Parsons' students' works, most of it, whether elaborative or revisionist, takes place within the school's research program. One need only think here of Bellah's *Tokugawa Religion* (1957) and *Beyond Belief* (1970), Smelser's *Social Change in the Industrial Revolution* (1959) and *Theory of Collective Behavior* (1962), and Eisenstadt's *The Political Systems of Empires* (1963). In each of these works there is a powerful challenge to an element in the tradition's ambiguous core (Alexander 1979a, 1983b), but it is expressed in the mode of an implicit revision of explanatory apparatus, not in the framework of general discourse.[13]

When generalized discourse does emerge in this initial period, it is almost entirely affirmative, its aim being to explain the intricacies of a difficult text to students or outsiders. Good illustrations of such occasional discursive references are the Devereux (1961) and Williams (1961) contributions to the Max Black volume on Parsons, various sections in Harry Johnson's (1960) once popular introductory textbook, and the initial chapters to the seminal books by Parsons' students we have listed above. Only in the waning days of functionalism's initial period, when Parsons came under increasing attack, did consistent exercises in generalized discourse appear. Victor Lidz's (1970, 1972) rejoinders to Albert Syzmanski's (1970a, 1970b, 1972) attacks on the value-laden character of Parsonian theory are a case in point. For the first time, Lidz raised the metamethodological underpinnings of Parsons' work in an explicit way. His rejoinders were brilliant elaborations and generalized defenses of Parsons' value-neutral stance, strictly from within the confines of the technical theory. The editors' introductions to the various sections of the two-volume Free Press *festschrift* for Parsons can be read in much the same way, as the last attempts by the last generation of "real Parsonians" to develop a general discourse that could affirm, elaborate, and revise the founder's work (Loubser et al. 1976).

Neofunctionalism can be distinguished from functionalism by its effort to reconstruct the core of the Parsonian tradition. Elaborative and revisionist efforts remain; indeed, the emergence of reconstructive efforts have relegitimated these more moderate, internalist lines of development. It is reconstruction, however, that has established the framework for a "neo" functionalism in the contemporary phase. Among those loosely associated with this movement, there is virtually no effort to return to the research program or discourse of the earlier period. A surprisingly large portion of earlier peripheral criticism has been accepted, just as the core itself is being reshaped in a responsive way. From this perspective, neofunctionalism is post-Parsonian. Its aim is to go beyond both the first and second phase of postwar sociology and to construct a new synthesis on the basis of the contributions of each.

It should not be surprising, then, that in contrast to the earlier phase of functionalist theorizing, generalized discourse has been central in the development of neofunctionalist work. Primarily, this has been in the service of reconstructive arguments about the core, but it has appeared also in the more affirmative practices of revisionism and even elaboration. Alexander's (1983b) work has explicitly attacked the idealist tendencies in Parsons' approach to action and argued that this reduction was responsible for many defects in Parsons' work, such as its tendency to see change in teleological terms and its relative slighting of economic rewards and political coercion. In a series of articles and working papers, Gould also sought to reemphasize material factors, in order similarly to reconstruct a more truly multidimensional tradition. His explicit challenge to Parsons remained reserved for his more specific and explanatory work (Gould 1987); in this more generalized domain, he chose revisionism, arguing that Parsons had issued an "earnest warning" against neglecting the material domain (Gould 1981).

In the initial period of neofunctionalism, the order issue seemed less salient. Here too, however, explicitly reconstructive discourse had strongly emerged. Alexander (1988c) has sharply criticized Parsons for his failure to bring contingency back into his theorizing of collective order. In response to this "black box" of individual action, Alexander has suggested formulations that are modeled on theories of individual exchange, interpretation, and pragmatic experience. In complementary efforts, Colomy (1985, 1990a, 1990b) has argued against the lack of attention to open-ended group processes in the functionalist understanding of change; in a series of theoretical and historical papers, he has developed systematic theories integrating work on collective behavior with structural approaches to social differentiation. Motivated by a similar interest to bring the individual back into functionalist work, Sciulli (1986, 1988) has argued that the early and the later Parsons himself understood voluntarism in a manner that emphasized its protean and individualistic qualities. Strongly criticizing Parsons' emphasis on socialization in his middle period work, Sciulli has argued for a convergence between Blumer's understanding of public negotiation and a neofunctionalist theory of public political life. Finally, though Munch's (1981, 1982) early articles on Parsons' neo-Kantian core were couched in the language of affirmative revision rather than reconstruction,[14] they, too, can be seen as a powerful attempt to bring effort and individual will back into the center of functionalist work.

There has also been an efflorescence of general and often polemical discussions about the model level of functional theory. Alexander (1983b) made a series of criticisms about the reification of functionalist and systems reasoning in Parsons' work. He also criticized the conflation between the AGIL divisions in the model and the empirical differentiation of contemporary society. Because these problematic applications of the model made it difficult to avoid the identification of functionalism with stasis and conflation, Alexander called for a return to the more concrete, group-oriented, early-middle phase of Parsons' work, in which the institutional content of a particular social system was clearly differentiated from its abstract mechanisms.

While in Germany it is actually the functionalized Weberianism of Schluchter and the Parsonian Marxism of Habermas that comes closest to this ideal, the German neofunctionalists have also altered Parsons' model in a revealing way.[15] Luhmann (1982), too, has criticized Parsons for reducing the dynamism of systems analysis by reifying it as a fourfold table; with his insistence on the tension between the internal and external environments of systems, he has developed a more supple and dynamic model.[16] Munch (1987a, 1988) has also changed the model forcefully, renaming the four subsystems in a manner that emphasizes contingency and the ideological and cultural imperative of rational communication.

Powerful and complementary challenges to Parsons' systems model have come from Gould and Colomy. In an ambitious challenge to Parsons, Gould (1985) has argued that functional models, drawn from systems or organicist theories, are necessary but limited. Developmental models must also be employed: abstract sketches of phases through which particular historical societies must pass if specified levels of development are to be achieved. Finally, in an argument that parallels Alexander's criticism of conflation, Gould insists that neither of these models should be confused with the actual structure of historical societies. This is provided by a "structural" model of particular institutional and group relations in a given period. For his part, Colomy (1985) has directed his efforts at altering Parsons' differentiation theory in a neofunctionalist way. He has argued that differentiation should be treated as a sharply delimited model; it is a "master trend" rather than an actual empirical description, much less an explanation for change. Within this altered framework, Colomy has offered a series of specific models of the structure and process of social change.

In the realm of ideology, the most radical break with orthodox funtionalism has simply been to make the ideological dimension of this tradition explicit. While arguing for the generally progressive and humanistic thrust of Parsons' work, Alexander has agreed with many of Parsons' critics about some of its conservative features. He himself has sought to politicize functionalism and tie it to the normative issues of the day. In his eulogy for Parsons in *The New Republic*, Alexander (1979b) described Parsons as providing "a sociology for liberals," stressing the normative and critical potential of Parsons' concepts of inclusion, differentiation, and value-generalization. Since that time he has tried to push neofunctionalism in a left-leaning but not radical direction. In an independent contribution to this effort, Colomy (1990c) has discussed this neofunctionalist orientation under the rubric of "critical modernism." Mayhew's (1982, 1984, 1990) work on the centrality of the public in democratic polities elaborates a similar normative-cum-empirical claim, as does Robertson's (1988) developing theory of globalization, which argues simultaneously for a new worldwide cosmopolitanism and for an increased tolerance for national variance, which, he suggests, Parsons' own modernization theory overlooked.

Sciulli and Gould have staked out more radical ideological claims. Operating in the space provided by his voluntaristic interpretation of Parsons' macrosociology, Sciulli (1989) has developed empirical criteria for evaluating democratization in his theory of "societal constitutionalism." Arguing that modern industrial societies are threatened by political and economic oligarchies, on the one hand, and by a pacified citizenry on the other, he finds a countervailing force in Parsons' understanding of the increasing importance of collegial, self-governing communities. Gould (1987, 1985) embraces an even more restrictive and critical conception of capitalist political economy, and he has reconstructed a model of contemporary societies whose strains can be alleviated only through the transformation of property relations.

The most ambitious effort to transform disciplinary understandings of the functionalist *Weltanschauung* can be found in Holton and Turner's (1986) work. Describing Parsons as the only major theorist rooted in a society that did not experience the damaging transition from feudalism to capitalism, they argue that he has been the only theorist to conceptualize the positive possibilities of a progressive and stable modernity. Compared to Marx, Weber, and Durkheim, Parsons escapes from nostalgia because he sees the moral and pluralistic possibilities of *Gesellschaft*.

> An alternative option is to consider the possibility that *Gesellschaft* permits authentic expressions of values, rather than the "false," or "fetished" forms of consciousness as diagnosed by exponents of the Frankfurt school. In addition, value-pluralism under *Gesellschaft* need be considered neither as a series of narcissistic worlds, in retreat from the public domain, nor as an irreducible battle of Nietzschian wills. Rather it can be conceived as generating a normative basis for the orderly resolution of pluralism and diversity.
>
> (Holton and Turner 1986, pp. 215–16)

In the second phase discourse of postwar work, Parsons was a conservative because he was not a radical. Arguing against the picture of Parsons as "an apologist for that kind of crass economic individualism that is often taken to underlie the capitalist economy," Holton and Turner portray Parsons' optimism, to the contrary, as reflecting "a profoundly moral and political identification with liberal democratic values" (pp. 216–17). In their view, it is Parsons, not his second phase critics, who now must be seen as occupying the higher moral ground.

> Parsons emerges from most confrontations with his critics as both
> morally engaged and politically committed, not as an apologist for
> capitalism, but as an anti-elitist and anti-Utopian social theorist. This
> standpoint moves us beyond the ambivalence of the classical sociolo-
> gists toward modernity.... In all these respects Parsons' social theory
> announces the end of the classical phase of sociological thought.
>
> (Holton and Turner 1986, p. 218)

Earlier in this chapter we spoke of the significance of the new
ideological and political environment in generating the contemporary,
third phase of sociological work. For neofunctionalism, the effect of
this altered environment has been most powerfully crystallized by
Holton and Turner; indeed, they present an argument that simply
could not have been made at any earlier point. While offered as an
affirmative elaboration and revision of the original rather than its
reconstruction, their argument can take this position only because it
is neofunctionalism, not orthodoxy, that now provides the framework for discourse in the Parsonian mode.[17] The powerfully reconstructive effects of their Parsons' portrait helps to renew the kind of
critical modernism that is necessary to reform and sustain a liberal
and democratic society.

The interpretive mode of generalized discourse is intimately tied to
the expository mode we have just discussed. We have earlier pointed
to the affirmative quality of the orthodox Parsonians' elaborations
and revisions of their founder's texts. More interesting, perhaps, was
this group's approach to classical texts outside the home tradition.
Parsons (1937) had set the tone in *The Structure of Social Action*,
when he stressed convergence within the work of his "group of recent
European writers." That Parsons had himself constructed this convergence through powerful interpretation was never acknowledged,
nor was the crucial fact that what they converged with was Parsons'
emergent social theory rather than their own. Parsons often "revisited"
Durkheim, Weber, and Freud, as his theory continually evolved. He
needed to incorporate new elements from their work, but he could
do so only by presenting these elements as if they converged with the
new elements in his own. Between those theorists admitted to the
classical canon of sociology there could be no fundamental strains,
nor could there be any unresolvable strains between these theories and
Parsons' own. This affirmative approach to interpretation – its expression as elaboration and revision – reached its apogee in Parsons and
his collaborators' *Theory of Societies* (1961). In its depiction of the

convergence of the entire history of social thought with action theory, this work was either extraordinarily naive or disingenuous.

Still, interpretive discourse did not flourish in the orthodox phase of functionalism any more than did discourse in the expository mode. When Parsonians engaged in interpretation, moreover, they modeled their discussions on Parsons' convergence model. Bellah's (1959) penetrating early article on Durkheim as a differentiation theorist is a case in point. Smelser's (1973) edition of Marx, Eisenstadt's (1971) of Weber, and the Lidz brothers' (1976) treatment of Piaget are similarly powerful examples.

Interpretation in the contemporary phase has, by contrast, been much more central and aggressively reconstructive. We have indicated above how Parsons' own work has been the object of several neofunctionalist critiques. In discussing classical works outside the home tradition, neofunctionalists have adopted a decidedly un-Parsonian line. They have stressed divergence rather than convergence, for they have need of theoretical resources beyond the home tradition itself.

We will take up the neofunctionalist dialogue with the classics of macrosociology first. Where Parsons not only neglected but in effect tried to repress Marx, Alexander (1982b) makes Marx paradigmatic of the material and instrumental theorizing that he criticizes Parsons for trying to ignore. He (1983a) sets Weber against Parsons in much the same way, arguing that Parsons underplayed the objectification that for Weber was the necessary underside of individuation. In a similar vein, Alexander (1988b) has stressed the symbolic and culturalistic elements in Durkheim, playing them off against the culturally reductionist tendencies in the orthodox functionalist concentration on "value." Gould (1987) has treated Marx, Hegel, Keynes, and Piaget in much the same way, stressing their distance from Parsons in the first instance, and the need to incorporate their "antifunctionalism" in the second. His theory of revolution and radical collective behavior has emerged from this reconstructed mix. For Sciulli (1985), the absence that interpretation must overcome is Habermas. While stressing in a revisionist mode the areas of convergence between Parsons and Habermas, he has also interpreted Habermas in a manner that exposes the self-limitations of Parsons' orthodox work. He has interpreted the legal theorist Lon Fuller in the same reconstructive way. Both Habermas and Fuller (Sciulli, 1989, 1990) provide critical resources for Sciulli's neofunctionalist theory of societal constitutionalism

There has also emerged within neofunctionalist interpretation a significant dialogue with the central texts of the microsociological tradition. Because Parsons did not recognize the problem of contingent action, it is not surprising that his relation to these traditions never went beyond ceremonial remarks on their convergence with his own. For neofunctionalism, by contrast, it has become important to understand the divergence between microsociology and the orthodox tradition, in order to develop theoretical resources for opening neofunctionalism up to contingency in the ways we have discussed above.

Alexander (1985b, 1987c, pp. 195–280) has emphasized, for example, a collective thrust in Mead, Peirce, and Goffman, and also in the phenomenological theory of Husserl, Schutz, and the early Garfinkel, arguing that such theoretical resources have been largely ignored by these traditions' contemporary interpreters. While Munch (1986, 1987b) and Sciulli (1988), by contrast, do not refer to this thrust in their interpretations of interactionist theory, all three theorists agree that neofunctionalism must draw upon these traditions in order to incorporate considerations of contingency and voluntarism. These theoretical appropriations are openly presented as remedies to the acknowledged shortcomings of orthodoxy, and defended as a means by which the more original, creative, and synthesizing project of neofunctionalists can be advanced.

Within the new environments of the third postwar phase, and in response to the opportunities and provocations provided by the new generalized discourse, there has been an outpouring of neofunctionalist research that, if this term is taken in its broad rather than restricted sense, can be called a research program. Earlier functionalist research was guided by a reaffirmative strategy, envisioning a single, all-embracing conceptual scheme that tied areas of specialized research into a tightly wrought package. What neofunctionalist empirical work points to, by contrast, is a package loosely organized around a general logic and possessing a number of rather autonomous "proliferations" and "variations" at different levels and in different empirical domains (Wagner 1984, Wagner and Berger 1985).

A Note on Research Programs in Neofunctionalism

In the preceding sections we have described the emergence of neofunctionalism, treating it as a central feature of the third phase of postwar sociology and identifying the intellectual and sociopolitical grounds for its resurgence. Neofunctionalism's discursive elements – its pre-suppositions, ontology, epistemology, and ideological implications – have been outlined. But neofunctionalism is more than generalized discourse. It also seeks to explain particular facets of the social world.

The most developed neofunctionalist research programs have emerged in the areas of social change, cultural sociology, political sociology, mass communications, feminist studies, the professions, and economic sociology. While a detailed examination of these programs cannot be presented here, an overview highlighting the most prominent contours of this work is in order.[18]

Much of neofunctionalist research has charted a decidedly revisionist course. Studies of structural differentiation, for instance, revise orthodox functionalism's approach to change in four ways: First, they supplement descriptions of the "master trend" toward increasingly specialized institutions by developing models of patterned departures from that trend (e.g., Alexander 1981, Lechner 1984, 1985, 1990, Tiryakian 1985, 1990, Champagne 1990, Colomy 1985, 1990a, 1990b, Hondrich 1990, Surace 1982, Smelser 1985, 1990, Colomy and Tausig 1988). Second, they move beyond purely systemic and evolutionary explanations of differentiation toward accounts that stress contingency, concrete groups, conflict, and social movements and collective behavior (e.g., Eisenstadt 1980, Colomy 1985, 1990a, 1990b, Colomy and Rhoades 1988, Colomy and Tausig 1988, Rhoades 1990, Mayhew 1990, Alexander 1980, Smelser 1985). Third, they recognize that the orthodox emphasis on adaptive upgrading, inclusion, and value generalization represent but one configuration among a much broader array of the possible outcomes of social differentiation (e.g., Luhmann 1982, 1990a, 1990b, Alexander 1978, 1983b, 1984, Eder 1990, Rhoades 1990, Munch 1981, 1982, 1983, 1987a, 1988, 1990a, 1990b, Sciulli 1985, 1990, Mayhew 1984, 1990). Fourth, they replace a complacent liberal optimism concerning the process and consequences of differentiation with a critical modernism that is more attuned to the dark sides that are ineluctably related to it (e.g., Sciulli 1990, Mayhew 1984, 1990, Munch 1987a, 1988, Colomy 1990c).[19]

Conventional functionalist research into the culture–society relation has also been critiqued and revised. The orthodox approach posited a cultural system neatly institutionalized in the social system through values that the personality internalized via socialization. Archer (1985, 1988) argues that this model is guilty of "downward conflation," for it holds that an integrated cultural system engulfs the social and personality systems. Alexander (1984) suggests that this conventional approach to institutionalization, which he calls the cultural specification model, represents only one form culture–society relations can assume. He proposes two additional modes. In cultural refraction, conflicting social groups and functions produce antagonistic subcultures that continue to draw upon a value system that is integrated at the cultural level. In cultural columnization, by contrast, there are fundamental antagonisms in both the social and cultural systems, interest groupings have no significant common beliefs, and genuinely antagonistic political cultural groupings emerge.[20]

In their effort to develop a broadly neofunctionalist feminist sociology, Miriam Johnson and her colleagues (Johnson 1975, 1977, 1981, 1982, 1988a, 1988b, Johnson et al. 1975, 1981, Gill et al. 1987, Stockard and Johnson 1979) reappropriate and revise elements of the Parsonian legacy others have left behind. They reconceptualize the traditional distinction between instrumentality and expressiveness, the structural differentiation model of the family, socialization, and Parsons' particular application of his culture, society and personality model to account for the origins and reproduction of gender inequality. When considered in isolation, each of their reconceptualizations can be accurately characterized as revisionist. Taken together, however, it is readily apparent that this research program is animated by a reconstructionist thrust. It aims not at describing how the family "produces" human personalities capable of assuming adult roles in a complex, differentiated society – the orthodox Parsonian issue – but at explaining the radically different question of how a cultural and social system subordinates and distorts a particular class of personalities.

Johnson and her colleagues not only revise and reconstruct Parsons, they also wed their reconfiguration of orthodox functionalism to other intellectual traditions, especially psychoanalysis and feminist scholarship. Jeffrey Prager (1986) has extended and revised the functionalist treatment of political sociology in an analogous way. He draws on Parsons' discussion of a differentiated societal community to devise a neofunctionalist conception of the public sphere. He ties that structural concept to the more concrete and processual symbolic interactionist approach that emphasizes the content, dynamics and effects of actual public discourse. With the aid of this powerful theoretical link between functionalism and interactionism, Prager's investigation of Ireland's movement toward democracy demonstrates not only how democratic institutions operate, but also how they are created in the first place.

In addition to its reconstructionist and revisionist thrust, neofunctionalist research also contains an elaborationist current. For instance, Robertson's (1985, 1986, 1987, 1990, Robertson and Chirico 1985, Robertson and Lechner 1985) analyses of the relationship between globalization and cultural change carries the Parsonian theme of value generalization to the level of the world system. At the same time, because he is sensitive to the wide diversity of cultural responses engendered by globalization, Robertson revises Parsons by eschewing the notion that these changes amount merely to a global version of cultural specification and normative integration.

More recently, such elaborative research has occurred less against the backdrop of earlier orthodox functionalism, but in relation to the rapidly developing body of neofunctionalist theory itself. Rothenbuhler (1986a, 1986b, 1987, 1988a, 1988b, 1988c, 1989, n.d., Peters and Rothenbuhler 1988) draws on general statements of the neofunctionalist position as well as on neofunctionalist treatments of culture to fashion an impressive research program in mass communications. Drawing upon highly abstract neofunctionalist discussions of the micro–macro link, Colomy and Rhoades (1988) develop a series of ideal-typical models and causal hypotheses to explain educational change in the late nineteenth century United States. In a similar way, Lehman (1988) uses Alexander's analysis of presuppositions about action and order to generate a new and more complex empirical research program on political power and the state. Rambo's (1988) work in economic sociology elaborates neofunctionalist treatments of culture, while Edles (1988) draws on the same neofunctionalist literature to analyze Spain's civil religion and its recent transition to democracy.

In sum, while a central part of neofunctionalism has been carried out at the level of general theory, there is a complementary, and rapidly growing, body of more empirically oriented work. This work supplements the reconstructionist thrust of neofunctionalist metatheory with several significant revisions of orthodox functionalism and has even begun to elaborate neofunctionalist general theory itself.

Conclusion

Our task in this chapter has been to demonstrate that neofunctionalism is delivering on its promissory notes. Today, neofunctionalism is much more than a promise; it has become a field of intense theoretical discourse and growing empirical investigation. We have conducted this demonstration within the framework of the model of social scientific knowledge we elaborated in chapter 2. Because sociological knowledge is generated by traditions, the most compelling criteria for evaluating scientific progress is comparative, in terms of different phases in the life of a particular tradition and in terms of the relations between competing traditions. By making such comparisons we can measure social scientific progress, although, to be sure, this is progress in a postpositivist sense.

In this chapter, we assessed neofunctionalism's advances primarily by comparing them to the older orthodoxy. Toward that end several terms – reconstruction, expropriation, revision, and elaboration – have been employed. Our thesis has been that, at both discursive and more empirical levels, neofunctionalism has produced significant advances relative to earlier renditions of the tradition. We have tried to show that the reconstructions, revisions, and elaborations that compose neofunctionalism have been directed precisely at those areas of the orthodox tradition that critics, both internal and external, earlier identified as theoretically or empirically suspect. If neofunctionalism represents theoretical progress – and we think it does – this reflects its ability to produce satisfactory reconstructions and revisions in response to critiques that once threatened to destroy the functionalist tradition altogether.

Of course, theoretical progress cannot be judged on internal grounds alone. Comparisons must also be made with competing traditions. Certainly the "critics of functionalism" will respond with new kinds of ripostes. Some will try to ignore the vast changes that neofunctionalism has wrought. Others will recognize that fundamental shifts have occurred and will reformulate the nature of their critiques. We eagerly await these reformulations. The conventional debates have become stale and dry. We are in the midst of a sea change in sociological theory. Old alignments are dissolving; new configurations are being born. "Neofunctionalism" cannot be stuffed back into the old box.

Notes

1   When the second volume of Habermas' *Theory of Communicative Action* was translated into English (Habermas 1987), the seriousness of his encounter with Parsons was clearly seen. We would argue, in fact, that the framework Habermas employs in both volumes of this work can be seen as a neo-Marxist revision of Parsonian concepts.

2   But not revised enough, from our point of view. Ritzer (1988), for example, simply places "neofunctionalism" as the concluding section to "functionalism," following it with sections on conflict theory and so forth. We will argue below that the vitality of neofunctionalism casts doubt on this conventional division of theory texts. Neofunctionalism has taken as its project to open itself up to social conflict and contingent interaction. Insofar as it does so, then certainly "conflict theory" and "ethnomethodology" cannot be presented as responses to contemporary functionalist work. These reified divisions were never theoretically accurate ones (Alexander 1982a), but they did represent at least the historical self-consciousness of the profession in what we will below call the second phase of postwar sociology. At this point, we believe, they do not even do that. Sociology is embarked upon a third phase of postwar development which is in the process of making these textbook divisions obsolete.

3   After making this claim, we want immediately to stress that neofunctionalism, while a genuine intellectual movement, is not an integrated theory. There is much disagreement between those whom we would classify under this rubric, and some, in fact, do not welcome the general designation as such. We will talk more openly about this unformed and emergent character below.

4   We have limited our discussion only to developments within what American sociologists consider to be the matrix of their discipline. Outside of it, of course, there are also extremely important illustrations of this third phase. In France, for example, we would point to the poststructuralist movement, where cultural structures – discursive formations (Foucault 1984), cultural capital (Bourdieu), and political narratives (Lyotard 1984) – have replaced material ones.

5   In the next two pages we are presenting, in an abbreviated and condensed form, the arguments we made in chapter 2, pp. 33–42.

6   After Marx, there are the elaborations and revisions of writers like Engels, Kautsky, Otto Bauer, Labriola, and others. These specifications were interrupted, however, by the more radical reconstructionist efforts of the World War I generation, theorists like Lenin, Gramsci, Lukács, Korsch, and others. Subsequent specification of Marxism often occurred within these reformulated Marxian traditions of Lenin–Marx, Gramsci–Marx, Lukács–Marx, etc., whether or not the reconstruction was explicitly recognized. Later in the history of the Marxian tradition, thinkers like Sartre, Althusser, E. P. Thompson, and those associated with the Frankfurt School introduced a new round of more radical reformulation.

7   Thus, theorists who created new traditions were at an earlier point usually important reconstructors of the traditions out of which their new theories were formed. Marx is a case in point. In the early 1840s he was a "Young Hegelian," which was a radical, quasi-religious movement of Hegel's last students to reopen the master's theory to critical strands of the Enlightenment and even to socialist thought. When Marx

encountered political economy, he felt compelled to leave the Hegelian fold and created historical materialism. Interesting parallels can be drawn for Parsons. For the first ten years of his scholarly life, through the very publication of *The Structure of Social Action*, he seemed devoted to reconstructing the classical sociological traditions. He became more ambitious only at a later point in his career. One should be careful not to see the ideal-typical sequences – elaboration, revision, reconstruction, tradition-creation – as a scale of theoretical contribution. Most of the greatest minds in social science, for example, never make the transition from reconstruction to tradition creation, and many who have made the transition were much the worse for it. The works of Von Wiese are long forgotten, but the writings of Gramsci, Lukacs, Mannheim, and Mauss continue to be intently pursued.

8   Vico's work represents just such an example from classical traditions, Spencer's from the sociological.

9   For an excellent discussion from a very similar point, see the detailed critiques Bryan Turner makes of the efforts at theoretical cumulation that comprise the collection of ASA miniconference papers Jonathan Turner (1989) has collected in *Theory Building in Sociology*. Bryan Turner (1989, p. 132) concludes: "In sociology, we appear to have more dispersal and fragmentation of approaches than cumulation and organized growth, and these theoretical fragmentations are products of institutional fragmentation and competition between intellectuals for audience and patronage. . . . Analytical rupture rather than theory cumulation is the decisive aspect of sociology's history in the twentieth century."

10 Think here of vulgar Marxism, which actually encompasses most of what has been accepted as legitimate Marxist work, or of the reductionistic and mechanistic applications of Durkheim and Weber, which have been offered by some of their most devoted followers. It need hardly be said that Parsonian functionalism had its own large share of simplifiers.

11 For a discussion that highlights the concept of "sensibility" in the investigation of the shifting commitments of a major contemporary theorist, see Alexander (1986).

12 This is by no means always true, however. Bernstein's empirical challenge to the reigning Marxist proposition about the falling rate of profit – an issue of research program rather than generalized discourse – struck at the core of the tradition and initiated the reconstruction that came to be called the "social democratic" tendency in Marxism. This tendency was accompanied, however, by a great deal of generalized discourse.

13 Bellah's essays for "symbolic realism" would have to be read as an exception in this regard: they were discursive, generalized arguments. Yet they remained revisionist. Rather than critically confronting Parsons' cultural theory, Bellah argued symbolic realism was one clear implication of it.

14   In this regard, Munch's articles of this period, and some of his later work as well, resemble Alexander's (1978) own earlier discursive defense of Parsons. Though clearly engaging in revision, Alexander did not choose to confront Parsons' theory in a reconstructive way. In the late 1970s, the second phase of postwar theorizing was still a vigorous rising tide, and those sympathetic to Parsons' tradition confronted his critics in the polemical spirit of the time. It may have been Parsons' death in 1979, as well as the changing theoretical and political climate, that allowed a less defensive and more reconstructive posture to be assumed.

15   It might be useful, in fact, to introduce the concept "expropriation" to refer to the incorporation by one tradition of key elements of an opposing tradition in order to elaborate, revise, and reconstruct the home tradition itself. Thus, while Schluchter and Habermas express a sharp antipathy to functionalism, in this third phase of theorizing they have expropriated Parsons' theory in creative and quite thorough-going ways. Expropriation is one sign of the expansionary phase of a tradition.

16   The problem for Luhmann is quite different: he has not developed a theory of institutions, groups, and concrete interaction. The differences between Luhmann's and Munch's work, on the one hand, and the American and English neofunctionalists', on the other, is a topic briefly taken up in chapter 1. The differences stem less from differences in national traditions, perhaps, than from the contrasts in the disciplinary environments from within each emerged. In Germany, neither conflict nor "micro" sociology ever became as strongly institutionalized.

17   "Since the death of Talcott Parsons in Munich in 1979, it has become clear that a significant re-appraisal of Parsons' sociology and his impact on modern sociology is well underway. . . . This volume . . . may appropriately be regarded as part of this new wave of re-evaluation" (Holton and Turner 1986, p. 1). The movement beyond affirmative revision is demonstrated by the fact that in his review of Holton and Turner's book in the *American Journal of Sociology*, Lechner (1988) – himself an active theorist in the reconstructionist movement – offers the criticism that it is "too positive" about Parsons!

18   For a detailed discussion of one of the most elaborated of these research programs, see our discussion of Eisenstadt in Alexander and Colomy (1988).

19   For a much more detailed analysis of recent developments in differentiation theory, see Colomy (1986, 1990c). For discussions that situate the emergence and development of differentiation theory in a broader historical and theoretical context see Giesen (1988, 1990) and Alexander (1988d).

20   Our discussion here has focused only on the primordial issue of culture–society boundary relations. Once the possible attenuation of this boundary relation has been acknowledged, however, a more internalist and

less socially circumscribed understanding of the cultural system can begin to be developed. In his efforts to incorporate semiotic and hermeneutic models, and to elaborate the "late Durkheimian" approach to cultural studies, Alexander's research has recently moved in this direction (1988b). See also Edles (1988) and Rambo and Chan (1990).

References

Alexander, J. C. 1978, Formal and substantive voluntarism in the work of Talcott Parsons: a theoretical and ideological reinterpretation. *American Sociological Review*, 43, pp. 177–98.

—— 1979a, Paradigm revision and "Parsonianism." *Canadian Journal of Sociology*, 4, pp. 343–57.

—— 1979b, Sociology for liberals. *The New Republic* (June 2), pp. 10–12.

—— 1980, Core solidarity, ethnic outgroups, and social differentiation: a multi-dimensional model of inclusion in modern societies. In J. Dofny and A. Akiwowo (eds), *National and Ethnic Movements*. Beverly Hills: Sage, pp. 5–28.

—— 1981, The mass media in systemic, historical and comparative perspective. In E. Katz and T. Szeckso (eds), *Mass Media and Social Change*. Beverly Hills: Sage, pp. 17–51.

—— 1982a, *Theoretical Logic in Sociology*, vol. 1: *Positivism, Presuppositions, and Current Controversies*. Berkeley: University of California Press.

—— 1982b, *Theoretical Logic in Sociology*, vol. 2: *The Antinomies of Classical Thought: Marx and Durkheim*. Berkeley: University of California Press.

—— 1983a, *Theoretical Logic in Sociology*, vol. 3: *The Classical Attempt at Theoretical Synthesis: Max Weber*. Berkeley: University of California Press.

—— 1983b, *Theoretical Logic in Sociology*, vol. 4: *The Modern Reconstruction of Classical Thought: Talcott Parsons*. Berkeley: University of California Press.

—— 1984, Three models of culture and society relations: toward an analysis of Watergate. *Sociological Theory*, 2, pp. 290–314.

—— 1985a, Introduction. In J. Alexander (ed.), *Neofunctionalism*. Beverly Hills: Sage, pp. 7–8.

—— 1985b, The individualist dilemma in phenomenology and interactionism: toward a synthesis with the classical tradition. In S. N. Eisenstadt and H. J. Helle (eds), *Perspectives on Sociological Theory*, vol. 1. Beverly Hills: Sage, pp. 25–57.

—— 1986, Science, sense, and sensibility. *Theory and Society*, 15, pp. 443–63.

—— 1987a, Action and its environments. In J. C. Alexander, B. Giesen, R. Munch, and N. J. Smelser (eds), *The Micro–Macro Link*. Berkeley: University of California Press, 289–318.

—— 1987b, On the centrality of the classics. In A. Giddens and J. Turner (eds), *Social Theory Today*. London: Polity Press, pp. 11–57.

—— 1987c, *Twenty Lectures*. New York: Columbia University Press.

—— 1988a, Between progress and apocalypse: social theory and the dream of reason in the twentieth century. Paper presented at the conference "Social Progress and Sociological Theory: Movements, Forces, and Ideas at the End of the Twentieth Century", Krakow, Poland.

—— 1988b, Culture and political crisis: Watergate and Durkheimian sociology. In J. C. Alexander (ed.), *Durkheimian Sociology: Cultural Studies*. New York: Columbia University Press, pp. 187–224.

—— 1988c, *Action and its Environments*. New York: Columbia University Press.

—— 1988d, Durkheim's problem and differentiation theory today. In J. C. Alexander, *Action and its Environments*. New York: Columbia University Press, pp. 49–77.

—— 1995, General Theory in the Postpositivist mode: the "epistemological dilemma" and the search for present reason. In J. Alexander, *Fin de Siècle Social Theory*. New York: Verso, pp. 90–127.

Alexander, J. C., and Colomy, P. 1988, Social differentiation and collective behaviour. In J. C. Alexander, *Action and its Environments*, New York: Columbia University Press.

Alexander, J. C., and Giesen, B. 1987, From reduction to linkage: the long view of the micro–macro debate. In J. C. Alexander, B. Giesen, R. Munch, and N. J. Smelser (eds), *The Micro–Macro Link*, Berkeley: University of California Press, pp. 1–44.

Archer, M. S. 1985, The myth of cultural integration. *British Journal of Sociology*, 36, pp. 333–53.

—— 1988, *Culture and Agency: The Place of Culture in Social Theory*. Cambridge: Cambridge University Press.

Becker, H. 1982, *Art Worlds*. Berkeley: University of California Press.

Bellah, R. N. 1957, *Tokugawa Religion: The Values of Pre-Industrial Japan*. Glencoe, IL.: Free Press.

—— 1959, Durkheim and history. *American Sociological Review*, 24, pp. 447–61.

—— 1970, *Beyond Belief*. New York: Harper and Row.

—— 1973, Introduction. In R. N. Bellah (ed.), *Emile Durkheim: On Morality and Society*. Chicago: University of Chicago Press, pp. ix–lv.

Blau, P. M. 1977, *Inequality and Heterogeneity: A Primitive Theory of Social Structure*. New York: Free Press.

Calhoun, C. 1982, *The Question of Class Struggle: Social Foundations of Popular Radicalism during the Industrial Revolution*. Chicago: University of Chicago Press.

Camic, C. 1986, The return of the functionalists. *Contemporary Sociology*, 15, pp. 692–5.

Champagne, D. 1990, Culture, differentiation, and environment: social change in Tlingit society. In J. C. Alexander and P. Colomy (eds), *Differentiation Theory and Social Change: Historical and Comparative Perspectives*, New York: Columbia University Press, pp. 52–87.

Coleman, J. S. 1986a, Social theory, social research, and a theory of action. *American Journal of Sociology*, 91, pp. 1309–35.

—— 1986b, *Individual Interests and Collective Action: Selected Essays*. New York: Cambridge University Press.

—— 1987, Microfoundations and macrosocial behavior. In J. C. Alexander, B. Giesen, R. Munch, and N. J. Smelser (eds), *The Micro–Macro Link*. Berkeley: University of California Press, pp. 153–73.

Collins, R. 1975, *Conflict Sociology: Toward an Explanatory Science*. New York: Academic Press.

—— 1981, On the micro-foundations of macro-sociology. *American Journal of Sociology*, 86, pp. 984–1014.

—— 1987, Interaction ritual chains, power and property: the micro–macro connection as an empirically based theoretical problem. In J. C. Alexander, B. Giesen, R. Munch, and N. J. Smelser (eds), *The Micro–Macro Link*. Berkeley: University of California Press, pp. 193–206.

—— 1988a, *Theoretical Sociology*. San Diego: Harcourt Brace Jovanovich.

—— 1988b, The Durkheimian tradition in conflict sociology. In J. C. Alexander (ed.), *Durkheimian Sociology: Cultural Studies*. New York: Cambridge University Press, pp. 107–28.

Colomy, P. 1985, Uneven structural differentiation: toward a comparative approach. In J. C. Alexander (ed.), *Neofunctionalism*. Beverly Hills: Sage, pp. 131–56.

—— 1986, Recent developments in the functionalist approach to change. *Sociological Focus*, 19, pp. 139–58.

—— 1990a, Uneven differentiation and incomplete institutionalization: political change and continuity in the early American nation. In J. C. Alexander and P. Colomy (eds), *Differentiation Theory and Social Change: Comparative and Historical Perspectives*. New York: Columbia University Press, pp. 119–62.

—— 1990b, Strategic groups and political differentiation in the antebellum United States. In J. C. Alexander and P. Colomy (eds), *Differentiation Theory and Social Change: Comparative and Historical Perspectives*. New York: Columbia University Press, pp. 222–64.

—— 1990c, Revisions and progress in differentiation theory. In J. C. Alexander and P. Colomy (eds), *Differentiation Theory and Social Change: Comparative and Historical Perspectives*. New York: Columbia University Press, pp. 465–95.

Colomy, P., and Rhoades, G. 1988, Specifying the micro–macro link: an application of general theory to the study of structural differentiation. Paper presented at the Annual Meeting of the American Sociological Association, Atlanta, Georgia.

Colomy, P., and Tausig, M.   1988, The differentiation of applied sociology: prospects and problems. Manuscript presented at the Annual Meeting of the Society for Applied Sociology, 1987.

Darnton, R.   1982, *The Literary Underground of the Old Regime*. Cambridge, MA: Harvard University Press.

Devereux, E. C., Jr.   1961, Parsons' sociological theory. In M. Black (ed.), *The Social Theories of Talcott Parsons*. Carbondale and Edwardsville: Southern Illinois University Press, pp. 1–63.

Eder, K.   1990, Contradictions and social evolution. In H. Haferkamp and N. J. Smelser (eds), *Social Change and Modernity*. Berkeley: University of California Press, pp. 320–49.

Edles, L. D.   1988, Political culture and the transition to democracy in Spain. Ph.D. dissertation, University of California, Los Angeles.

Eisenstadt, S. N.   1963, *The Political Systems of Empires*. New York: Free Press.

—— 1971, Introduction. In S. N. Eisenstadt (ed.), *Weber on Charisma and Institution Building*. Chicago: University of Chicago Press, pp. ix–lvi.

—— 1980, Cultural orientations, institutional entrepreneurs, and social change: comparative analyses of traditional civilizations. *American Journal of Sociology*, 85, pp. 840–69.

—— 1986, Culture and social structure revisited. *International Sociology*, 1, pp. 297–320.

Fine, G. A.   1984, Negotiated orders and organizational cultures. *Annual Review of Sociology*, 10, pp. 239–62.

—— 1988, Symbolic interactionism in the post-Blumerian age. In G. Ritzer (ed.), *Frontiers of Social Theory*. New York: Columbia University Press, pp. 117–57.

Foucault, M.   1984, *The Foucault Reader*, ed. Paul Rabinow. New York: Pantheon.

Friedrichs, R.   1970, *A Sociology of Sociology*. New York: Free Press.

Geertz, C.   1973, *The Interpretation of Cultures*. New York: Basic Books.

Giddens, A.   1971, *Capitalism and Modern Social Theory*. Cambridge: Cambridge University Press.

—— 1984, *The Constitution of Society*. Berkeley: University of California Press.

Giddens, A., and Turner, J. (eds)   1987, *Social Theory Today*. London: Polity Press.

Giesen, B.   1988, The autonomy of social change. *International Review of Sociology*.

—— 1990, The change in "Change": an evolution theoretical view on the history of the concept. In H. Haferkamp and N. J. Smelser (eds), *Social Change and Modernity*. Berkeley: University of California Press.

Gill, S., Stockard, J., Johnson, M., and Williams, S.   1987, Measuring gender differences: the expressive dimension and critique of androgyny scales. *Sex Roles*, 17, pp. 375–400.

Goffman, E. 1974, *Frame Analysis*. New York: Harper and Row.

Goode, W. 1978, *The Celebration of Heroes: Prestige as a Social Control System*. Berkeley: University of California Press.

Gould, M. 1981, Parsons versus Marx: an earnest warning. *Sociological Inquiry*, 51, 197–218.

—— 1985, Prolegomena to any future theory of societal crisis. In J. C. Alexander (ed.), *Neofunctionalism*. Beverly Hills: Sage, pp. 51–71.

—— 1987, *Revolution in the Development of Capitalism*. Berkeley: University of California Press.

Habermas, J. 1975, *Legitimation Crisis*, tr. Thomas McCarthy. Boston: Beacon Press.

—— 1984, *The Theory of Communicative Action*, vol. 1: *Reason and Rationalization of Society*, tr. Thomas McCarthy. Boston: Beacon Press.

—— 1987, *The Theory of Communicative Action*, vol. 2: *Life-world and System: A Critique of Functionalist Reason*, tr. Thomas McCarthy. Boston: Beacon Press.

Heritage, J., and Greatbatch, D. 1986, Generating applause: a study of rhetoric and response at party political conferences. *American Journal of Sociology*, 92, pp. 110–57.

Holton, R. J. 1986, Talcott Parsons and the theory of economy and society. In R. J. Holton and B. S. Turner, *Talcott Parsons: On Economy and Society*. London: Routledge and Kegan Paul, pp. 25–105.

Holton, R. J., and Turner, B. S. 1986, *Talcott Parsons: On Economy and Society*. London: Routledge and Kegan Paul.

Hondrich, K. Otto 1990, World society versus niche societies: paradoxes of undirectional evolution. In H. Haferkamp and N. J. Smelser (eds), *Social Change and Modernity*. Berkeley: University of California Press, pp. 350–66.

Johnson, H. M. 1960, *Sociology: A Systematic Introduction*. New York: Harcourt, Brace.

Johnson, M. M. 1975, Fathers, mothers, and sex typing. *Sociological Inquiry*, 45, pp. 15–26.

—— 1977, Androgyny and the maternal principle. *School Review*, 86, pp. 50–69.

—— 1981, Heterosexuality, male dominance, and the father image. *Sociological Inquiry*, 51, pp. 129–39.

—— 1982, Fathers and femininity in daughters: a review of the research. *Sociology and Social Research*, 67, pp. 1–17.

—— 1988a, *Strong Mothers, Weak Wives: The Search for Gender Equality*. Berkeley: University of California Press.

—— 1988b, Feminism and the theories of Talcott Parsons. Paper presented at the American Sociological Association meeting, Atlanta, GA.

Johnson, M. M., Stockard, J., Acker, J., and Naffziger, C. 1975, Expressiveness reevaluated. *School Review*, 83, pp. 617–44.

Johnson, M. M., Stockard, J., Rothbart, M. K., and Friedman, L. 1981, Sexual preference, feminism, and women's perceptions of their parents. *Sex Roles*, 7, pp. 1–18.

Knorr-Cetina, K., and Cicourel, A. V. (eds) 1981, *Advances in Social Theory and Methodology: Toward an Integration of Micro- and Macro-Sociologies*. Boston: Routledge and Kegan Paul.

Lechner, F. 1984, Ethnicity and revitalization in the modern world system. *Sociological Focus*, 17, pp. 243–56.

—— 1985, Modernity and its discontents. In J. C. Alexander (ed.), *Neofunctionalism*. Beverly Hills: Sage, pp. 157–76.

—— 1988, Review of Holton and Turner, *Talcott Parsons: On Economy and Society, American Journal of Sociology*, 94 (no. 2), pp. 404–5.

—— 1990, Fundamentalism as path away from differentiation. In J. C. Alexander and P. Colomy (eds), *Differentiation Theory and Social Change: Comparative and Historical Perspectives*. New York: Columbia University Press, pp. 88–118.

Lefort, C. 1986, *The Political Forms of Modern Society: Bureaucracy, Democracy, Totalitarianism*, ed. and with an introduction by John B. Thompson. Cambridge, MA: MIT Press.

Lehman, E. W. 1988, The theory of the state versus the state of theory. *American Sociological Review*, 53, pp. 807–23.

Lewis, D. J., and Smith, R. L. 1980, *American Sociology and Pragmatism: Mead, Chicago Sociology, and Symbolic Interaction*. Chicago: University of Chicago Press.

Lidz, C. W., and Lidz, V. M. 1976, Piaget's psychology of intelligence and the theory of action. In J. Loubser et al. (eds), *Explorations in General Theory in Social Science*. New York: Free Press, pp. 195–239.

Lidz, V. 1970, Values in sociology: a critique of Szymanski. *Sociological Inquiry*, 40, pp. 13–20.

—— 1972, On the construction of objective theory: rejoinder to Syzmanski. *Sociological Inquiry*, 42, pp. 51–64.

Loubser, J. J., Baum, R. C., Effrat, A., and Lidz, V. M. (eds) 1976, *Explorations in General Theory in Social Science*, vols 1 and 2. New York: Free Press.

Luhmann, N. 1982, *The Differentiation of Society*, tr. Stephen Holmes and Charles Larmore. New York: Columbia University Press.

—— 1990a, The paradox of system differentiation and the evolution of society. In J. C. Alexander and P. Colomy (eds), *Differentiation Theory and Social Change: Comparative and Historical Perspectives*. New York: Columbia University Press, 409–40.

—— 1990b, The direction of evolution. In H. Haferkamp and N. J. Smelser (eds), *Social Change and Modernity*, Berkeley: University of California Press, pp. 279–93.

Lyotard, J. F. 1984, *The Postmodern Condition: A Report on Knowledge*, tr. Geoff Bennington and Brian Massumi. Minneapolis: University of Minnesota Press.

Mayhew, L. (ed.) 1982, *Talcott Parsons: On Institutions and Social Evolution*. Chicago: University of Chicago Press.

—— 1984, In defense of modernity: Talcott Parsons and the utilitarian tradition. *American Journal of Sociology*, 89, pp. 1273–1305.

—— 1990, The differentiation of the solidary public. In J. C. Alexander and P. Colomy (eds), *Differentiation Theory and Social Change: Comparative and Historical Perspectives*. New York: Columbia University Press, pp. 294–322.

Meyer, J. W., and Scott, W. R. 1983, *Organizational Environments: Ritual and Rationality*. Beverly Hills: Sage.

Molotch, H. L., and Boden, D. 1985, Talking social structure: discourse, domination and the Watergate hearings. *American Sociological Review*, 50, pp. 273–88.

Moore, B. Jr. 1978, *Injustice: The Social Bases of Obedience and Revolt*. New York: Pantheon.

Munch, R. 1981, Talcott Parsons and the theory of action I: the structure of Kantian lore. *American Journal of Sociology*, 86, pp. 709–49.

—— 1982, Talcott Parsons and the theory of action II: the continuity of development. *American Journal of Sociology*, 87, pp. 771–826.

—— 1983, Modern science and technology: differentiation or interpenetration? *International Journal of Comparative Sociology*, 24, pp. 157–75.

—— 1986, The American creed in sociological theory. *Sociology Theory*, 4, pp. 41–60.

—— 1987a, *Theory of Action*. London: Routledge and Kegan Paul.

—— 1987b, The interpenetration of microinteraction and macrostructures in a complex and contingent institutional order. In J. C. Alexander, B. Giesen, R. Munch, and N. J. Smelser (eds), *The Micro–Macro Link*. Berkeley: University of California Press, pp. 319–36.

—— 1988, *Understanding Modernity*. London: Routledge and Kegan Paul.

—— 1990a, Social change in the United States: the system of equality and inequality. In H. Haferkamp and N. J. Smelser (eds), *Social Change and Modernity*. Berkeley: University of California Press, pp. 147–76.

—— 1990b, Differentiation, rationalization, interpretation: the emergence of modern society. In J. C. Alexander and P. Colomy (eds), *Differentiation Theory and Social Change: Comparative and Historical Perspectives*. New York: Columbia University Press, pp. 441–64.

Orru, M. 1988, Review of *Talcott Parsons: On Economy and Society* (by Robert J. Holton and Bryan S. Turner) and *The Integration of Economic and Sociological Theory* (The Marshall Lectures, University of Cambridge, 1953). *Contemporary Sociology*, 17, pp. 115–17.

Page, C. H. 1985, On neofunctionalism. *Footnotes*, 13, p. 10.

Parsons, T. 1937, *The Structure of Social Action.* New York: Free Press.

Parsons, T., Shils, E., Naegele, K. D., and Pitts, J. R. (eds) 1961, *Theories of Society.* New York: Free Press.

Peters, J. D., and Rothenbuhler, E. W. 1988, The reality of construction. In H. Simons (ed.), *Perspectives on the Rhetoric of the Human Sciences.* London: Sage, pp. 11–27.

Prager, J. 1986, *Building Democracy in Ireland: Political Order and Cultural Integration in a Newly Independent Nation.* Cambridge: Cambridge University Press.

Rambo, E. 1988, Economic culture. PhD dissertation, University of California, Los Angeles.

Rambo, E., and Chan, K. 1990, Text, structure and action in cultural sociology, *Theory and Society*, 19, pp. 635–48.

Rhoades, G. 1990, Political competition and differentiation in higher education. In J. C. Alexander and P. Colomy (eds), *Differentiation Theory and Social Change: Comparative and Historical Perspectives.* New York: Columbia University Press, pp. 187–221.

Ritzer, G. 1975, *Sociology: A Multiple Paradigm Science.* Boston: Allyn and Bacon.

—— 1985, The rise of micro-sociological theory. *Sociological Theory*, 3, pp. 88–98.

—— 1988, *Sociological Theory*, 2nd edn. New York: Knopf.

Robertson, R. 1982, Parsons on the evolutionary significance of American religion. *Sociological Analysis*, 43, pp. 307–26.

—— 1985, The sacred and the world-system. In P. Hammond (ed.), *The Sacred in a Post-Secular Age.* Berkeley: University of California Press, pp. 347–58.

—— 1986, Sociological theory and images of world order: a working paper. Paper presented at the American Sociological Association and German Sociological Association Conference on Development and Change, Berkeley, California.

—— 1987, Globalization theory and civilizational analysis. *Comparative Civilizations Review*, 17, pp. 20–30.

—— 1988, The sociological significance of culture: some general considerations. *Theory Culture and Society*, 5, pp. 3–23.

—— 1990, Globality, global culture and images of world order. In H. Haferkamp and N. Smelser (eds), *Social Change and Modernity.* Berkeley: University of California Press, pp. 395–411.

Robertson, R., and Chirico, J. 1985, Humanity, globalization and worldwide religious resurgence. *Sociological Analysis*, 46, pp. 219–42.

Robertson, R., and Lechner, F. 1985, Modernization, globalization and the problem of culture in world-systems theory. *Theory, Culture and Society*, 2, pp. 103–18.

Rothenbuhler, E. W.   1986a, A cross-national analysis of communication in social conflict. Paper presented to the Annual Convention of the American Association for Public Opinion Research, St Petersburg Beach, Florida.

——   1986b, Media events and social solidarity: an updated report on the living room celebration of the Olympic Games. Paper presented to the Annual Convention of the International Communication Association, Chicago.

——   1987, Neofunctionalism and mass communication. In M. Gurevitch and M. R. Levy (eds), *Mass Communication Review Yearbook*, vol. 6. Newbury Park, Cal.: Sage, pp. 67–85.

——   1988a, Live broadcasting, media events, telecommunication, an social form. In D. R. Maines and C. Couch (eds), *Information, Communication, and Social Structure*. Springfield, IL.: Charles C. Thomas, pp. 231–43.

——   1988b, The liminal flight: mass strikes as ritual and interpretation. In J. C. Alexander (ed.), *Durkheimian Sociology*. New York: Columbia University Press, pp. 66–89.

——   1988c, The living room celebration of the Olympic Games. *Journal of Communication*, 38 (no. 4), pp. 61–82.

——   1989, Values and symbols in public orientations to the Olympic media event. *Critical Studies in Mass Communication*, 6 (no. 2), pp. 138–58.

——   n.d. Collective action and communication. Paper, Department of Communication Studies, University of Iowa.

Schegloff, E. A.   1987, Between macro and micro: context and other connections. In J. C. Alexander, B. Giesen, R. Munch, and N. J. Smelser (eds), *The Micro–Macro Link*. Berkeley: University of California Press, pp. 207–34.

Schluchter, W.   1979, The paradox of rationalization. In G. Roth and W. Schluchter, *Max Weber's Vision of History*. Berkeley: University of California Press, pp. 11–64.

——   1981, *The Rise of Western Rationalism: Max Weber's Developmental History*. (Translated by Guenther Roth.) Berkeley: University of California Press.

Sciulli, D.   1985, The practical groundwork of critical theory: bringing Parsons to Habermas (and vice versa). In J. Alexander (ed.), *Neofunctionalism*. Beverly Hills: Sage, pp. 21–50.

——   1986, Voluntaristic action. *American Sociological Review*, 51, pp. 743–67.

——   1988, Reconsidering interactionism's corrective against the excesses of functionalism. *Symbolic Interaction*, 11, pp. 69–84.

——   1989, Theory of societal constitutionalism: foundations of a non-Marxist critical theory. Manuscript.

——   1990, Differentiation and collegial formations: implications of societal constitutionalism. In J. C. Alexander and P. Colomy (eds), *Differentiation Theory and Social Change: Comparative and Historical Perspectives*. New York: Columbia University Press, pp. 367–405.

Sewell, W. Jr. 1980, *Work and Revolution in France: The Language of Labor from the Old Regime to 1848*. Cambridge: Cambridge University Press.

―― 1985, *Structure and Mobility: The Men and Women of Marseilles, 1820–1870*. Cambridge: Cambridge University Press.

Skocpol, T. and Finegold, K. 1982, State capacity and economic intervention in the early new deal. *Political Science Quarterly*, 97, pp. 255–78.

Smelser, N. J. 1959, *Social Change in the Industrial Revolution*. Chicago: University of Chicago Press.

―― 1962, *Theory of Collective Behavior*. New York: Free Press.

―― (ed.) 1973, *Karl Marx: On Society and Societal Change*. Chicago: University of Chicago Press.

―― 1985, Evaluating the model of structural differentiation in relation to educational change in the nineteenth century. In J. C. Alexander (ed.), *Neofunctionalism*. Beverly Hills: Sage, pp. 113–29.

―― 1990, The contest between family and schooling in nineteenth century Britain. In J. C. Alexander and P. Colomy (eds), *Differentiation Theory and Social Change: Comparative and Historical Perspectives*. New York: Columbia University Press, 165–86.

Stockard, J., and Johnson, M. M. 1979, The social origins of male dominance. *Sex Roles*, 5, pp. 199–218.

Stryker, S. 1980, *Symbolic Interactionism: A Social Structural Version*. Menlo Park, CA: Benjamin Cummings.

Surace, S. 1982, Incomplete differentiation. In P. Colomy (ed.), *Dynamics of Social Systems*, pp. 93–119.

Swidler, A. 1986, Culture in action. *American Sociological Review*, 51, pp. 273–86.

Syzmanski, A. 1970a, Toward a radical sociology. *Sociological Inquiry*, 40, pp. 3–13.

―― 1970b, The value of sociology: an answer to Lidz. *Sociological Inquiry*, 40, pp. 21–5.

―― 1972, Dialectical functionalism: a further answer to Lidz. *Sociological Inquiry*, 42, pp. 145–53.

Tiryakian, E. A. 1985, On the significance of dedifferentiation. In S. N. Eisenstadt and H. J. Helle (eds), *Macro-Sociological Theory: Perspectives on Sociological Theory*, vol. 1, Beverly Hills: Sage, pp. 118–34.

―― 1990, Dialectics of modernity: Reenchantment and dedifferentiation as counter processes. In H. Haferkamp and N. J. Smelser (eds), *Social Change and Modernity*. Berkeley: University of California Press, pp. 78–94.

Turner, B. S. 1986a, *Citizenship and Capitalism*. London: Allen and Unwin.

―― 1986b, Personhood and citizenship. *Theory, Culture, and Society*, 3, pp. 1–16.

―― 1987, Marx, Weber, and the coherence of capitalism. In N. Wiley (ed.), *The Marx–Weber Debate*. Beverly Hills: Sage, pp. 169–204.

—— 1989, Commentary: some reflections on cumulative theorizing in sociology. In J. H. Turner (ed.), *Theory Building in Sociology*.

Turner, J. H. (ed.) 1989, *Theory Building in Sociology*. Beverly Hills: Sage.

Turner, J. H., and Maryanski, A. 1988, Is "Neofunctionalism" really functional? *Sociological Theory*, 6, pp. 110–21.

Wagner, D. G. 1984, *The Growth of Sociological Theories*. Beverly Hills: Sage.

Wagner, D. G., and Berger, J. 1985, Do sociological theories grow? *American Journal of Sociology*, 90, pp. 697–728.

Williams, R. M., Jr. 1961, The sociological theory of Talcott Parsons. In M. Black (ed.), *The Social Theories of Talcott Parsons*. Carbondale and Edwardsville: Southern Illinois University Press, pp. 64–99.

Wippler, R., and Lindenberg, S. 1987, Collective phenomena and rational choice. In J. C. Alexander, B. Giesen, R. Munch, and N. J. Smelser (eds), *The Micro–Macro Link*. Berkeley: University of California Press, pp. 135–52.

Wuthnow, R. 1988, *Meaning and Moral Order: Explorations in Cultural Analysis*. Berkeley: University of California Press.

4

Parsons' *Structure* in American Sociology

At the annual meeting of the American Sociological Association in 1987, a session held to commemorate the fiftieth anniversary of the publication of the *The Structure of Social Action* drew a large and interested audience. Had the commemoration been held 20 years earlier, it is quite likely that it would have occurred entirely within the framework of *Structure* itself. Speakers would have treated the work as an exercise in general theory, as a hugely successful attempt to provide an explanatory framework for empirical sociology. They would have assessed the box score of empirical and theoretical "progress" since its publication in 1937; spoken about "recent developments" in the field; and probably would have concluded – with an important dissent registered here and there – that in the 30 years following its appearance significant accumulation and elaboration had occurred. The *Structure*, in other words, would at that time have been taken as a founding event in a relatively consensual, proto-scientific discipline. For even as late as the mid-1960s, *Structure* was still seen as Parsons had originally presented it: as a framework of accumulated theoretical knowledge, on the basis of which predictions could be made and compared (favorably) with what social scientists had subsequently discovered about empirical fact.

In the late 1970s, by contrast, such a commemoration would not have taken place. The profession at that time was involved in a massive effort to overthrow *Structure* and, in doing so, to free itself from what was thought to be the pernicious influence of functionalist thought. *Structure* was still viewed as an exercise in general explanatory theory – though as an ideological document as well – but it was now widely felt by many that contemporary empirical reality no longer fit the model, if ever it had. Those leading this struggle – theorists like Gouldner, Garfinkel, Blumer, Giddens, Collins – believed that the theory articulated by *Structure* was something social science should, and probably would, safely leave behind.

Yet here we are, in the late 1990s, still talking about *Structure* and, indeed, commemorating it. The announcement of *Structure*'s death turns out to have been premature, as was the announcement of Parsons'. In fact, it is possible that, with the exception of Habermas, no postclassical sociological theorist is more talked about today in Europe and the United States than Parsons himself, though this talk is certainly more reflective and selective than it was in the late 1960s. And since I have brought up Habermas, let me make the obvious point: Who could possibly know what in the devil Habermas is talking about if they did not know Parsons' work? In the last decade Habermas has decided that Parsons must not only be his Hegel but his Ricardo, that it is Parsons whose ideas he must internalize and dispute (Alexander 1985, cf. Sciulli 1985), if his new version of critical theory is going to fly.

Why now, why still? To honor the publication of *Structure* – Parsons' first and finest single work – we must answer these questions. The first answer is rather obvious: we find that sociologists are still talking about their empirical problems in explicit relation – both positive and negative – to the problems that *Structure* first posed. Jonathan Turner, one of my partners in that 1987 ASA symposium, published *The Structure of Social Interaction* in 1988. His title is not fortuitous. It signals that Turner has written his new book to argue against what he claims to be a monistic bias in the Parsonian approach to action. Turner is confident, moreover, that Parsons' title of 1937 is still so well known that his play on words will be immediately recognized. The same evidence that *Structure* remains our contemporary can be found in the work of Harold Garfinkel, my other partner on the platform of the ASA commemoration. As Garfinkel attests (1988), it is impossible to understand the theoretical significance of ethnomethodology without understanding that it has developed in dialogue with Parsons' early work. Indeed, Garfinkel still insists that to properly understand the microfoundations of social order we must understand just why *Structure* explained it in the wrong way. As I will suggest later in this chapter, there are numerous other contemporary works that continue to present and justify their findings in the same way.

But there are even more important reasons for the continuing contemporary relevance of Parsons' early work. It is not only that there continue to be important discussions about, and in relation to, *Structure*'s earlier concepts. It is also that we can now understand the influence of *Structure* in a more reflective and more accurate way. Armed with the postempiricist philosophy, history, and sociology of science, we understand theorizing differently than we once did. We are less inclined to see theory as a pragmatic test shot at empirical targets, the reality of which are taken for granted. To the contrary, we now understand that theory has an important role in *creating* the objects as well as their explanation.

Twice removed from the period in which the concepts of *Structure* were taken to be identical with society as such, we are beginning to appreciate that it was *Structure* that itself helped to invent – not simply discover – the empirical universe within which postwar sociology lived and within which, by and large, it continues to live today. Sociology, therefore, has not escaped from *Structure* by arguing against its propositions, concepts, or even its intellectual history. The reason is that it has done so largely within the frame of reference that *Structure* had such a huge part in establishing. If contemporary sociology is a language game, albeit one with rational and scientific aspirations, it was *Structure* that gave to this language some of its most important words.

By virtue of its intrinsic power and extrinsic intellectual influence, *Structure* played a key role, perhaps the key role, in establishing the base line vocabulary for modern sociology. It is in the post-World War II period that this contemporary, "modern" sociology may be said to have begun. Published in the no man's land between this postwar era and the close of the classical age, *Structure* functioned both as dividing watershed and integrating bridge. It did so in two distinctive ways. First, it constructed – through selection and interpretation – the classical heritage from which subsequent theoretical and empirical sociology would draw. Second, it translated the "classics" into a particular conceptual vocabulary, one which is still largely in force today. It is for both of these reasons that *Structure* is still a living and vital theoretical work. It has, indeed, become a classic in its own right.[1]

I will take up each of these pathways to classical ascension in turn. I begin with the translation of earlier theorizing – what *Structure* taught us to call "classical" theorizing – into a new and eventually omnipresent theoretical vocabulary. Parsons' goal in *Structure* was not simply to recount, either historically or hermeneutically, the "real meaning" of Durkheim, Weber, Pareto, and Marshall. He wanted, rather, to demonstrate that they had established a new conceptual scheme. It is revealing that, before he ever got to these writers, Parsons spent more than one hundred pages laying this scheme out. He made three points.

1   Sociology is about the problem of order. What Parsons called the Hobbesian problem can be understood in the following way: What holds "society" together? Is it force and fraud – in which case the Hobbesian problem is avoided – some common commitment to values, or both?

2   Any solution to the order problem involves an approach to action. To avoid Hobbes' Leviathan, the essential liberty of action, what Parsons called "voluntarism," must be maintained. This can only be done if the interpretive (nonrational) character of action is accepted: actors strive for meaning.

3   Parsons' third point ties together his first and second. If actors strive for meaning, they orient themselves toward norms that provide standards of evaluation. Insofar as these standards are shared, they can be called values. Insofar as values are internalized, they solve the problem of order in an anti-Hobbesian way.

Parsons went on to demonstrate ingeniously and brilliantly, if often quite mistakenly, that Durkheim, Weber, Pareto, and Marshall each discovered and promulgated these very points.

In the half century after *Structure*, Parsons' answers to these three central questions became three of the most central and contentious notions in empirical and theoretical sociology. That the relation of these concepts to classical sociology has become just as central and vexing to the emerging field that is called the history of sociology is a topic to which I will return. I want initially to take up the argument generated by these concepts in and of themselves.

According to an understanding of this conceptual scheme that became increasingly widespread, *Structure* had addressed these points in a manner that created two central dichotomies.

The first was conflict versus order. Before Parsons wrote *Structure*, there was no such beast as "conflict theory." Certainly there were theorists who emphasized conflict, like Marx, and others who emphasized order and consensus, like Durkheim. But the problem had never been posed in terms of "theories of" either one. While this was not how Parsons himself had actually posed the problem, there is a powerful subtext in his argument that does allow this dichotomy between order and consensus to be drawn.

Between 1950 and 1960, Ralf Dahrendorf, David Lockwood, John Rex, Alvin Gouldner, and C. Wright Mills wrote that there were conflict theories and order theories and that the choice between them defined the future of macrosociology.[2] Order theories, in their view, talked exclusively about nonrational action, values and equilibrium;

conflict theories, by contrast, emphasized instrumental action, power, and disorder. In the next generation, macrosociologists like Michael Mann, Randall Collins, Charles Tilly, and Theda Skocpol elaborated conflict and "structural" sociologies that sought to build exclusively upon this antivoluntaristic, anticultural base. Their results are open to debate. In my own work (e.g., Alexander 1988a), I have argued that in dismissing culture and subjectivity these theorists have made serious mistakes. What is important in this context, however, is to see that the sources of the "structuralism" so hegemonic in contemporary macrosociology are directly if dialectically linked to Parsons' publication of 1937.

The second dichotomy that *Structure* appeared to have established was between action and order. Through his notion of value internalization, Parsons tied individual effort to the ordering power of social structure. Was there, his critics wondered, any truly individual action left? In my view, once again, this is by no means an accurate rendition of what Parsons was up to. The theorist whose intention was to save subjectivity, and who called his work "the theory of action," could hardly have intended to eliminate individual action as such. Still, it is quite possible to read *Structure* in this way and, again, an entire generation of microsociologists did just this.[3]

For Herbert Blumer, George Homans, the early Erving Goffman, the later Garfinkel, Ralph Turner, and Aaron Cicourel, the only way to emphasize the importance of individual, contingent action was to neutralize the influence of values and prior social structure as such. The result was a brilliant body of work that elaborated the interactive strategies, rational and interpretive intentions, and creative structuring capabilities of individual actors. This work decisively illuminated a whole range of empirical domains. It did so, however, by cutting sociology in half. Because they understood *Structure* in a distinctive way, these studies of individual interaction significantly deepened and reinforced the micro–macro divide. Still, in the present context, whether they misunderstood Parsons is not the point; without the framework of *Structure*, they would not have formulated their revolutionary ideas in anything like the same way.[4]

I have suggested that contemporary theorizing and research in macro and microsociology has been generated within the rubric of Parsons' founding work. The dichotomies around which this theorizing revolves continue to inspire, and to confuse, new theoretical efforts today. For example, a new subdiscipline of cultural sociology is in the course of being established. If sociologists working in this area want to emphasize contingent activity and social conflict, will they feel that they have to sacrifice a focus on values and cultural structure? Following the polemically constructed dichotomies of macro and microsociology, many have argued (e.g., Swidler 1986) that this must, indeed, be the case.

If these false dichotomies in macro and microtheorizing rest upon partially flawed interpretations of Parsons' work, efforts to go beyond them will continue to draw upon, criticize, and revise Parsons' founding effort as well. It should not be surprising, therefore, that in opposing arguments that deny the centrality of values, Archer's (1988) effort to formulate a theoretical framework for cultural sociology returns to Parsons' fundamental distinction between culture and social system (cf., Eisenstadt 1986 and Alexander 1984).[5]

I argued earlier that the influence of Parsons' conceptual translation of earlier thought was not the only reason for *Structure*'s classical status. There is also the fact that, in the course of this great book, Parsons selected and interpreted what came to be sociology's classical pantheon. It is important to understand that Parsons did not present *Structure* as an interpretation but as an empirical discovery. In calling it an interpretation, I am making the contrary claim: Parsons' portraits of classical writers were constructed, not discovered. His theorizing about these writers, therefore, must be deconstructed in turn.

The theorists who were the subjects of *Structure* were not accorded classical status, in English-speaking sociology at least, before Parsons wrote. Parsons made them so and he read them in a creative, contingent, and highly variable way. Social science disciplines are hermeneutic, not only discovering enterprises. Their explanatory, discovering theories are embedded in earlier, conventionalized understandings of pivotal texts. To put it another way, social science discoveries are textually mediated by classics. It follows that debate about who the classics are and what their works mean is critical to the development of even the most empirical social science field.

Structure came to be seen as the most sophisticated history of sociology for several decades after its publication. This meant that any alternative version of sociological theory and research had to challenge its interpretive claims. This is precisely what has ensured since the mid-1960s (Alexander 1987b). The battle has been waged not only, as Derrida would say, against the presences in Parsons' text, but also against the absences (see chapter 6, below).

It was in part because Marx and Simmel were notably absent from *Structure* that it became very difficult in the immediate post-war period to do Marxist and Simmelian sociology. The purpose of writers like Gouldner, Giddens, and Zeitlin, on the one side, and Levine, Wolff, and Coser, on the other, was to make it possible to engage in these sociologies by reestablishing the legitimacy of their classical exemplars. Thrust and counter-thrust can be followed in the long decades of interpretive argument about Marx's and Simmel's work (see chapter 5, below). Suffice it to say that, eventually, it became impossible to keep them out of the pantheon's central core. My own book on Marx (Alexander 1982), for example, starts from just this "anti-Parsonian" premise, even while I criticize Marx's mature sociology in a manner that complements what I take to be *Structure*'s central concerns.

More interesting than the efforts to overcome the absences in *Structure* are the attempts to redefine the presences. Despite the fact that Durkheim and Weber had lost their centrality in their own national traditions, Parsons succeeded in establishing them at the center of sociology in a disciplinary sense. Rather than seeking to dislodge these theorists, later challengers to Parsons worked at reinterpreting them. Every major theoretical tradition in post-Parsonian sociology has justified itself via some anti-Parsonian reinterpretation of Weber and Durkheim, even those positivist traditions that have entirely rejected the scientific validity of interpretation.

Typically, these new interpretations are presented as readings that have no axe to grind. They seek to establish their validity as "objectively better" interpretations rather than interpretations that have been inspired by different theoretical interests. They have done so by emphasizing their greater access to new texts, the accumulation of scholarly facts, the advancement of interpretive methodology. It is not very difficult, however, to deconstruct these interpretive discussions. When we do so, we can see that they are neither neutral nor objective, in the positivist sense of these terms. Indeed, they are as far from these ideals as Parsons' originating interpretation itself. These encounters with the classics never, in fact, confronted the "classics" in and of themselves. They are themselves textually mediated. The text is Parsons' *Structure*.

Parsons' (1937, pp. 473–694) "Weber" was constructed through a brilliantly selective reading. Weber is said to have been preoccupied with values: his *Economy and Society* received from Parsons only cursory treatment. Parsons argued, moreover, that Weber's concepts of "charisma" and "legitimation" were homologous with the concepts "sacred" and "moral authority" in Durkheim's work. Shils (1982) made these interesting but rather far-fetched claims central to his later theoretical program of macrosociology, despite the fact his Weber interpretation was no more textually substantiated than Parsons' own. Eisenstadt continues to theorize within this "Weberian" justification, arguing (e.g., Eisenstadt 1968) that in Weber's work institution building has a sacred and charismatic basis.

Bendix launched and organized the more strategic, conflict-oriented reading of Weber. It takes nothing away from the grandeur of his "intellectual biography" of Weber (Bendix 1962) to say that it was a brief for this anti-Parsonian position. Later, Roth (1968) took on the burden of this scholarly agenda, his introduction and translation of *Economy and Society* marking its exegetical apotheosis. Collins' (1968) early political sociology rested upon Bendix's and Roth's interpretation. When the Indiana group "de-Parsonsized" Weber in the early 1970s (Cohen et al. 1975), they merely formalized the most widely consensual of these claims.

Parsons' (1937, pp. 301–450) Durkheim interpretation was as important for establishing the normative, functional framework for postwar sociology as his reading of Weber. The interpretive challenge in this case took two forms. Scholars like Bendix (1971), Tilly (1981), and Collins, accepting the gist of Parsons' portrait, argued that the Durkheimian approach was pernicious to any effective macrosociology. Interpreters like Gouldner (1958), Giddens (1972), and Traugott (1978), on the other hand, argued that Parsons had ignored the real, institutional Durkheim, who had supposedly embraced a materialistic conflict approach hardly different from Marx's own. Once again, the Indiana group (Pope 1973) represented the apotheosis of this line of interpretation in the effort to "de-Parsonsize" Durkheim.

If I am right that that postwar interpretation of Weber and Durkheim has been a sotto voce, and not so sotto, dialogue with *Structure*, it should not be surprising that recent efforts to reestablish the cultural dimension of macrosociology should have turned more positively to Parsons' original arguments. Insofar as structural conflict theory wanes, Weber takes on a different character. Thus, the recent German interpretations of Weber – by Schluchter, Munch, and Habermas – are heavily indebted to Parsons, not only to his framework in *Structure* but to his later, evolutionary history as well. The current revival of the "late Durkheim" as an exemplar for cultural sociology (e.g., Alexander 1988d) also takes off from Parsons' insight into the increasingly symbolic path of Durkheim's later work. Collins (1988), for example, takes a very positive line on this later writing of Durkheim, to the point of endorsing, with conditions, some key elements in Parson's Durkheim-inspired political sociology.

The Structure of Social Action is one of the truly exemplary works of twentieth century social theory. Like virtually all of this century's seminal social thinkers, Parsons began this work with an alarming sense of the crisis of his time. Disillusioned with the shallow progressivism of nineteenth century thought, he distrusted reason in its narrowly positivist sense. He was also suspicious of idealism in its naive, organicist form. His goal was to establish the possibility of reason on a more realistic base.[6] Keynes's goal was much the same, and his *General Theory*, published one year before *Structure*, resembles Parsons' own book in crucial ways. Wittgenstein's *Philosophical Investigations*, composed over roughly the same period, questions rationalistic theories from a remarkably similar point of view and proposes a conventionalized and interpretive alternative that exhibits distinctive parallels to Parsons' own. Husserl's *Cartesian Meditations* presents another interwar approach to rationality that *Structure* resembles in critical ways, despite its equally clear departure in others. All these great works argued that freedom and rationality can be explained theoretically, and sustained socially, only if earlier frameworks – materialistic, individualistic, idealistic – are abandoned. If the anxiety that surrounded the creation of these works has abated, it has by no means disappeared. Their call for a new kind of social theory remains as relevant today. That is why sociologists continue to read, to grapple with, and to celebrate Parsons' first great work.

Notes

1 For an analysis of how social science disciplines are constructed via discourse about the writings and subsequent interpretations of figures who are given a classical status, see Alexander (1987b).

2 In his early essays, Gouldner (e.g., 1960) tried to draw the line in a more subtle way, developing a "left functionalism." He (1970) later adopted the more conventional line. Lockwood's developing theory goes in the opposite direction, drawing back from the overly simple dichotomy between conflict and order he asserted so forcefully in his earliest work (Lockwood 1956) to the later distinction between system and social integration, which criticized Parsons' treatment of order in a more nuanced and sophisticated way and, indeed, actually stood on the shoulders of Parsons' earlier work (Lockwood 1964). While Coser (1956) accused Parson himself of being simply an order theorist, he argued that functionalism in a more generic form could successfully handle the problem of social conflict (see especially Coser 1967).

3   See *Twenty Lectures: Sociological Theory since World War II* (Alexander 1987a) for an extensive analysis of the dialogue between Parsons' action theory and his micro critics, on the one side, and his macroconflict critics, on the other. I argue that while critical problems in Parsons' work made these criticisms partially legitimate, and the counter-programs they offered partially progressive, these critics made Parsons into a straw man and offered one-dimensional theories in turn. Future progress in sociological theory, I suggest, must go beyond these critics and Parsons' himself. Efforts at developing a new synthesis is what the contemporary, "third phase" of postwar macrosociological theorizing is all about (see Alexander 1988b).

4   Garfinkel continues the argument (1988), arguing that in *Structure* Parsons ignored the "concrete" individual and that he recommended that sociology focus only on the analytically abstracted "unit act." In my view, what Parsons intended to argue was something very different. His point was that, when the "concrete" – living, breathing, irredeemable, ect. – individual is the topic of empirical analysis, it must be conceived in a manner that does not identify it with an atomized asocial individual. It was the latter that Parsons called the "analytical individual," and it was only this he wanted to avoid. Parsons used the notion of analytic individualism, in other words, to restore to the concrete individual – the real social actor – a fuller depth. Still, neither in *Structure* nor at any later point in his work did Parsons actually examine the manner in which this real social actor acts. I explore this paradox – which gives some credence to Garfinkel's critique while avoiding its damaging reductionism – in my introduction and substantive contribution to *The Micro–Macro Link* (Alexander 1987c, Alexander and Giessen 1987, cf. Alexander 1988c). For an extensive discussion of the slide toward reductionism in Garfinkel's work, see Alexander 1987a: 238–80.

5   Wuthnow's effort to establish a theoretical framework for cultural sociology clearly falls within this second approach, for while Wuthnow emphasizes the significance of social structure he argues for the need to construct relatively autonomous cultural patterns which interact with it (see especially Wuthnow 1988: 66–96).

6   Parsons (1937, p. 5) writes that "various kinds of individualism have been under increasingly heavy fire [and] the role of reason, and the status of scientific knowledge . . . have been attacked again and again." From the right, the threat was Nazism – "we have been overwhelmed by a flood of anti-intellectualist theories;" from the left, it was communism – "socialistic, collectivistic, organic theories of all sorts."

References

Alexander, J. C.   1982, *Theoretical Logic in Sociology*, vol. 2: *The Antinomies of Classical Thought: Marx and Durkheim*. Berkeley and Los Angeles: University of California Press.

—— 1984, Three models of culture and society relations: toward an analysis of Watergate. *Sociological Theory*, 2, pp. 290–314.

—— 1985, Habermas' new critical theory: its promise and problems. *American Journal of Sociology*, 91, pp. 400–25.

—— 1987a, *Twenty Lectures: Sociological Theory since World War II*. New York: Columbia University Press.

—— 1987b, On the centrality of the classics. In A. Giddens and J. Turner (eds), *Social Theory Today*, Stanford: Stanford University Press, pp. 11–57.

—— 1987c, Action and its environments. In J. C. Alexander, B. Giessen, R. Münch, and N. J. Smelser (eds), *The Micro–Macro Link*, Berkeley and Los Angeles: University of California Press, pp. 289–318.

—— 1988a, Social structural analysis: presuppositions, ideologies, empirical debates. In J. C. Alexander, *Action and its Environments: Toward a New Synthesis*. New York: Columbia University Press, pp. 11–35.

—— 1988b, The new theoretical movement. In N. J. Smelser (ed.), *The Handbook of Sociology*. Los Angeles: Sage, pp. 77–101.

—— 1988c, *Action and its Environments: Towards a New Synthesis*. New York: Columbia University Press.

—— 1988d, (ed.) *Durkheimian Sociology: Cultural Studies*. New York: Cambridge University Press.

Alexander, J. C., and Giessen, B.   1987, From reduction to linkage: the long view of the micro–macro link. In J. C. Alexander et al., *The Micro–Macro Link*, Berkeley, University of California Press, pp. 1–44.

Archer, M.   1988, *Culture and Agency*. London: Cambridge University Press.

Bendix, R.   1962, *Max Weber*. New York: Doubleday.

—— 1971, Two sociological traditions. In R. Bendix and G. Roth, *Scholarship and Partisanship: Essays on Max Weber*, Berkeley and Los Angeles: University of California Press, pp. 282–98.

Cohen, J. Hazelrigg, L. E., and Pope, W.   1975, De-Parsonizing Weber: a critique of Parson's interpretation of Weber's sociology. *American Sociological Review*, 40, pp. 229–241.

Collins, R.   1968, A comparative approach to political sociology. In R. Bendix et al., *State and Society*, Berkeley and Los Angeles: University of California Press, pp. 42–67.

—— 1988, The conflict tradition in Durkheimian sociology. In J. C. Alexander (ed.), *Durkheimian Sociology: Cultural Studies*. New York: Cambridge University Press, pp. 107–28.

Coser, L.   1956, *The Functions of Social Conflict*. New York: Free Press.

—— 1967, Introduction. In L. Coser, *Continuities in the Study of Social Conflict*, New York: Free Press, pp. 1–14.

Eisenstadt, S. N.   1968, (ed.) *Max Weber on Charisma and Institution Building*. Chicago: University of Chicago Press.

—— 1986, Culture and social structure revisited. *International Sociology*, 1, pp. 278–320.

Garfinkel, H. 1988, Evidence for locally produced, naturally accountable phenomena of order, logic, reason, meaning, method, etc., in and as of the essential quiddity of immortal ordinary society (I of IV): an announcement of studies. *Sociological Theory*, 6 (no. 1), pp. 103–9.

Giddens, A. 1972, *Capitalism and Modern Social Theory*. London: Cambridge University Press.

Gouldner, A. 1958, Introduction. In E. Durkheim, *Socialism and Saint-Simon*, Yellow Springs, Ohio: Antioch, pp. v–xxix.

—— 1960, The norm of reciprocity. *American Sociological Review*, 25, 161–78.

—— 1970, *The Coming Crisis of Western Sociology*. New York: Equinox.

Lockwood, D. 1956, Some remarks on "the social system." *British Journal of Sociology*, 7, pp. 134–46.

—— 1964, Social integration and system integration. In G. K. Zollschen and W. Hirsch (eds), *Explorations in Social Change*, Boston: Little, Brown, pp. 244–57.

Parsons, T. 1937, *The Structure of Social Action*. New York: Free Press.

Pope, W. 1973, Classic on classic: Parsons' interpretation of Durkheim. *American Sociological Review*, 38, pp. 399–415.

Roth, G. 1968, Introduction. In G. Roth and C. Wittich (eds), *Max Weber, Economy and Society*, New York: Bedminster Press, pp. xxxiii–cx.

Sciulli, D. 1985, The practical groundwork of critical theory: bringing Parsons to Habermas (and vice-versa). In J. C. Alexander (ed.), *Neofunctionalism*, Beverly Hills and London: Sage, pp. 21–50.

Shils, E. 1982, *The Constitution of Society*. Chicago: University of Chicago Press.

Swidler, A. 1986, Culture in action. *American Sociological Review*, 51, pp. 273–86.

Tilly, C. 1981, Useless Durkheim. In C. Tilly, *As Sociology Meets History*. New York: Academic Press, pp. 95–108.

Traugott, M. 1978, (ed.) *Emile Durkheim on Institutional Analysis*. Chicago: University of Chicago Press.

Turner, J. 1988, *The Structure of Social Interaction*. Stanford: Stanford University Press.

Wuthnow, R. 1988, *Meaning and Moral Order*. Berkeley and Los Angeles: University of California Press.

5

"Formal Sociology" is Not Multidimensional: Breaking the "Code" in Parsons' Fragment on Simmel

As with any disputation about a sociological "classic," to engage in an interpretation of Parsons is to talk about the nature of contemporary society. While certainly textual rather than empirical, such generalized discourse is no less important than research programs in the development of sociology (see chapter 2). Textual disputation, in other words, is a primary means of doing sociological theory.

After many years of often extremely distorted interpretation, from friend and foe alike, some first-rate studies of Parsons are beginning to appear that are interpretative-theoretical contributions in their own right (Holton and Turner 1986, Robertson and Turner 1991, Wearne 1989, Wenzel 1990). The publication by *Teoria Sociologica* of "George Simmel and Ferdinand Tönnies: Social Relationships and the Elements of Action" – the long sought "lost fragment" from an early draft manuscript of Parsons' *The Structure of Social Action* – presents an opportunity to complement this recent work by laying to rest one of the earlier period's most persistent disputes.

It is well known that Parsons was not content to legitimate the "theory of action" he developed in *Structure* on discursive, analytic, or hermeneutic grounds alone. He committed himself also to offering what he described as an "empirical proof." He claimed that the theories of the greatest social scientists of the time had all "converged" on the same action elements. This ambitious historical claim left a door wide open to Parsons' critics. They had only to prove that there were great theorists other than the ones Parsons discussed whose work did not converge with the analytic elements he laid out.[1] One obvious challenger of classical status was Marx, but he was not of the same generation as the thinkers – Weber, Durkheim, Marshall, and Pareto – whom Parsons had highlighted in his 1937 work. A better candidate was Simmel. He was a great theorist of the same generation, and he was left out. This is where our story begins.

From the 1950s until the present day, critics of Parsonian theory have argued that leaving Simmel out was, in fact, profoundly consequential. His absence from *Structure*, they have argued, cut Parsons off from an important branch of the turn-of-the-century intellectual movement that it was his professed goal to synthesize. Because Parsons did not have Simmel, he could not speak, or at least not speak properly, about a number of vital matters that Simmel had brought to light, about the structural and material aspects of society, about phenomena of conflict, exchange, and hierarchy, about reification, and about interaction as it relates to social structure and social change. Levine (e.g., 1980, cf., Alexander 1989) is the best-known interpretor to make this claim, but Coser's extremely influential *The Functions of Social Conflict* (1956) rested on similar grounds, as did Bendix's and Wolff's early translations of Simmel's essays, *Conflict and the Web of Group Affiliations* (Simmel 1955). For Coser, Wolff, and Bendix, if not for Levine, Simmel provided a non-Marxist version of the newly conceived "conflict theory" that was the first challenger to Parsonian thought in the 1950s. Simmelian conflict theory, they believed, could be an alternative to the neo-Marxist conflict theories of Dahrendorf, Lockwood, and Rex.

For more than 30 years the case for the importance of the "missing Simmel" has been argued hypothetically, in the manner of most such discussions in the history of social thought. Sometimes Parsons' critics argued that Parsons didn't know Simmel; at other times they suggested that he was afraid to speak of him because to do so would have proved his early theory to have been wrong. But something unusual has happened. What Parsons actually thought about Simmel, and came very close to publishing, is now available. Its existence allows the claims about the consequentiality of the "missing Simmel" to be examined more realistically, if not, of course, to be settled once and for all.

I begin by noting one of the peculiarities of these critical claims. Although they were issued by critics of Parsons' discussion in *Structure*, these critics themselves accepted the empiricist epistemology of convergence that was perhaps that great work's weakest claim (Alexander 1989). In effect, they argued that if only Simmel had been included, Parsons' database would have been different. The new data would have changed the results of Parsons' induction, and a new theory would have been the result. This argument follows Parsons' own self-presentation in suggesting that he was conducting an empiricist rather than hermeneutic exercise. It assumes that Parsons did not already have at least the outlines of his "action theory" well in hand before *Structure* was written. It assumes, too, that "Simmel" is an object whose theoretical implications are available for observation or interpretation in an unambiguous way.

The publication of this fragment demonstrates that neither of these assumptions is true. Parsons' theory would not have changed if he had included Simmel as an object of his interpretative ambition. For Parsons did not ignore Simmel; he disagreed with him in a fundamental way. This is the reason he excluded Simmel from *Structure*. Parsons could weave a narrative of convergence only if he included theorists whom, he believed, had converged in the right way. This was a matter of belief, which itself rested on interpretation. Indeed, I will suggest toward the end of this chapter that, differently interpreted, Simmel could just as easily have been grist for Parsons' convergence mill.

Original theorists write and think in a code they have themselves invented. If one is not familiar with their writing, it can seem like mystifying gibberish. Parsons not only developed his own intricate code but had the lamentable tendency, inherent in systematic thinkers, to camouflage his theoretical tastes behind objective-seeming elements in the code. In this way the code could signal implications and judgments of which he himself was afraid to speak.

Parsons' fragment on Simmel is permeated by this camouflaging and objectifying strategy. Because of it, Parsons appears to use most of his ammunition indicting Simmel on relatively trivial grounds, ignoring the themes in Simmel's theory which should have drawn his best shots. The theoretical tone is evasively neutral. Parsons is hiding behind his code. If we learn its language, however, we can see that the signals Parsons sends out do, in fact, indict Simmel for having committed theoretical errors of the most fundamental kind.

Parsons' criticism of Simmel's formal sociology seems to turn on the abstract, relatively restricted issues of scientific methodology and disciplinary boundary maintenance. He claims that Simmel misunderstands the nature of "emergentism" in science;[2] that because of this error Simmel is unable to develop an explanatory theory; that this failure in turn reduces formal theory to mere description; and that, for all these reasons, Simmel's theory cannot defend sociology against the other social sciences.

These arguments are formalistic rather than substantive; they are also tendentious. We will see that there are passages where Parsons himself acknowledges the emergent status of Simmel's "forms," which do provide a new level of causality in an explanatory sense. So constructed, formal theory can hardly be mere description. While Parsons' efforts to legitimate sociology by analogy with natural science practice were sophisticated, moreover, they appear thoroughly anachronistic to us today, as does his effort to build upon this status to defend the distinctive scientific status of the field.

These discourses on science and sociology, then, were not compelling arguments in themselves. They were, however, vital elements in the complex code that Parsons developed in his early work. In this context, they functioned simultaneously to obscure and to signal the more fundamental, substantive, and legitimate reservations that Parsons had about Simmel's formal sociology.

The way in which methodological and theoretical issues, form and content, were guardedly intertwined in the Parsonian code is well illustrated by the phrase that Parsons employed in *Structure* to sum up everything he disliked in his theoretical enemies – "positivistic utilitarianism." As the coupling implies, Parsons saw positivism as an integral part of the individualistic and rationalistic approach to action and order he was fighting against. For positivism, Parsons believed, fooled theorists into accepting appearances without reconstructing them analytically, that is, according to their own prior, theoretical reasons. It was this failure at analytical reconstruction that led people to adopt the rationalistic individualism upon which utilitarianism was based.

Adopting a less mirroring and empiricist view of the relation between observation and theory building, Parsons argued against individualistic social theory that theorists should not be fooled by appearances into believing that "concrete," or "empirical," actors were actually individuals in an analytical sense. Empirical individuals must be understood, rather, as social constructions that have emergent properties at the level of contingent action and personality, formed particularly from building blocks provided by the value elements of society. Parsons argued against rationalistic theory on similar grounds. Actions like economic exchange appeared to be throughly utilitarian only because theorists looked at them from the outside, in an empiricist way. Seen from a more analytic point of view, every "unit act" is composed of several different elements, not only the rational ones. Norms, values, means, ends, and effort are all present, in tension with one another and with various kinds of physical and nonphysical environments.

Parsons' aim in making these criticisms was ostensibly to construct a more truly scientific, less positivistic version of the human studies, an achievement which would also defend sociology against the imperialism of economics. More deeply, however, it is clear that he utilized these methodological arguments, much as he used historical ones, to build a case against rationalistic, materialist, and individualistic thinking which he opposed on more substantive, presuppositional grounds. In analytical terms, Parsons did not believe that the objective and the subjective, the individual and the collective, were nearly as dichotomized as did the reigning theories of his day, although he acknowledged the presence of powerful social forces that were pushing the empirical referents of these terms farther apart. On normative grounds, moreover, Parsons believed that rationalist, materialist, and individualist theories played an insidious social role, undermining not only social theory but the learning capacities, the intellectual reflexivity, of industrial society itself.

It is clear, in other words, that methodological and disciplinary issues were, ultimately, signifiers rather than signifieds in Parsons' theoretical code. They were analogically (and sometimes not altogether logically) related to compelling substantive issues and to ultimate values. The terms of the debate between Parsons and his enemies were theoretical, social, and ideological. For Parsons, synthetic social theory was not only a means of creating a more integrated sociology but a more integrated society as well.

We must read Parsons' objections to Simmel, then, not only intrinsically, for the information they communicate, but symbolically, in terms of their referents in Parsons' overarching code. When we do so, we will see that Parsons objected to Simmel's methodological assumptions and his approach to theory-building because he believed they were the source of substantive commitments that were similar to the ones Parsons criticized throughout his early work. Indeed, very similar objections (briefly referred to in this fragment) emerged in Parsons' treatment of Weber. For, despite his intensive admiration for the "other" great German sociologist, Parsons recoiled from the objectified and instrumental elements in Weber's theory of modern society. Parsons traced these problems, not to substantive theoretical commitments or presuppositions, but to a methodological issue, to

Weber's use of "type" rather than "analytic" concepts in the con-struction of the explanatory units he employed (see, e.g., Parsons 1947, pp. 22–9, 58–60). He reproached Weber for thinking descript-ively rather than analytically, and he argued that Weber's genial historical insights could be saved only by reformulating them in terms of the nonempirical referents, the "action" variables, that lie beneath the typifications that make up the observational, interactional units of everyday life. Substantively, what Parsons objected to was Weber's conception of modern society as an "iron cage," but he explained this problem only in formal terms, as the result of Weber's methodological errors, his misunderstanding of theory-building in sociology.

When Parsons first discusses Simmel's work in this fragment, he actually acknowledges that his formal discussions do involve abstrac-tion from "concretely existent," that is, merely empirical, phenomena. He goes on to argue, however, that these early discussions are not truly abstract because Simmel begins with classes of "concrete motives." This empiricism means that Simmel can come up only with concepts that refer merely to "classes of concrete acts," which Parsons implicitly criticizes as an approach that reinforces the traditional, dichotomizing disciplinary boundaries between fields like economics, government, sociology, and religion.

Yet we know, and Parsons knew, that this was not, in fact, the ambition of Simmel's formal sociology, which actually intended to avoid disciplinary conflicts by creating sociology as a kind of post-substance, supradisciplinary method. Yet, when Parsons does come to terms with the actual drift of Simmel's work, he insists on restating his critique in the same coded terms.

Parsons now acknowledges that Simmel's "social relations," the object of his formal sociology, did in fact indicate emergent propert-ies, "forms" that seemed to have much in common with the analytical focus he himself was proposing for sociological theory. He moves on to vitiate this recognition, however, by what seems at first to be a most peculiar critique. Parsons accuses Simmel's forms of being "nothing . . . but the structural aspect of social relationship." He than claims that, while emergent properties, structures can be explained only by their parts. Because they do not constitute causal factors in and of themselves, they cannot function as independent variables or provide the basis for "explanatory theory." Parsons makes an analogy between Simmel's formal structures and a waterfall, claiming that "no scientist would think of [such] a form as an independent element." Because changes in a structure's form are attributable, not to its own emergent properties, but to changes in its parts, Parsons insists that Simmel's "forms" are "epiphenomenal."

This argument is surely wrong. It is wrong textually because it is contradictory. It goes against the initial recognition of emergentism and the later acknowledgment that social structures are, in fact, emergent properties. The critique is also wrong empirically; as Simmel convincingly demonstrates, formal aspects of social relations do possess structures – certainly size is one – that play an independent causal role in the explanation of social life.

Why does Parsons offer such weak arguments? He does so because they evoke central terms in his broader theoretical code. This broadening is illustrated when Parsons tries to argue that Simmel's structural formalism is not really analytical, but descriptive. "It is true," Parsons acknowledges, "that 'forms of relationship' is not a concrete descriptive category . . . but it is not in *our* sense an analytical element" (original italics). This is Parsons' problem. He recognizes the analytical status of Simmel's forms, but he also recognizes that they do not conform to the theoretical categories that Parsons claims an analytical theory implies. When he insists that Simmel's categories are not analytical in "our" sense, he is introducing a possibility for different kinds of analytic theory which he has never acknowledged before, or since. Indeed, he quickly closes this possibility off by saying that, if Simmel's forms are not descriptive, at least (perhaps because they are not analytic in "our" sense) they possess a "descriptive aspect." This residual category indicates that Parsons is struggling with something that challenges the formalism of his own theoretical code. His problem is that, while Simmel's sociology in analytical in a philosophical sense, it does not reveal the more substantive, presuppositional attributes that Parsons claimed that an antiempiricist position implied. Simmel emphasized conflict and exchange. Did this mean that an "antipositivistic utilitarianism" might be possible? Parsons confesses, indeed, that "in spite of the abstraction involved it [Simmel's formal theory] is a mode of abstraction which directly cuts across the line of analysis into elements of action which has been our main concern." Parsons theorized the "elements of action" in order to overcome individualistic and rationalistic theory. If we understand the larger code, then, we can see that what Parsons is really complaining about here is that Simmel's analytic sociology does not challenge rationalistic and individualistic thinking, at least in the same way as his own.

The submerged substance of this polemic begins to be revealed when Parsons likens Simmel's forms to the structural concepts "division of labor" and "exchange" in "ordinary economic theory." He argues that these concepts are abstractions, or "resultants," of smaller parts, or "interactions." These formal structures, in other words, must be seen as economic *actions*, which according to Parsons' theory are hybrids of rational *and* nonrational elements. He proceeds to insist, indeed, that because interactions may contain different weightings of the elements of action, processes like the division of labor, exchange, and contractual relationships – principal concepts in Simmel's formal sociology – do not have any consistent empirical shape. They are not, in other words, invariant social forms. As proof, Parsons evokes Durkheim's emphasis on the noncontractual elements of contract. He uses this to chide Simmel for thinking contract, or exchange, could be analyzed simply on the basis of its form. Once again, he implicitly points to nonrational elements: "For there to exist contractual elements in the relations of individuals on a large scale there must exist in the same social systems other elements of a different order not formulated in the conception of contractual relation." When Parsons insists that to think only in terms of contract is to think in terms of "the ad hoc interests of the contracting parties," he is linking Simmel's formal theory to individualism and rationalism. He argues that there must be an element that lies "above" such individual interests, and suggest he has established this in his other writings. It is the "institutional" element, which Parsons identifies in *Structure*, and elsewhere (Parsons 1990 [1934], Alexander 1990) with the normative element of action. What Parsons meant by "analytic in our sense" is now completely clear. It is the ability to differentiate between the economic elements (means, situation) and the noneconomic elements (ends, norms) of action.

Now that we have cracked the code, we can see exactly in what Parsons' objections to Simmel consist. Simmel's formal sociology must fail, by virtue of its very formality, to clarify whether, and to what degree, such fundamental processes as conflict, exchange, and contract-making are instrumental and inherently conflictual or normatively mediated and possibly integrative. As I will argue below, although the substance of Simmel's formal sociology emphasizes normative elements, his choice of forms seems to indicate, in fact, the very opposite, as its impact on contemporary sociological theory seems to suggest. Coser used Simmel to argue that virtually every important social process can be understood as one form of hostile strategy or another. Homans used Simmel to legitimate an exclusive focus on utilitarian exchange and a focus on individual interaction rather than group solidarity or institutions.

These Simmelian approaches, along with conflict and exchange theory in their non-Simmelian modes, suffer from exactly the problems that Parsons surmised. They take the forms for the reality of action, refusing to go beneath the one-sided appearance of conflict or exchange to discover the normative and collective elements beneath. For every conflict is mediated by social integration in a significant way. This is exactly why, as Ekeh (1974) argued more than two decades ago, social exchange theory has developed another tradition in addition to the individualistic and rationalist one, beginning with Mauss and continuing through Lévi-Strauss. The empirical process of exchange, in other words, can be interpreted in different, theoretically dependent ways. Parsons' ultimate reply to Simmel is that "in principle *all* the elements of action are relevant to the understanding of any particular 'social form'" (original italics). Is it any accident that, in his later writings, Parsons developed his own theory of the "generalized media of exchange" that exploded the rationalistic notion of simple exchange and elaborated the complexity of extraindividual controls?

At one point in this highly encoded essay Parsons praises Simmel for his "brilliant" essays, so "full of suggestion and insight" about "what *purported* to be specific social forms" (my italics).[3] At another point Parsons suggests that even Simmel was compelled, in these substantive essays, to refer to nonformal elements, particularly to historically specific factors and motives. It is a shame that Parsons concluded that these Simmel essays "are of relatively little help for our purposes" and failed almost entirely to discuss them, because in fact Parsons was more right than he knew. For in his theories of both exchange and conflict Simmel was compelled, despite the ostensibly formal quality of his theory, to go beyond the utilitarian and individualistic elements that the "forms" of these processes seemed so clearly to invoke.

For example, although Simmel could classify types of conflicts and communicate their distinctive structures in formal terms, he could not explain how they come to take the different forms they do without referring to the differential impact of historically variable cultural constraints. In such discussions Simmel actually developed an original theory of the mediating role of highly generalized, universalistic cultural elements. He called these "concepts," and described them as notions like "person," "women," "rights," and "worker." Simmel suggests, indeed, that it is the increasing importance of such widely shared and highly general ideas that allows conflict to be integrative and competitive rather than disintegrating and revolutionary. Empirically, Simmel was no doubt overly optimistic about the impact of such cultural constraints. Nonetheless, he was suggesting, in this line of his thinking, exactly the kind of interpenetration of culture and social system that Parsons' antidualistic action theory aimed to provide.

It is important to recall that "formal sociology" did not exhaust Simmel's intellectual ambition, which included also a proposal for cultural studies. Because it suggested that institutional analysis could proceed without formal attention to historically specific meaning, this split negatively affected subsequent sociological thought. It is possible to argue, nonetheless, that despite his prescriptive claims, Simmel's formal sociology was highly interpenetrated by his "cultural sociology." If Parsons had read Simmel more closely and with less scientistic baggage of his own, he might have been able to notice this interpenetration. If he had, he would have been able to mount a more imminent and sympathetic criticism. For, in fact, Simmel certainly was as involved as "the founding fathers" in the convergence that Parsons professed to discover in fin-de-siècle sociology. But Parsons was preoccupied with providing an alternative to the school of "formal sociology" (Parsons 1979) and he could not see anything in Simmel except the party line.

I began this brief chapter with the assertion that to interpret Parsons is also, at the same time, to explore contemporary society. I have suggested that Parsons' struggle with "Simmel" was an effort to integrate, enrich, and complexify society. At the end of this fragment, Parsons argues that Tönnies' dichotomy of *Gemeinschaft* and *Gesellschaft* represents a prime example of the dichotomizing, "type-theorizing" for which he has so sharply criticized Simmel. In the published section on Tönnies in *Structure*, Parsons showed how the famous conceptual antinomy undermined the ability of moderns to understand the continuing role of normative integration in modern "societal" (e.g., *gesellschaftlich*) life. It was this continuity that informed Parsons' theory of professions and modern collegiality, which showed how rational authority could form the reference for non-rational, solidary bonds that allowed modern, antiauthoritarian standards of legitimacy. In the 1960s and 1970s, this line of thought crystallized in Parsons' conception of the "societal community," arguably his single most important contribution to the macrosociology of contemporary life.

By societal community Parsons referred to an arena of contemporary societies that mediates the extremes of ultimate values and the
practical realities of money, power, individuation, and contingent
conflict. It was the realm of solidarity that provided regulative norms
which, to the degree they were differentiated from other spheres and
from ascriptive ties, could be a liberating, democratizing force in
social life.[4] With this theory, Parsons greatly enriched Marshall's
rather thin conception of citizenship and initiated a series of studies
on ethnic and racial conflict, religious tolerance, and the role of law.
It is here, I believe, that we find the practical embodiment of the
abstruse, even obfuscatory language that Parsons used to criticize
Simmel in the initial stages of his intellectual life.

Notes

1 They could, of course, also prove that one of the theorists Parsons had
   discussed did not actually converge. This, indeed, was the strategy of
   one of the most mechanistic challenges to Parsons' early work launched
   by Pope and his colleagues during the 1970s, the goal of which was to
   "de-Parsonsize" Weber and Durkheim.
2 All quotations from Parsons are taken from his article on Simmel
   (Parsons 1993).
3 "Purported" is extremely revealing. For Parsons, Simmel's essays could
   not be about the formalism of social organization and brilliant and illuminating at the same time. They could be positively evaluated only if they
   avoided formalism, hence only being "purportedly" formalistic.
4 In their very interesting and highly ambitious recent work, Cohen and
   Arato (1992) make a compelling argument that Parsons' theory of "societal
   community" should be viewed as a singular contribution to the line of
   thinking that emerged with Hegel's theory of civil society and which has
   crystallized in the new democratic social movements in Latin America and
   Eastern Europe today. It can be argued, indeed, that Parsons' theory of
   societal community provides the only viable take-off point for a sociological theory of civil society today. In recent years neofunctionalists have,
   in effect, been making precisely this argument, via a loosely connected
   series of theoretical, historical, and contemporary sociological studies.
   Mayhew (1992) rediscovers the origins of societal community in English
   Puritanism and early modern liberalism. Sciulli (1992) redefines societal
   community in terms of proceduralism, developing a theory of "societal
   constitutionalism" that tries to explain and evaluate problem of authoritarianism in public and private life. In my own work, I earlier made use
   of societal community to develop a neofunctionalist approach to news
   media (1988a) and ethnic exclusion (1988b). More recently (Alexander

1992, Alexander and Smith 1993), I have tried to broaden the concept in order to develop a more cultural, institutional, and agonistic theory of civil society. See chapter 9, below, especially pp. 221–8.

References

Alexander, J. C.   1988a, The mass news media in historical and comparative perspective. In J. C. Alexander, *Action and its Environments*, New York: Columbia University Press, pp. 108–52.

—— 1988b, Core group, ethnic outgroup, and social differentiation. In J. C. Alexander, *Action and its Environments*, New York: Columbia University Press, pp. 78–106.

—— 1989, Against historicism/for theory: reply to Levine. *Sociological Theory*, 7, pp. 118–21.

—— 1990, Commentary: structure, value, and action: on Parsons' "Prolegomena". *American Sociological Review*, 55, pp. 339–45.

—— 1992, Citizen and enemy as symbolic classification: on the polarizing discourse of civil society. In M. Fournier and M. Lamont (eds), *Where Culture Talks*, Chicago: University of Chicago Press, pp. 289–308.

Alexander, J. C., and Colomy, P.   1992, Traditions and competition: preface to a postpositivist approach to knowledge cumulation. In G. Ritzer (ed.), *Metatheorizing*. London and Los Angeles: Sage, pp. 27–52.

Alexander, J. C. and Smith, P.   1993, The discourse of American civil society: a new proposal for cultural studies. *Theory and Society*, 22, pp. 151–207.

Cohen, J., and Arato, A.   1992, *Civil Society and Political Theory*. Boston: Beacon Press.

Coser, L.   1956, *The Functions of Social Conflict*. New York: Free Press.

Ekeh, P.   1974, *Social Exchange Theory: The Two Traditions*, Cambridge, MA: Harvard University Press.

Holton, R., and Turner, B. S.   1986, *Talcott Parsons on Economy and Society*. London: Routledge and Kegan Paul.

Levine, D. N.   1980, Introduction to the Arno Press Edition. In D. N. Levine, *Simmel and Parsons*, New York: Arno Press, pp. iii–lxix.

Mayhew, L.   1992, Political rhetoric and the contemporary public. In P. Colomy (ed.), *The Dynamics of Social Systems*, London and Los Angeles: Sage, pp. 190–214.

Parsons, T.   1947, Introduction. In M. Weber, *The Theory of Social and Economic Organization*, New York: Free Press, pp. 3–86.

—— 1979, Letter to Jeff Alexander. Unpublished manuscript, January 19.

—— 1990 [1934], Prolegomena to a theory of social institutions. *American Sociological Review*, 55, pp. 319–33.

—— 1993, George Simmel and Ferdinand Tonnies: Social relationships and the elements of action. *Teoria Sociologica*, no. 1, pp. 45–71.

Sciulli, D.   1992, *Theory of Societal Constitutionalism: Foundations of a Non-Marxist Critical Theory*. New York: Cambridge University Press.

Robertson, R., and Turner, B. S. (eds)   1992, *Talcott Parsons: Theorist of Modernity*. London and Los Angeles: Sage.

Simmel, G.   1955, *Conflict and the Web of Group Affiliations* (translated by and introduced by Kurt Wolff and Reinhard Bendix, introduced by Everett Hughes.) Glencoe, IL: Free Press.

Wearne, B.   1989, *The Theory and Scholarship of Talcott Parsons to 1951*. Cambridge and New York: Cambridge University Press.

Wenzel, H.   1990, *Die Ordnung des Handelns: Talcott Parsons' Theorie des allgemeinen Handlungssystem*. Frankfurt am Main: Suhrkamp.

6

On Choosing One's Intellectual Predecessors: Why Charles Camic is Wrong about Parsons' Early Work

Co-written with Giuseppe Sciortino

In 1992, in the *American Sociological Review*, Charles Camic offered an intriguing and potentially important argument about the intellectual status of *The Structure of Social Action*. Expanding and refining an important series of works on Parsons, Camic (1987, 1989, 1990a, 1990b, 1991) suggested that the theorists with whom Parsons debated in that seminal work – Marshall, Pareto, Durkheim, and Weber – were "chosen" not because of their intrinsic theoretical relevance to Parsons' project but because of "reputational" factors. He claimed that other social scientists – specifically, the American institutional economists – were intrinsically just as relevant, but that Parsons ignored these figures because their prestige had been eclipsed in the United States, particularly among powerful figures in Parsons' "local" Harvard environment. Camic asserted that Parsons chose the Europeans as his ancestors – and, we would add, his debating partners – because they were much more powerfully reputed among those who controlled his fate.

If this analysis were correct, much of the current scholarship on Parsons' theory of action would have to be rewritten. But the implications of Camic's arguments go well beyond the relatively small group of Parsons scholars. If Camic's argument about Parsons were correct, central perspectives in the historiography of social thought and in the sociology of knowledge would have to be abandoned as well. Camic's research program is a *theoretical* one: Parsons' work is adopted as an empirical exemplar to demonstrate the need for a radical reorientation not only of sociological theory's beloved genealogies, but of the meaning and identity of the discipline itself. To confront Camic, then, means much more than confronting a particular interpretation of Parsons' biography and intellectual corpus. It means, on the methodological level, to analyze the claims of a strongly historicist approach to scientific ideas and, on the theoretical level, to confront a subtle new version of an instrumentalist approach to the sociology of knowledge.

We believe that such a complex and sophisticated research program deserves much more attention than it has received thus far. We contend that Camic's argument is fundamentally flawed, not only in the historical interpretation it proffers about Talcott Parsons but, more important, in the overall theory of intellectual formation upon which it relies and which it evokes.

In the following pages, we offer a critical summary of Camic's research program, discuss the sociological importance of the topic of predecessor selection, and summarize Camic's historical reconstruction of Parsons' early development. We then analyze in depth Camic's own account of how Parsons' selection of his predecessors took place. We question – mainly through the use of Occam's razor – Camic's historical interpretation of Parsons' biography and work, but we also highlight the often hidden theoretical assumptions that underlie this empirical endeavor. By the end of this analysis, we hope to have demonstrated, *in corpore vili*, that the differences between contending sociological readings of the classics generally are not – and in the present case surely are not – caused by differences in historical accuracy but rather by differences in the respective approaches to social theory.

Camic's Research Program: a Critical Summary

Since the late 1970s, Camic has developed an ambitious research program around Talcott Parsons' life, work, and theoretical heritage. Focusing mainly on the early phase, which culminates in *The Structure of Social Action* (1937; hereafter *Structure*), Camic has produced historical contextualizations of Parsons' theoretical and methodological proposals (Camic 1987, 1989), editions of previously unpublished materials (Camic 1991), systematic anthologies of little-known texts (Camic 1991), and, most important, inquiries into the sources of Parsons' maturing theoretical ideas (Camic 1979, 1992).

Taken together, this material surely constitutes one of the most innovative lines of work in the current, very active reappraisal of Parsons' contribution to sociology and social thought. It presents itself neither as the usual hero-worshiping genre practiced by disciples, nor as a critical attempt to reconstruct Parsons' project in order to repropose it as a contemporary theoretical option. Camic is not sympathetic with Parsons' ideas, and makes clear, in fact, that he believes key dimensions of Parsons' work to be fundamentally wrong.[1] At the same time, Camic's approach is very different from earlier attempts to sociologize Parsons' sociology (e.g., Mills 1959, Gouldner 1970). Less inclined to enter openly into the discipline's contemporary politics, Camic is apparently impartial and scholarly. Ideology and political correctness are not immediate concerns of his inquiries; his control of Parsons' corpus and biography is impressively rich and detailed, and his theoretical models present themselves as grounded generalizations fitting the available evidence. In short, Camic declares his intention to treat Parsons' life and work as empirical data, to consider them with all the care that any scrupulous researcher should give his object of study.

What are the basic aims of Camic's research? Camic pursues both a critical assessment of Parsons' intellectual heritage and a sociological analysis of the processes through which this heritage was constituted (Camic 1989, p. 39). He expresses his dissatisfaction with the current scholarship on Parsons in the clearest possible terms: It has produced "surprisingly little in the way of a broader appreciation of where sociology stands with regards to the arguments of *Structure*" (Camic 1989, p. 39). Parsons' early contributions, Camic suggests, have been either neglected or treated superficially. Interpreters have employed a teleological perspective on Parsons' early development derived from the later, more mature writing (Camic 1991); decisive passages in the early works have been radically misconstrued because interpreters have failed to employ contemporary historiographical standards that emphasize contextualization (Camic 1987); the reconstructions of Parsons' early intellectual choices have been distorted by an inadequate account of the full range of alternatives he actually faced (Camic 1979, 1992). In sum, contemporary assessments of the early period of Parsons' development are a consequence of "collective amnesia about sociology's actual past" (Camic 1987, p. 434).

However, Camic does not wish merely to correct and enlarge our historical understanding of Parsons' work and life. He views his studies, rather, as empirical efforts to validate the historicist position in the disciplinary debate that has evolved about the meaning and role of classical work (cf. Alexander 1987b). Placing sociological classics in the "vast historical fluidity of knowledge in a universe of groups and their diverse values, interests, relations and circumstances" (Camic 1987, p. 436) is the only legitimate way of putting classics to use. In fact, the goal is not historical reconstruction *per se*, but rather the capacity to understand sociological works "sociologically."[2]

Camic's big fish is the sociology of knowledge. He defines his goal as producing case studies that focus "on the specific social processes that affect the formulation of a theorist's distinct methodological stance" (Camic 1987, p. 421) and that illuminate how theorists' concerns are "structured by their social roles" (Camic 1979, p. 517). Camic uses historical analysis as a tool to pursue this more general sociology of knowledge, which he identifies in the most instrumental, power-oriented, and conflict-constructed way. He suggests that theoretical works can be interpreted only in their socioinstitutional context, and that the latter is structured by the relentless quest for academic placement, status, and recognition.[3]

There is, finally, another goal of Camic's endeavors, one that is significant, if less overt. He wishes to advocate a radically different conception of the nature of sociology from Parsons' own. To be sure, Camic does not want to expose the shortcomings of Parsons' understanding as such; nor does he wish – as the earlier wave of critics did – to substitute for Parsons' ideas theories of his own. Nonetheless, over and above the particular objections to this or that part of Parsons' theorizing, Camic strenuously objects to Parsons' effort to develop a common vocabulary for sociology at large. The problem with Parsons' presentation of his intellectual development, and contemporary presentations as well, is that they have successfully imposed a "pre-emptive suppression of methodological alternatives, intellectual legacies, conceptions of action and social structures and personality, approaches to the causes and solutions of the problem of order, and perspectives on human voluntarism" (Camic 1989, p. 95). By concealing the fundamental "social variety" of the world (Camic 1987, p. 434), Parsons gave to his theories "a peculiarly self-referential quality, [a] tendency to regard the ideas he personally encountered in local surroundings as those ideas most worth engaging and vesting with epochal import" (Camic 1991, p. xii). By deconstructing Parsons' work, by showing how socially contingent and how historically bounded his intellectual selections actually were, Camic proposes his alternative vision. He believes that we must abandon any vision of sociology as a coherent (even if decidedly nonconsensual) intellectual discipline and see it rather as a kind of catalogue. Instead of attempting to develop a generalized theoretical logic, we must resign ourselves to the reconstruction of historically dependent concepts and learn not merely to accept but to advocate the equal validity of theoretically irreconcilable lines of argument.

These arguments form the main lines of Camic's research on Parsons' early life and work. They also form the warp and woof of his 1992 paper on the mechanism of predecessor selection, which may in certain important respects be taken as the most systematic statement of Camic's research program. Our analysis of this particular paper on predecessor selection, then, should be considered in a representational way; it applies, *pari passu*, as much to Camic's larger research program as to the particular work whose details we take up here.

The Importance of Predecessor Selection Processes

The topic of predecessor selection can hardly be considered a small one. All significant intellectual work stands in complex relationship with a set of authors and problems, with what can loosely be called a "tradition." Any significant work is impregnated by past contributions, and any researcher sits "on the shoulders of giants" hoping to see farther and better.[4] This connective process, however, unfolds in sharply different ways from the cumulative mechanics so praised by positivists. Post-Mertonian sociology of science, and intellectual history more generally, have long since demonstrated that relationships with intellectual predecessors are creative ones: To relate to an intellectual tradition means always to interpret it. Readings of earlier authors and their problems change, often dramatically, in the light of new *Problemstellung*. Similarities are discovered between authors once considered diametrically opposed, just as differences are highlighted between authors once considered to have been intellectual bedfellows. Different strands – or "phases" or "works" – of the same *corpora* are played one against the other. This creative appropriation is highly consequential, for the reception of an influential intellectual work can radically alter the intellectual space provided by extant traditions, making new alternatives available to contemporary scholars and to emerging cohorts alike.

Camic is surely right, therefore, in pointing out the need for a better understanding of the predecessor selection process. He is also correct in insisting that to ignore predecessor selection is to miss an important resource for understanding the construction and evolution of disciplines. Whether he provides an adequate response to the problems to which he draws our attention is, however, another question.

Camic's point of departure is the analytical distinction between what he calls the study of "intellectual influences" – the general milieu of experiences and ideas within which writers are socialized – and what he rather ambiguously terms "predecessor selection," a process, apparently intentional, through which a writer identifies preceeding authors as explicit reference points.[5] Concentrating on the latter element, Camic believes that, although the identification of a theorist's *intellectual* predecessors is indeed a concern in current scholarship on sociological theory, it is usually based on a narrow understanding of the social processes involved. A vast majority of contemporary scholars, Camic believes, ascertain predecessors by looking simply at the relationship between the ideational content of the writer under scrutiny – most particularly "the thinker's own statements" (1992, p. 423)[6] – and the ideas of others whom the writer has quoted and referred to.

This model, where the relationship between scientist and predecessors is established mainly on the basis of intellectual content, Camic calls the "content-fit model." According to Camic, this model, although hegemonic, suffers from serious weakness, both substantive and methodological. It ignores the variability in the "historical and socioinstitutional circumstances," severs the "predecessor selection process from its socioinstitutional context," and neglects "the possibility of predecessor choices not based primarily on content" (p. 423). Methodologically, the content-fit model makes use only of the thinker's own statements "as the primary or exclusive evidence" and fails to "investigate adequately the dark side of predecessor selection," by which Camic means that there may be other potential predecessors whom the thinker did not choose (pp. 423–4).

Because of these weaknesses in the content-fit approach, Camic proposes an alternative model, concentrated not on ideational content but on "socioinstitutional circumstances,"[7] circumstances that highlight the role and force of reputational mechanisms. The operation of these mechanisms, according to Camic, is actually hidden by using the content-fit approach, for the latter concerns itself mainly with the explicit and self-established links expressed by the author. By accepting these statements at face value, the scholar does not take adequately into account the "published work prior to publications, unpublished papers, course materials, letters and so on, during the time [the author's] ideas were working out" (p. 422). Because explicit statements are "a poor indicator of the bases on which [the author] made these selections and decided to exclude other figures from among his predecessors" (p. 422, n. 2), they hide the reputational factors that have been the true causes of predecessor selection in sociology – "during much of its history" (pp. 439–40) at least. Camic offers the historical case study of Parsons as proof.

Parsons, the Institutionalists, and the Mechanisms of Predecessor Selection

Camic starts his case study by summarizing *Structure's* "substantive-theoretical argument," referring to one of his earlier papers for a discussion of its methodological claims (Camic 1987). He decomposes *Structure's* substantive-theoretical argument into two interrelated components: the critical (the attack on utilitarianism) and the constructive (the relevance of social components of the personality, ultimate values, the definition of society as a reality *sui generis*, the relevance of regulatory ethical rules).[8] Camic then posits that "nearly all interpretations of this famous theoretical argument have been conjoined to historical accounts of the process by which Parsons worked out his position, accounts that accord central significance to Parsons' relationship with the four turn-of-the-century European predecessors identified in *Structure*" (p. 426). According to Camic, there are two capital sins in such interpretations: the assumptions either that *Structure* was a synthesis of the predecessors' distinctive theoretical stances or that Parsons had been attracted to these earlier positions because of the similarities between their problems and his own. As a result, these interpretations have assumed that "Parsons did not draw upon" other earlier work – "of which he was aware" – because this "work [was] deficient in content-fit and therefore not pertinent to the project" (p. 426). But this assumption, Camic asserts, is nothing but a self-deception: Accepting at face value *Structure* and later retrospective accounts by Parsons himself, scholars have failed to investigate the actual selections Parsons made while *Structure* was just getting underway. If enough documentary materials are studied carefully enough, Camic argues, a very different story about predecessor selection can be told.

Which story? It is well known that Parsons had been exposed during his undergraduate years at Amherst to the influence of two teachers, Walton H. Hamilton and Clarence E. Ayres, both prominent figures in the second wave of institutional economics. This movement, which originated in Veblen's attack on neoclassical economics, stressed the limits of utilitarianism, criticized approaches that appealed to biopsychological forces, recognized the role of noncommercial incentives in economic behavior, paid cultural factors their due, and stressed interconnection and interdependence as valuable components of any social explanation (p. 429). In short, according to Camic, in "oppos[ing] utilitarian views of action," institutionalist ideas paralleled the general orientation of *Structure* in significant respects (p. 430). Camic stresses, moreover, that during his undergraduate years Parsons was deeply involved in institutionalist ideas and later in his career acknowledged that Hamilton and Ayres were the principal agents of his conversion to the social sciences (e.g., Parsons 1976). But Camic goes much further than simply stating that the institutionalists' ideas could easily fit the *Structure* project. He argues that, in fact, they were even more fit for this project than the ideas of the European foursome Parsons actually chose (p. 431).[9] Why, then, did Parsons not encompass them in his more mature professional work, paying them only marginal attention instead?

Here Camic's alternative model takes center stage: It was not a matter of content but of reputation. Beginning in the 1920s, institutionalists had an increasingly negative reputation in the academic world, for they were widely perceived as on the losing side in the ongoing conflict with neoclassical economics. Moreover, unlike institutionalist ideas, the neoclassical approach was deeply entrenched in the more prestigious academic institutions and leading departments. These considerations applied even more strongly to the Harvard environment that Parsons entered in 1927 as an instructor of economics. Harvard's leading figures were very critical of the institutionalists. At Harvard, Camic argues, "to attach one's ideas to those of the institutionalists was to ally oneself openly with a losing cause" (p. 435). Moreover, within the same Harvard intellectual network, Marshall, Pareto, Durkheim, and Weber – the foursome who were to form the core of *Structure* – were considered positively, or at least not considered in a negative light. Marshall and Pareto, of course, were major neoclassical thinkers. Durkheim was becoming a figure of major interest, and Weber was already held in high regard. In short, and here Camic enters into the more detailed brief for his alternative view, Parsons was "part of a well-signposted intellectual network that warned him of the defectiveness and uselessness of some lines of work while announcing the greatness, brilliantness [sic] and fruitfulness of other lines" (p. 437). Camic goes on to explain in some detail why he believes this signalling to have been theoretically wrong-headed, and he insists that institutionalism still has an important theoretical value (p. 438). Yet Camic's paper is less about vindicating institutionalism than about demonstrating the validity of his broader instrumentalist approach to the critical role that reputational networks play in the construction of science. With certain reservations, discussed below, it is upon this reductionist approach to the sociology of knowledge that Camic ultimately makes his case.

Camic's Sociology of Science: Variations on a Familiar Theme

Although Camic presents his constructions of the two modalities of predecessor selection as something new in the debates that surround the history of social thought, and in debates about the thought of Parsons in particular, the contrast merely supplies a new name for the venerable dispute between internalists and externalists that has been at the center of discussion in the history and philosophy of science for the last half century at least. Naive internalists take all thinkers at their word; assuming the truth and legitimacy of his or her predecessor-construction, they devote themselves primarily to reconstructing and interpreting the theorist's own rationales. Externalists typically make the opposite mistake. Assuming the ideational contents of a work to be unproblematic, they devote themselves to finding the so-called social – organizational, economic, or political – factors that "caused" the thinker to adopt such ideas.

By focusing on such factors as the contrasting reputations of Parsons' intellectual reference groups, Parsons' job market prospects, and the status structure of Parsons' local organizational environment at Harvard, Camic obviously takes the externalist position on Parsons' predecessor choice. We believe that his explanation of the interpretative shifts in Parsons' work suffers accordingly. External factors can never independently account for theoretical choice. Choices are certainly affected by external factors, and they are to some extent strategic; but, also, they always involve intentions in a broader sense, intentions that rest upon subjectivities.

This broader theoretical subjectivity must be explored. If we consider how theorists choose their predecessors, their colleagues, or even their enemies, we can understand subjectivity as supplying "selection criteria" that filter external factors. How can one study choice without studying criteria? Yet, we argue, this is precisely what Camic tries to do.

The Argument and its Self-Contradictions

Any criticism may be sustained through systematic argument (see, e.g., Alexander 1983); through discussion of what we view as alternative and more successful approaches to the study of classical figures (e.g., Wearne 1989 on the early Parsons, Taylor 1975 on the early Hegel); or through a disciplined confrontation with the empirical case study at hand. In what follows, we engage in each of these forms of criticism, but we initially pursue a different, more textual approach. We point out how the limitations of externalism produce debilitating contradictions in Camic's own argument. For the uncomfortable truth is that Camic cannot himself maintain the integrity of his reputational model. He abandons it in his most critical arguments, and takes up the very alternative his paper is intended to refute.

Camic's central claim, occasional ambiguities notwithstanding, is that Parsons ignored the American institutional economists in *Structure* and turned instead to the Europeans for one reason only: The former's reputation was too negative to help Parsons in his early efforts to establish his career, or at least to produce "a credible theoretical statement" (p. 437). This central claim we call Hypothesis 1 (H1), and we return to it in the closing pages of our discussion. The central claim, however, rests upon a secondary one, which we call Hypothesis 2 (H2): Institutionalist theory would have provided just as viable, as useful, and as complementary a platform for the theory that Parsons constructed in *Structure* as did the European theories with which Parsons actually engaged. It is upon the validity of this secondary claim (H2) that Camic's reputational argument (H1) rests. If H2 is refuted, H1 is decisively weakened, although it would still remain necessary to assess the reputational factor in and of itself. We must first devote ourselves, then, to Camic's secondary claim.

Our initial argument against H2 is to demonstrate that in his effort to verify it Camic employs the very methodology that he is engaged in trying to refute, namely, that of content fit.[10] Camic devotes much of his case study to an extensive, highly internalist interpretation of the similarities between the ideational contents of *Structure* and those of institutional economics. In fact, in his introduction to this discussion he goes so far as to acknowledge that "content factors cannot be excluded when examining Parsons' selections, [for] thinkers with solid reputations for work whose content was obviously irrelevant were outside the range of possible predecessors for him" (p. 436). Only after spending many pages to assure his readers that a content fit does exist, does Camic discuss the impact of reputational factors on Parsons' predecessor selection.

Judging from such perlocutionary actions rather than formal ill-ocutionary aims, one can only conclude that Camic actually believes that it is ideational congruity – content fit – that sets the agenda for arguments about the nature of predecessor selection. He would seem to be suggesting, in spite of himself, that analysts should begin by investigating content fit. Reputational factors are, perforce, reduced from primary to secondary considerations. They cannot explain the general field of selection, but only why, within an already highly restricted field, one rather than another viable predecessor was chosen. Once again, it is Camic himself who puts this argument very well, asserting that only "when it came to work not ruled out by this broad criterion [of content fit], [was] reputation . . . a decisive differential" (p. 436) for the early Parsons.

How could the substance of Camic's argument so contradict its formally stated aims? In fact, such self-contradictions are not at all infrequent in theoretical argument. They often reveal strains produced by unresolved, and unresolvable, theoretical claims. That Camic commits such a self-contradiction should be attributed not to a personal failing but to the inadequacies of the externalist position he seeks to uphold. In a certain sense, in fact, it is a testimony to Camic that he allows this contradiction to surface. His commitment to the historical materials he has uncovered, and his highly ambivalent yet still substantial sense for the integrity of Parsons' early project, lead him to insist that such ideational parallels in content can and should be found.

The Residual Categories

The best way to control for an interpreter's claim that a text is contradictory – our claim here – is to find statements indicating that the author is aware of these contradictions. Camic's text is helpful in this regard. It is clear that Camic senses the hole that he has dug for himself. He tries to dig himself out in two ways. First, immediately after the introduction to his discussion of content fit, quoted above, he issues a *mea culpa*: "This discussion of the topic of content fit should not be viewed as contradicting the argument just made *against* the current use of the content-fit model" (p. 424, italics in original). It is difficult to understand what "should not" means, for in the discussion that follows this statement, which sits at the heart of Camic's paper, Camic himself contradicts the argument against the content-fit model he has just made. Certainly, he "should not" have done so, but we are glad he did, for it is our claim that content references simply have to be made.

The manner in which Camic illustrates the logic of this *mea culpa* reveals the difficulties he has created. "Just as studies seeking to challenge class-based explanations of educational attainment require a careful examination of class factors before the effect of these factors can be qualified," he writes (p. 424), "so here I examine content-fit factors to demonstrate empirically the deficiency of the content-fit model and the need to supplement it with an alternative approach." We respond, first, by noting the linguistic anomaly: It is hard to see how an approach diametrically opposed to an alternative can be understood as being supplemented by it. More important than the linguistic slippage in this statement, however, is the logical fallacy the syllogism involves. Camic is not merely "examining" the alternative, content-fit model; he is incorporating it as a central part of his explanation. Challenges to class-based explanations of education do not begin by arguing that class factors actually provide the most important, indeed, the framing factor in explaining it!

This admission *faute de mieux* adumbrates the second move that Camic makes to dig himself out of the hole, an effort that only serves to dig him in deeper still. In the concluding section of his paper, Camic begins to speak of the two models not as theoretical alternatives, one of which is right and the other wrong, but as equally necessary empirical strategies whose employment depends merely on the nature of the facts at hand. Introducing the notion of "mutual dependence," he puts forward the thesis that the relevance of reputation versus content is empirically contingent on the organizational characteristics of intellectual disciplines. If a discipline is only loosely organized, he suggests, an original work will not need to "content fit," and reputational factors will count for more. In more tightly organized disciplines, however, fitting with the contents of predecessors is more important, and reputation will count for less.

No doubt this is sometimes the case. Camic does not seem to realize, however, that his own study has demonstrated something quite
different. Writing about a period of only loose disciplinary dependence, he has shown that reputation analysis must be subordinated to
content-fit models – that it is the latter that must be used as the
principal frame.[11] At any rate, each of these positions – mutual
dependence, empirical variation, subordination – contradicts the strong
claim for reputation with which Camic's paper began and upon
which his broad and ambitious claims for a new sociology of knowledge relies.

It is difficult to understand how the central argument of Camic's
essay could be allowed to change its meaning so fundamentally in
such a short space. Our explanation is that the theoretical logic of
the originating argument was impossible to sustain. As a result of the
tensions generated by an untenable position, Camic's reputational
model wavers between the theoretically significant claim that it may
account for predecessor selection as such and the much more modest
allusion to its utility in explaining a subset of choices among a larger
set of predecessors that has already been selected on entirely different
grounds.

Selection Criteria: the Missing Factor

H2 asserts that institutional theory would have provided a viable
theoretical reference for Parsons' foundational work. Our first argument against H2 has been indirect; we have shown that in trying to
sustain it Camic has employed the very method, content fit, that his
entire exercise is designed to dispute. Our second argument against
H2 is more direct. We argue that Camic has not demonstrated that the
contents actually fit at all. Camic's interpretive method, we suggest,
is not up to the hermeneutic task at hand. He is using blacksmith's
tools for a carpenter's job.

Indeed, if "content fit" is an appropriate goal for comparative
cultural analysis, it can hardly be an appropriate means, or method;
it is simply too general and vague. Only the most casual intellectual
historians have ever suggested that a fit between categories as broad
as "the common moral foundation of human action" or the "limits
of theories based only on self-interest" (phrases Camic invokes in the

section from pp. 424–30, passim) can provide the basis for evaluating intellectual influence.[12] It is necessary to point to the intervening factor of cognitive selection. But this intervening factor is precisely what is lacking from Camic's account.

Social scientists and theorists are agents. They possess, protect, and nurture subjectivities that allow them to select, consciously and unconsciously, among the internal and external pressures of their environments, whether these be the reputations of other scientists or the idioms of broad cultural traditions. Some simple thought experiments allow us to see just how important these selection criteria turn out to be. For example, one has many colleagues, both locally and elsewhere, whose reputations are attractive and high. Just so, there is a wide range of broadly congenial "ideational contents" from which to choose. The critical issue, then, is not selection *per se* but the criteria of relevance one applies. It is the latter that must be a primary topic of inquiry if actual predecessor selection is to be understood.

Who would deny that, painted in broad brush, there are many striking similarities between some of Parsons' ideas and some of the institutionalists'? There are also striking similarities between Parsons' ideas and those of many other important thinkers such as Comte, Hegel, Tocqueville, or Troeltsch. Camic himself points to Hobhouse and Laski as equally likely candidates for the identity of excluded predecessor (p. 439), going so far as to suggest that, because they too were thinkers with whose ideas Parsons was familiar, they should not have been ignored!

This is a game everyone can play. As Zeitlin (1968) and Gouldner (1970, pp. 150, 185–9) once asked in outraged tones about Parsons' canon, why not Marx? As Levine still asks, why not Simmel?[13] The game is too easy. Not only can everyone play but, actually, everybody has.[14] Thus, our first response to Camic's argument for content fit on the basis of broad similarities is to stress the importance of differences. Simmel, after all, departed in fundamental ways from Parsons' agenda (Alexander 1993, Sciortino 1993). Why should the American have built his theoretical base, or legitimated it, vis-à-vis the German thinker's work?

Our second response cuts deeper, and moves more directly to the issue of the selection criteria themselves. One cannot argue for the plausibility of including or excluding this or that thinker in the interpretative (re)construction of predecessors merely on the basis of this or that piece of content fit. Every work has similarities and differences with every other. Beef soup and vegetable soup have many similarities, meat apart. Yet, for those who have any developed sense of taste, it is precisely the absence of meat that matters. In the end, it is not the broad category of the work but the selection criteria that matters. We must be prepared to analyze the intellectual development of the thinker in a close and detailed way in order to understand the theoretical interests that result.

Structure was never meant to be, and was not presented as, an exhaustive survey of the contemporary literature in European or American social theory. It was presented as a precise statement of theoretical axioms developed in relation to the work of a small number of authors whom Parsons considered the most significant for his theoretical aims. It is active consideration that is precisely the point. Camic suggests that a work may be considered likely predecessor material simply if "the thinker was aware of relevant previous lines of work and [if] the quality of this *work met contemporary standards for publishability*" (p. 423, italics added). But this standard is absurdly broad. To ascertain the relevance to an intellectual of preceding work, we must ask a question more like the following: When Parsons was preparing *Structure*, what did he think he was doing, and why?

One way to answer this question might be to find out what Parsons actually said about the institutionalists, in his pre-*Structure* papers, in *Structure* itself, and in his later phases – to examine, in other words, the statements that Camic either studiously ignores or underrates. The first, and most crucial, thing Parsons said was that the institutionalist position was untenable because it confused analytic and concrete approaches to social facts (1937, pp. 122, 125).[15] Why was this distinction important to him? Because, by this time in his development, Parsons was a neo-Kantian, concerned with producing an analytic, structured, quasi-a priori framework for theoretical analysis. This was indeed one of the bigger tasks of *Structure*, as Camic (1987) himself has clearly recognized.

Whether or not this was a good choice is not our concern here. Maybe Parsons would have benefited from a more open attitude to pragmatism and historicism or, indeed, to empiricism. The fact is that he did not make this choice. His selection criteria were different in decisive ways.

Looking at what Parsons actually said about the institutionalists also demonstrates that Camic is wrong to suggest that Parsons "never recognised any substantive similarity between his approach and that of his two teachers" at Amherst. In fact, Parsons stressed several times that some of the institutionalists' critiques of neoclassical economics were sound,[16] and he always recognized the relevance of institutionalism in his intellectual formation (Parsons 1959, 1970, 1976). At the same time, on these occasions and others, he also remarked that, in his opinion, institutionalism had taken the wrong path. Institutionalists had argued against utilitarianism in an empirical way, whereas in *Structure* Parsons was determined to make an analytical critique. Although institutionalism advocated sociology as an encyclopedic science of holistic phenomena, virtually every section of *Structure* is intended to demonstrate the limits of this conception, and to suggest, in contrast, the need to differentiate sociology analytically, not empirically, from the other social sciences. The institutionalists had, in a sense, done the right deed for the wrong reasons, and reasons are what *Structure* is all about.

Camic, in fact, may be aware of such possible consequences; if so, the ad hoc statements that appear at various points in his essays are attempts to ward them off. As we have seen, in the very beginning of his discussion of Parsons' intentions in *Structure*, Camic introduces a distinction between "substantive-theoretical" and "methodological views," including in the latter Parsons' discussion of the "analytical" problem. Because he has dealt with the former issue in another publication, Camic writes, he will not deal with it here, except when "these methodological issues . . . bear directly on the analysis" (p. 424). This move, understandable as it may seem for theoretical economy and simple consideration of space, is, however, highly problematical. First, it makes invisible the fundamental and crucial difference between Parsons and the institutionalists, a difference, after all, that is the very *experimentum crucis* of Camic's paper. Second, this invisibility of what Camic calls the methodological issue in *Structure* obscures the relationship between the institutionalist position and what for Parsons were the book's real theoretical stakes. For Parsons, "analytic" was not only an epistemological position, but also a kind of flag that stood for just about everything important he believed at the time. Deeply affected by the neo-Kantian movements in Germany and France, which were fundamentally removed in both spirit and empirical thrust from American pragmatism, Parsons had become opposed to the very philosophy that inspired the most important American social theory. In these terms, the apparently "mere" epistemological issue was strongly connected with a substantive thrust. It suggested for Parsons not only the importance of morality *sui generis* and religiosity, but also the whole range of methodological and theoretical tools that would allow one to produce empirical explanations of these phenomena in a comparative and historical frame, without having to give up the rigorous and cumulative character of scientific constructs.[17] Whatever the theoretical problems such an overemphasis produced, this very conceptual inflation suggests that ignoring Parsons' invocation of "analytic" can have disastrous consequences for interpreting the rationale of his early work and the predecessor selection involved.

These were some of Parsons' theoretical interests, his criteria of theoretical relevance for choosing the predecessors with whom he would engage. Given these presuppositions, in our view, it cannot seriously be suggested that institutionalism could have provided the same kind of intellectual resources to answer Parsons' questions as did Durkheim's religious sociology or his study of suicide, much less Weber's comparative studies of the world religions.[18] Yet, even if one disagrees with this judgment – and Camic, characteristically, both does and does not – any serious appreciation of the more general orientation from which Parsons viewed the world leads one to understand why Parsons would have rejected the contributions of the institutionalists in a very emphatic way, on intellectual grounds alone. It was not their reputations he objected to but, as we will see more clearly in the next section, their ideas.

Speculation from Fragmentary Evidence: Distorting Parsons' Intellectual Career

It should be clear by this point how evidence about Parsons' dissatisfaction with institutionalism – the lack of content fit between his emerging ideas and theirs (H2) – seriously undermines the claim (H1) that reputation rather than ideas inspired Parsons' attachment to the European predecessors he eventually chose. Before considering H1 more directly, in fact, we examine one final piece of evidence that Camic invokes to demonstrate H2. This concerns the impact of Parsons' attachments to institutionalism in his undergraduate years. By this path, we will be led, finally, to the central reputational claim itself.

Camic emphasizes that Parsons was deeply affected by his undergraduate courses with Walton H. Hamilton and Clarence E. Ayres, and that Parsons decided to move from the biological to the social sciences as a result of these experiences. On the basis of these early connections and influences – to which Parsons himself freely attested (e.g., 1959, 1970, 1976) – Camic argues that institutionalism must have had a continuing effect on Parsons' thinking in the years between Amherst and *Structure*.[19]

This does not seem to us highly compelling evidence. Although Parsons no doubt was a highly precocious 21 year old, must we insist the selection criteria he employed at that tender age remained intact for another decade hence? Many social scientists "discover" social science in their initial college courses. How many feel themselves compelled to forever evaluate relevance according to the approaches they learned on those occasions, despite the fact that they may continue to agree with their general claims? Such a thesis posits an imprinting factor stronger than any of those identified in Konrad Lorenz's geese!

In fact, the evidence Camic quotes, the detailed biographical information now available on Parsons (to which Camic himself partly contributed), and the essays Parsons published before *Structure* (which Camic himself has rendered easily available) tell us something quite different, and they amount to a not uncommon story. A brilliant student initially exposed to a compelling stream of social theory discovers quickly that there are other compelling theories available, and decides, over the course of a few years, to opt for what he now thinks to be a more sensible one. This maturing student, in such a situation, may not reject some of the general ideas associated with the theory of his early youth; he may retain and refine an interest toward some topic associated with the former approach. Yet, in his later work, after acknowledging that "the controversy between the orthodox and the institutionalists has played a decisive part in the development of the discussion" in which he was interested, he may decide that "the present discussion must be concerned with pointing to satisfactory ways out rather than warning against false paths" (Parsons 1932, p. 87). In light of available evidence, we would suggest that this reconstruction seems more likely to survive Occam's razor than Camic's reputational account.

Indeed, Camic produces in this paper no evidence even for Parsons' enthusiastic endorsement of institutionalist ideas after he left Amherst. On the contrary, he acknowledges that Parsons appears to have had fundamental misgivings about institutionalist ideas long before the idea of *Structure* ever had crossed his mind: Parsons "went to Harvard in 1927 . . . to study" (p. 434) with the neoclassical economists who were the theoretical enemies of his former Amherst teachers. Before arriving at Harvard, in other words, Parsons was already persuaded that his prior economics training was inadequate, indeed "way off of the main track" (Parsons 1959, p. 5).

We have finally come to Camic's central contention (H2). Do not these last pieces of biographical evidence, introduced by Camic himself, run directly counter to his critical claim that it was the impact of Harvard and its neoclassical economists' reputation that induced Parsons' turn away from institutionalism? Even Camic's own selective reconstruction of Parsons' progress makes clear that the young theorist's negative judgment of institutionalism had been formed before, not after, Parsons entered into the reputational networks of his Harvard years.[20] Indeed, there is very good reason to suspect that Parsons selected that network according to his intellectual interests, rather than having his relevance criteria shaped by it. Camic writes as if we should be astonished that "Hamilton, Ayres, and the other younger institutionalists were not even encompassed by Parsons in his work *in the late 1920's and early 1930's*" (p. 430, italics added). To the contrary, we would be astonished if they were. Our suspicion that Parsons may have possessed, even at that early age, a capacity for independent intellectual choice (see Wearne 1989) is reinforced when we consider the impact of the character-forming experience that Camic inexplicably leaves entirely out of his biographical reconstruction. We refer here, of course, to the two years that Parsons spent as a student in European universities, first in England, then in Germany, after leaving Amherst on a travel and study fellowship in October 1924. This period was not exactly unimportant, after all: It amounted to the only graduate training program Parsons ever had. Moreover, while Parsons never hesitated in asserting that his year at the London School of Economics (with Hobhouse, Laski, and Malinowski partly excepted) was an intellectual disappointment, his experience of a year of study in Heidelberg, in 1925–6, where "the ghost of Max Weber" was still very much in evidence, made on him a profound and lasting impression (Parsons 1970, 1980).

Camic not only neglects to consider the consequences of this intellectual *Bildung*, but he fails entirely to mention that it was this same young Parsons who during the summer of 1927 began revising the translation of Weber's *Protestant Ethic*, which was published three years later. Weber, we can be sure, was not one of the institutionalists, despite the fact that his views in certain ways converged – content fit – with their own. To the contrary, Webers' acceptance of the importance of marginal utility theory was fundamental to his sociological ideas (Holton and Turner 1985), and he considered himself, in the latter part of his career at least, to be contributing to the development of an analytically differentiated social science. Reading Parsons's lucid and admiring introduction to that first English translation of a major Weber work, one can hardly doubt the direction in which the young American's intellectual interests lay. He did not need to be led astray by the fame of Harvard neoclassical thought, nor by the fortune that association with them supposedly was to provide. He was already becoming "Weberian," and it was certainly this interest that lay at the heart of *Structure* itself.[21]

Why not respect the young Parsons as capable of making his own decisions, as drawing selectively from his intellectual environments, and as directing his own intellectual path? Precisely because he was deeply exposed to institutionalism as an undergraduate, one can assume that Parsons understood its position very well. If his Harvard colleagues had been sending him the wrong signals about institutionalism (p. 437), as Camic assumes, would Parsons not have been able to realize their error? It is Camic, in fact, who believes these signals to have been wrong, claiming that Parsons' colleagues were "misinformed" (p. 439). Obviously, Parsons did not feel the same way, and he certainly was in a position to judge for himself.[22]

The author who was accused, not so long ago, of portraying actors as cultural dopes (Garfinkel 1967) stands accused by Camic of being a reputational dope, unable to evaluate information according to his own relevance criteria, accepting automatically and unthinkingly the ideas of whoever was most prestigious in his intellectual environment at the time.

Reputational Reduction as Behaviorism

By discounting Parsons' capacity as an agent, his capacity for judging, interpreting, and processing his experience, Camic has arrived at his central claim that reputation, not intellectual content, was responsible for the predecessor choices Parsons made. This implicitly behaviorist understanding of the manner in which institutional factors affect intellectual creation betrays the kind of quasi-rationalistic exchange theory perspective that saturates, and undermines, Camic's understanding of how reputation works. Claiming that Parsons would have been irrational "in choosing as predecessors locally disreputable thinkers like the institutionalists" (p. 435), Camic cites Goode's proposition that "to admire openly the 'wrong' person or achievement can be costly if one's boss is likely to feel less respect for anyone who holds such an opinion" (p. 435, n. 15).

Finally, Camic insists on the point that has been at the heart of his reductionist interpretations of Parsons all along (e.g., Camic 1987, 1989). Noting that "several institutional factors made it especially important to avoid these associations" (p. 435) with the institutionalists, Camic emphasizes the singular and overriding importance of Parsons' position in the stratification system. In a number of key dimensions – job security, professional prestige, departmental power – Parsons' status was low; by contrast, in each of these same dimensions, the position of analytical, as compared with institutional, economics was high. *Ipso facto*: The insecure disciplinary status of sociology is supposed to have made it necessary for Parsons to gain credible allies from the discipline of economics, dominated by the anti-institutional approach; the low status of Harvard's own sociology department allegedly pushed Parsons in the same direction locally; "the uncertainty about his prospects for promotion in the Sociology Department" (p. 435) induced Parsons to make allies outside of it.

If we assume behaviorist motives internally and the stratification of every environment externally, then such "evidence" seems obviously to prove H1. It could only have been because Parsons so desperately "needed the backing of the economists and other local influentials" (p. 435) that he turned away from institutionalism! And what about the Europeans? Why did Parsons turn to them instead? Camic provides, as always, an instrumentalist explanation for this as well. It was "because they were not 'liabilities'" (p. 435). *Homo economicus theoreticus.*[23]

All of this is not to say that reputation does not matter, or that intellectuals are not influenced by the environments in which they live. It is to suggest, however, that the flow of reputation, its origins, and its impacts cannot be understood simply from the perspective of exchange. It is intellectual actors who do the exchanging, actors who have subjectivities that inform their intentions, intentions that establish criteria for choice. Intellectuals make efforts to select from their environments in ways that are consistent with these criteria, although certainly they do not always succeed. The point is not to deny that intellectual projects are often also political and disciplinary actions, nor to forget that essay writing is often also an occasion for building alliances and acknowledging debts. The point is to argue that the relevance of intellectual works to one another should not be judged primarily upon these grounds.

In his early work on the scientific community, Warren Hagstrom (1965) wrote that scientists exchange information for recognition. The exchange theory he employed, however, was that of Marcel Mauss, not Homans or Goode. In the Durkheimian tradition, the search for recognition, no matter what is exchanged for it in return, is regulated by some prior understanding of moral force. Camic claims to have made use of Hagstrom's work. It is a shame he did not understand it.

Conclusion: on the Deconstruction and Destruction of Classics

Camic claims great originality for focusing attention on Parsons' choice of intellectual predecessors. "To date," he writes, "research in the theory area has treated the inclusion of certain intellectual predecessors without regard to the exclusion of other writers" (p. 424). We will leave aside the intriguing question of just what "research in the theory area" can mean. Does the century-long inquiry into Marx's predecessors not count as research or not count as theory work? However, we insist that this statement is fallacious even if it is taken as applying only to the narrow area of theoretical discussion of Parsons himself.

From the very beginning of *Structure*'s public life, one of the principal strategies of those who have disagreed with its central tenets – and Camic has made no secret of his own disagreement – has been to emphasize the self-serving and particularistic manner in which Parsons chose his predecessors. From Coser's (1956) outrage over Parsons' exclusion of early American sociology, an outrage later echoed by Hinkle (1963), to countless indignations that Parsons had excluded Marx (Rex 1961), to Levine's ([1957] 1980) insistence that Simmel deserved to be in the pantheon too, Parsons's critics have consistently disputed his predecessor choice. In ways very similar to Camic's, they attacked Parsons for excluding those whose work they judged to be equally relevant, or they accused him of ignoring figures whose theories, in their view, would have been damaging to his argument. It requires only a modest extension of such arguments to include those interpreters who have argued, not that Parsons actually excluded a theorist from *Structure*, but that he neglected one or the other – invariably the most important – part of that theorist's work. Bendix and Roth launched serious arguments of this sort about Parsons's relation to Weber. The spate of subsequent "de-Parsonsizing" articles (Pope 1973, Cohen et al. 1975) continued this approach in a fundamentally less serious way.

All of which is to say that no one except Parsons himself and his early and most ardent followers have described him as an "impartial bricoleur, searching out and drawing on any relevant intellectual resources" (p. 432). This straw man does more, however, than create a misleading impression of Camic's originality. Camic also employs it to suggest that the kind of behaviorist and reductionist emphasis on reputation he proffers is the only way that the exclusion of predecessors – the "dark side" (p. 424) – can be explained. Yet many of the most severe critics of Parsons' exclusion of this or that predecessor never found the need to evoke a reputational claim; they launched explanations of exclusion on intellectual grounds alone or upon broader understandings of the impact on Parsons of society at large. Perhaps even more tellingly, some of the interpreters whom Camic criticizes most consistently for their concentration on "content fit," and who have made an effort to promote a more complex and appreciative understanding of Parsons in recent years (e.g., Gould 1981; Alexander 1983, 1988), have themselves written at length about the dark, exclusionary holes in his selection of predecessors. Gould has extensively discussed, and criticized, Parsons' exclusion of Marx. Alexander (cf. 1987a) makes Parsons' exclusions – of Marx, of the materialist Weber, of pragmatism and phenomenology, and of the later Durkheim's religious turn – central to his reading of the entire postclassical tradition in sociology.

Because he has so persistently tried to interpret the theoretical arguments of Parsons' first and most important book as reflections of the author's personal and institutional ambitions, it is fair to say that Camic's inquiries into the construction of *Structure* have had a destructive intent. We have argued that Camic's search for Parsons' predecessor choice is not original and that his substantive arguments are not correct. It is well to remember, however, that every discussion of a classic has much more than an empirical aim. It is theorizing by another name (Alexander 1987b).

It might be that Camic has tried to destroy the integrity of *Structure* because he fundamentally disagrees with its arguments for the centrality of moral regulation, for the independent integrity of moral choice, for the necessity of theoretical synthesis and an analytical approach to theory as such. Certainly in his own explanations he has proposed to substitute for such emphases a behavioristic understanding of motives and an instrumental approach to the external pressures of institutional life, and a relativistic conception according to which, once they meet "contemporary standards of publishability" (p. 423), pushpin is as good as poetry. Because our own approach to social theory is very different, and because we understand action and order in a very different way, our empirical evaluation of Camic's arguments about the classics have had a different theoretical aim.

The deconstruction of our discipline's classics need not necessarily have a destructive aim. Sociology is mature enough today to disagree with its own founders without having to fantasize on their evil and covert intentions. Sounder arguments and better conceptual frameworks may advance and tighten theoretical debates. "Prior publication, unpublished papers, course materials, letters, and so on" are surely helpful in gaining a better understanding of the legacies of great theorists and the history of our discipline. They cannot, however, be used to substitute for genuine theoretical arguments, and they should never be used to conceal them.

Notes

1   See Camic 1987, pp. 434–6; 1989, p. 95. As far as *Structure* is concerned, Camic contends that "it holds its greatest present-day utility only when its original meaning is benignly overlooked" (Camic 1989, p. 40).

2   Critics have noted the fuzziness in Camic's definition of "sociological" (Tiryakian 1990, p. 452). Unfortunately, this critique has not received from Camic an adequate answer: "He [Tiryakian] asks what I mean for sociological, assuming (as Parsons himself) that the desideratum is a fixed definition that rules some things in and some things out. As my paper should have made clear, this is not my point of view.... The history of sociology presents (to quote Levine) 'a gallery of sociologies' and definitions of sociological are context dependent" (Camic 1990b, p. 458). As we will see in the discussion of his 1992 paper, however, our problem is not so much in the fuzziness of Camic's definition of "sociological" as with its reductionism.

3   Camic's essays do include occasional sentences pointing in the opposite direction. However, these ambiguities, as we show below, are more attempts to overcome the intrinsic weaknesses of reductionism by the resort to residual categories than real theoretical openings.

4   Merton (1965) has demonstrated in loving and copious detail how this metaphor – standing on the shoulders of giants – has been reconstructed continuously over centuries, acquiring new meanings in the process.

5 Camic's definition is ambiguous because, although the term "selection" seems to imply a conscious intention, the issues of consciousness and intentionality are, as we will see, some of the principal points Camic glosses over. The complexity of the very concept of "intention" in this regard is well illustrated by the thoughtful and very revealing essay on intellectual historiography by Jones and Kibbee (1993), which can be read as an autocritique of the kind of narrow reading of intention stressing conscious intent that had earlier informed Jones's work, and which continues to inform Camic's work today.

6 Unless otherwise cited, henceforth all page numbers refer to Camic 1992.

7 Cf., p. 423. This alternative is elsewhere defined as "social-organizational" (p. 439) or, more simply, "social" (p. 433).

8 In this chapter, we cannot treat adequately the peculiarities of Camic's reading of *Structure*. A detailed and powerful confrontation with Camic's thesis may be found in Gould's essays (1989, 1991).

9 On this point, Camic seems to point especially toward Pareto (p. 438; see also Camic 1987). Perhaps precisely because he refuses to confront analytical theory seriously, Camic seems unable to understand what Parsons did find of interest in Pareto.

10 Here are Camic's own words describing the empirical case study upon which H2 rests: "[T]his example involves a review of the content of *Structure* and an examination of its fit with the content of American institutional economics" (p. 424).

11 It could still be argued, of course, that while Camic's own analysis of Parsons emphasizes the primacy of content fit, Parsons himself did not use this approach to choose his predecessors. It seems highly implausible, however, that Camic should rely so heavily on content selectivity while arguing that great social theorists themselves either cannot or do not avail themselves of the same technique. Insofar as Camic proposes these techniques as scientific methodologies, he is contending that they correspond to strategies intellectual actors themselves employ. To suggest anything else would be enormously condescending.

12 Such an assertion reminds one, in both form and content, of the spurious claims that Nisbet made, time and time again (e.g., Nisbet 1966), for the conservative origins of Durkheim's work. Nisbet justified these assertions by pointing to the fact that such terms as "morality" and "integration" appeared not only in the work of conservatives like De Maistre and but in Durkheim's work as well. With such broad brush strokes, he ignored the fact that such concepts also appeared in the works of Enlightenment figures. This was precisely the point of Seidman's (1983) important early work, which focused much more precisely on the actual theoretical and ideological intentions of the social theorists themselves.

13 See Levine ([1957] 1980). A coordinated claim is actually common to Levine and Camic. Both impute to Parsons' *Structure* a responsibility for

the later reputational misfortunes of their preferred earlier theorists (Sciortino 1993). By removing them from his creative 1937 work, so this argument goes, Parsons concealed them from the attention of later sociologists (see chapter 5, above). However, both Camic and Levine admit that the influence of the pre-Parsons theorists they prefer was decreasing long before *Structure* was written, and both acknowledge – indeed, insist – that neither *Structure* nor Parsons himself were influential among sociologists for quite a long time after 1937.

14   Indeed, this is not the first time that Camic himself has played this game. His first published essay on Parsons' *Structure* was devoted to asking, why not the true utilitarians? (Camic 1979). Arguing that Adam Smith surely qualified for the criteria Parsons had laid out for inclusion, Camic thus committed the same mistake – a disregard for Parsons's analysical intentions – that he was to repeat in the later, more historicist work we are considering here.

15   Some examples: "I do not consider institutionalism a genuine solution of Marshall's predicament, while I do so regard Pareto and Weber [. . . .] Insofar as they do not repudiate theory altogether, which is fatal, they tend to fall back into 'psychologism' and 'survivalism,' which Marshall successfully avoided" (Parsons [1932] 1991, p. 87); "The institutionalists' repudiation of the conceptual tools of orthodox economic theory is an excellent example of this [confusion between analytic and concrete]. Though often empirically right in their criticism of conclusions arrived at by the use of these concepts, they are none the less disastrously wrong on a theoretical level in failing to see the possibility of avoiding these consequences by using the same tools in the context of a different conceptual framework" (Parsons 1937, p. 125). Thirty-nine years later, in a contribution to a Festschrift for Clarence Ayres, a leading institutionalist (see below), Parsons made exactly the same point: "I think, in retrospect, that I had two major theoretical objections to the institutional point of view. The first was that, in the name of a generalized radical empiricism, it denied the legitimacy of analytical abstraction – a conception I found running through all of the principal authors whose work was treated in my [1937] study" (Parsons 1976, p. 178).

16   Some examples: "These [critiques] do not mean of course that many of the Institutionalists' criticisms of the orthodox, especially the more dogmatic [neoclassical economists], are not well taken" (Parsons [1932] 1991, p. 87); "There can be no doubt that in large measure these unorthodox theories are empirically right" (Parsons [1935] 1991, p. 212); "Thus, in a *positivistic* context, there is a good deal of truth in the "institutionalist' charge that orthodox economic theory is logically bound up with hedonism" (Parsons 1937, p. 122, original italics).

17   In terms of theoretical logic, indeed, Parsons often employed the term "analytic" in an overly broad way (Alexander 1983). At various times,

especially in his earlier work, he conflated the Kantian metamethodological commitment with other levels of the scientific continuum in
an almost talismanic manner. Parsons attributed Weber's overrationa-
lized understanding of late modernity, for example, to the fact that
he had adopted an ideal-typical rather than analytical approach to
bureaucracy.

18 Durkheim and Weber, of course, were leading representatives of the neo-
Kantian revival in their respective milieux. It is interesting that in his
brief 1976 retrospective on Ayres, Parsons insists at two different points
that the institutionalist had not prepared him to understand Durkheim's
religious writings, which, he notes, had in fact been assigned to him
as an undergraduate by Ayres himself: "I shudder to think how little
I understood about what Durkheim was trying to do in those first
readings from his work [. . . .] In my earlier days at Harvard I was
thus exposed . . . on my own to Emile Durkheim, to whose work I
had originally been introduced by Ayres, but understanding of whom
required far more study than I devoted to it in my undergraduate days"
(Parsons 1976, pp. 175, 178).

19 On the one hand, Camic acknowledges that "it would be absurd to
question the selection of Weber and Durkheim, which the subsequent
history of the discipline has strongly vindicated" (p. 438). On the other
hand, he argues that "European figures like Durheim and Weber were by
no means his [Parsons'] only options from the standpoint of a fit in intellectual content" (p. 438). Both statements cannot be true.

20 Since part of Camic's reasoning for this early influence, and its significance, evidently is based on some of Parsons' college papers and earliest
essays, it is important to note that he does not confront the fact that
another scholar (Wearne 1989, pp. 26–38), using the same published
and unpublished materials, has been able to identify a breaking away of
Parsons from the institutionalists' legacy already in his last year as an
undergraduate student. E.g.: "From these two [undergraduate] essays we
detect the influence of Veblen and Sumner. But did he [Parsons] acquiesce
in their views? There is sufficient reason to suggest that even in these early
years Parsons was attempting to diverge from their patterns of thought"
(Wearne 1989, p. 36).

21 It is possible that Camic does not mention Weber's relevance because of
his belief that Parsons' Weber is not the true one (Camic 1987, pp. 434–
6). Whether or not he is correct on this score, as far as Parsons' project
construction is concerned, it is Parsons' Weber and not Camic's that
should be taken into account.

22 It also seems relevant to make the obvious observation that the differences between Hamilton and Ayres, on the one hand, and Schumpeter,
Knight, and Henderson (and Whitehead, we would add), on the other,
certainly involve more than reputation and intellectual disagreement.

The latter represented intellectual teachers of an entirely different stature and quality.

23   In a move that is all too familiar, Camic betrays the misgivings he has about the position he has taken by denying that he has taken it. Parsons' turn toward the Europeans, he explains, "does not mean that his selection of the four European thinkers was an instrumentalist maneuver that set aside content factors in an effort to cater to the opinions of the local crowd" (p. 436). No, what he actually means, Camic informs us, is that "Parsons' serious intellectual commitment" to the Europeans' position was merely "heightened by institutional factors" (p. 436). If this were an accurate self-description, of course, Camic would have to explain where the prior, intellectual commitment came from; unable to attribute it to reputational factors, he would have to acknowledge the primary role of intellectual ones! This is the opposite of what he actually does.

References

Alexander, J. C.   1983, *Theoretical Logic in Sociology*, vol. 4: *The Modern Reconstruction of Classical Thought: Talcott Parsons*. Berkeley: University of California Press.

——   1987a, *Twenty Lectures: Sociological Theory since World War II*. New York: Columbia University Press.

——   1987b, On the centrality of the classics. In A. Giddens and J. Turner (eds), *Social Theory Today*, New York and London: Basil Blackwell, pp. 1–60.

——   1988, Parsons' "Structure" in American Sociology. *Sociological Theory*, 6, pp. 96–102.

——   1993, Formal sociology is not multidimensional: breaking the code in Parsons' fragment on Simmel. *Theoria Sociologica*, 1, pp. 101–14.

Camic, C.   1979, The utilitarians revisited. *American Journal of Sociology*, 85, pp. 516–50.

——   1987, The making of a method: a historical reinterpretation of the early Parsons. *American Sociological Review*, 52, pp. 421–39.

——   1989, *Structure* after 50 years: the anatomy of a charter. *American Journal of Sociology*, 95, pp. 38–107.

——   1990a, Interpreting *The Structure of Social Action*: a note on Tiryakian. *American Journal of Sociology*, 99, pp. 445–50.

——   1990b, An historical prologue. *American Sociological Review*, 55, pp. 313–45.

——   1991, Introduction. In C. Camic (ed.), *The Early Essays*, by Talcott Parsons, Chicago: University of Chicago Press, pp. ix–lxix.

——   1992, Reputation and predecessor selection: Parsons and the institutionalists. *American Sociological Review*, 57, pp. 421–45.

Cohen, J., Hazelrigg, L., and Pope, W. 1975, De-parsonizing Weber: a critique of Parsons' interpretation of Weber's sociology. *American Sociological Review*, 42, pp. 229–41.

Coser, L. A. 1956, *The Functions of Social Conflict*. New York: Free Press.

Garfinkel, H. 1967, *Studies in Ethnomethodology*. Englewood Cliffs, NJ: Prentice-Hall.

Gould, M. 1981, Parsons versus Marx: "An Earnest Warning." *Sociological Inquiry*, 51, pp. 197–218.

—— 1989, Voluntarism versus utilitarianism: a critique of Camic's history of ideas. *Theory, Culture and Society*, 6, pp. 637–54.

—— 1991, *The Structure of Social Action*: at least 60 years ahead of its time. In R. Robertson and B. S. Burner (eds), *Talcott Parsons: Theorist of Modernity*, Los Angeles: Sage, pp. 85–107.

Gouldner, A. W. 1970, *The Coming Crisis of Western Sociology*. New York: Equinox.

Hagstrom, W. O. 1965, *The Scientific Community*. New York: Basic Books.

Holton, R., and Turner, B. 1985, *Max Weber on Economy and Society*. London: Routledge and Kegan Paul.

Hinkle, R. 1963, Antecedents of the action orientation in American sociology before 1935. *American Sociological Review*, 28, pp. 705–15.

Jones, R. Alun, and Kibbee, D. A. 1993, Durkheim, language, and history: a pragmatist perspective. *Sociological Theory*, 11, pp. 152–70.

Levine, D. N. [1957] 1980, *Simmel and Parsons*. New York: Arno Press.

Merton, R. K. 1965, *On the Shoulders of Giants*. New York: Free Press.

Mills, C. W. 1959, *The Sociological Imagination*. New York: Oxford University Press.

Nisbet, R. 1966, *The Sociological Tradition*. New York: Free Press.

Parsons, T. [1932] 1991, Economics and sociology: Marshall in relation to the thought of his time. In C. Camic (ed.), *The Early Essays*, Chicago: University of Chicago Press, pp. 69–94.

—— [1935] 1991, Sociological elements in economic thought. In C. Camic (ed.), *The Early Essays*, Chicago: University of Chicago Press, pp. 181–230.

—— 1937, *The Structure of Social Action*. New York: Free Press.

—— 1959, A short account of my intellectual development. *Alpha Kappa Delta*, 29, pp. 3–12.

—— 1970, On building social system theory: a personal history. *Daedalus*, 99, pp. 828–81.

—— 1976, Clarence Ayres's economics and sociology. In W. Breit (ed.), *Science and Ceremony*, Austin: University of Texas Press, pp. 175–9.

—— 1980, The circumstances of my encounter with Max Weber. In R. K. Merton and M. W. Riley (eds), *Sociological Tradition from Generation to Generation*, Norwood, NJ: Ablex, pp. 37–43.

Pope, W.   1973, Classic on classic: Parsons' interpretation of Durkheim. *American Sociological Review*, 38, pp. 399–415.

Rex, J.   1961, *Key Problems in Sociological Theory*. London: Routledge and Kegan Paul.

Sciortino, G.   1993, Un capitolo inedito de *La Struttura dell'azione sociale*. *Teoria Sociologica*, 1, pp. 13–41.

Seidman, S.   1983, *Liberalism and the Origins of European Social Theory*. Berkeley: University of California Press.

Taylor, C.   1975, *Hegel*. New York: Oxford University Press.

Tiryakian, E. A.   1990, Exegesis or synthesis? Comments on 50 years of *The Structure of Social Action*. *American Journal of Sociology*, 96, pp. 425–55.

Wearne, B. D.   1989, *The Theory and Scholarship of Talcott Parsons to 1951*. Cambridge: Cambridge University Press.

Zeitlin, I.   1968, *Ideology and the Development of Sociological Theory*. Englewood Cliffs, NJ: Prentice-Hall.

7

Structure, Value, Action: What Did the Early Parsons Mean and What Should He Have Said Instead?[1]

Every sociologist leaves manuscripts unpublished. It is only classical figures whose unpublished manuscripts will eventually be published again. Historical interest is often the pretext. Perhaps this once-hidden or forgotten text can finally tell us what this important person was thinking at a crucial time, and why. In our discipline, however, historical interest is always a Trojan horse. It camouflages and promotes contemporary concerns – theoretical, empirical, ideological. This, after all, is why we make certain theorists classical (Alexander 1989). We have decided that they can help us out. By interpreting their works, we find that what they "really said" clarifies what we ourselves would or would not like to say today (see chapter 2, above). Finding an early, unpublished work might be a way for us to say something new.

This is not to deny that historical or properly hermeneutical questions are involved. We do not read an earlier text simply in terms of today's theoretical questions. Contemporary questions are often mediated by debates about the historical development of a thinker's corpus and by complex discussions about the character of this or that dimension of his or her work. For these reasons, I begin my commentary on Parsons' "Prolegomena" (Parsons 1990) by examining what light it sheds on the historical disputes over his work. Next, I look at the text to see how it confirms or denies current interpretive versions of this work. While the contemporary theoretical and empirical relevance of these discussions will be apparent, it is only in the third section of this chapter that I address my own basic interest, the text as a contribution to sociological theory today.

Historicist Claims

When historical approaches to canonical work demarcate an "early" period, they do so either to make invidious contrasts with the classical figure's "later" material, or to suggest that from this initial seed the problems or achievements of later work have grown.

The first strategy has been exemplified in the claim – which has stretched from Scott (1963) to Habermas (1988) via Menzies (1976) – that Parsons' early work emphasized individual autonomy and individual interaction, in contrast to the functionalist and systemic emphases of the later work which stressed socialization and institutional control. The point has been to suggest an antipathy between these two modes of explanation, not only in Parsons' oeuvre but in the conceptual construction of reality itself. However, this historical interpretation fails to recognize that the "unit act" in Parsons' early work was an analytical scheme, not an empirical generalization about the actions of real individuals. In "Prolegomena", for example, Parsons utilizes an analytic conception of action to describe it as a process that involves various dimensions of rationality. By doing so, Parsons can describe complexes of "means–ends chains" of wealth, power, and esteem – complexes that are regulated, in the ideal-typical case, by value complexes of meaning. Given this purely analytical status of "action," it should not be surprising that this early essay is permeated by concepts like *system* and *function*, and that one can even find here the language of ultimate ends and ultimate conditions that was to reappear in cybernetic form 30 years later. With the publication of "Prolegomena," it is difficult to believe that historical arguments about an action/system axis in Parsons' work can be sustained any longer.

The second strategic reason for demarcating an early period, what might be called the "original sin" argument, has been exemplified by Camic's (1987, 1989) contention that the specificities of Parsons' theory – for example his failure to emphasize conflict and power, his lack of concern with institutional forces – can be traced back to the decisive influence on his early work of the analytical, antihistoricist approach advocated by his Harvard economics colleagues (see chapter 6, above). "Prolegomena" suggests, however, that Camic may have emphasized concrete networks at the expense of more fundamental intellectual influences. After all, before he came under the influence of Harvard economists, Parsons had translated *The Protestant Ethic and the Spirit of Capitalism*, introducing it with an essay that emphasized its antieconomic character and praising Weber for his insight into the nonrational – spiritual and emotional – quality of human motivation. One of the most striking emphases in the "Prolegomena" is Parsons' insistence that people have "transcendental" interests, that there are nonempirical, invisible ends that material and instrumental explanations of motivation overlook (p. 321).[2] To preserve the transcendental and metaphysical reference of human action, to theorize the faith in systems of value and meaning that such reference implies, is the very point of the institutional theory he tries to develop. If Parsons *did* adopt an analytic approach, he did so not to extend the economic style of social theorizing, but to explode the economic theory of society at its roots (cf. Gould 1989).

Interpretive Disputes

While historicists try to resolve interpretive disputes by looking at social and intellectual contexts, most scholars try to understand the meaning of a classical canon by entering into the thicket of interpretation itself. In the debate over Parsons, two issues have long been disputed.

One is the question of "functionalism." Habermas (1988) is the most recent and influential example of critics who have argued that Parsons' references to system and function reveal a mechanistic tendency that negates his self-proclaimed concern with meaning, voluntary action, and the interpenetration of material and organizational structures by cultural codes. "Prolegomena" provides direct evidence against this interpretation. Its treatment of "system" is direct and unequivocal. Parsons introduces the term to emphasize that the subjective ends of individual actors are socially organized in a nonrandom way. For Parsons a system of ends is a value pattern. Indeed, rather than implying mechanism and coercion, Parsons thinks that the concept of system is necessary to preserve the morality of free will. He insists that "a choice of ends [is] involved" only if one can conceive of "an organized *system* of ends" (p. 323, original italics). If some system were not organizing ends, ends would be random. This would negate the very notion of a reasoned and conscientious choice.

While "Prolegomena" contains contradictory treatments of "function," the most important discussion occurs in Parsons' justification for a functional approach to institutional classification over what he calls a structural or relational one. Parsons believes that the functional approach is the only one consistent with the "subjective" point of view – it allows sociologists to make fine-grained distinctions not simply between different kinds of institutions and concrete actions, but among the "rather different elements *in* concrete action" (p. 331, italics in original). Parsons makes this kind of intra-action distinction so he can point out that within any concrete action there are elements, like means and conditions, that promote efficiency and practicality, and other elements, like ends and norms, that are more subjective. Using this distinction in a metaphorical way, Parsons suggests four different kinds of "functions" for institutions, the technological-economic-political, the symbolic, the artistic and expressive, and the educational (p. 330). Resorting to "functionalism" in this early work, then, hardly betrays a mechanistic bent.

"Prolegomena" sheds light on a second major interpretive issue – Parsons' idealism. In four decades of debate over Parsons' work, his supporters generally defended the anti-idealist or synthetic character of his work, while most of his critics, from Dahrendorf (1959) to Gouldner (1970), attacked what they viewed as his exclusive emphasis on normative control. There is a clear sense in which "Prolegomena" supports the former interpretation. After all, this is an essay about institutionalization, not about values or ideas in themselves. In fact, Parsons spends a great deal of time elaborating upon what he calls "the intermediate sector" that lies between the "system of ends" on the purely normative side, and the "system of means" on the techno-logical (p. 323). This intermediate sector is one of means–ends interrelations – a sphere composed of technology, economy, and power in which ideals are continuously mediated by practical concerns. Whereas an idealist approach would deny the existence of this inter-mediate sector, Parsons sees it as presenting the major challenge for social organization. It is precisely the remoteness of this world of concrete ends from the idealized, transcendent values of a society's "system of ends" that creates the need for what Parsons calls institu-tionalization. Parsons insists that congruence between the intermedi-ate sector and the more idealized system of ends cannot be guaranteed by the direct involvement of ultimate ends in individual acts. He resists this "solution," perhaps, because it would lead to the kind of conceptual dichotomy Weber introduced between a purely pragmatic "purposive-rationality" (*Zweckrationalität*) and an extremely idealistic rationality of absolute values (*Wertrationalität*).

On the basis of this dichotomy, Weber argued that values rarely in-trude on the mundane activity of modern society, which he understood as assuming a purely purposive, instrumental form. Parsons thinks about everyday life in a different way, as typically occupying an intermediate zone where the pursuit of wealth, power, technology, and prestige is neither entirely self-interested nor entirely altruistic. It is to conceptualize this gray zone that he introduces the "system of normative regulation." Parsons insists that norms are "related to . . . specific actions [but] not in the form of ends" (p. 324). This is a crucial point, for it indicates that Parsons does not conceptualize norms as entering directly into the process by which actors form their own, self-interested and individualized ends. What norms do, rather, is present "regulatory" standards that define "limits within which the choice both of immediate ends and of means to their attainment is permissible" (p. 324). Norms, then, are intermediate – between ultimate ends and concrete situations of interest. It is within this intermediate zone that Parsons chooses to define institutions.

This first approach to institutionalization might be called a nesting theory; it is derived from the conception of norms as vertically integrated with ultimate values on the one hand, and with immediate situational interests on the other.

However, after going to great lengths to establish this intermediate zone for institutions, Parsons proceeds to negate it. First, he introduces an asymmetry between what he calls the primary ("disinterested") and secondary ("calculation of advantage") motives for institutional conformity, a distinction that gives priority to cultural rather than practical motives (p. 326). Moreover, Parsons also suggests that norms are not only integrated upward and downward with more general values and more specific interests, but that they are integrated horizontally with the norms of most other actors. Thus, there is not only nesting but intertwining as well. However, it is one thing to say that because institutional norms are not horizontally shared there will be social conflict; it is quite another to *define* norms as shared by the entire community. While the goals of most conflict groups are nested, they are not intertwined. They are structured by the normative mediation of practical and ideal interests – that is, they are quite integrated in the vertical sense – but they are *not* consensual. This is only to say that, in Parsons' multidimensional rather than idealistic sense, social conflict is often highly institutionalized.

"Prolegomena" demonstrates that, once again, in their interpretation of Parsons' idealism, neither his fervent sympathizers nor his harshest critics are right. Indeed, it is a mistake to see Parsons' theory, or the "theory" of any other classical canon, as exhibiting a particularly

high degree of internal consistency. Parsons articulates a multidimensional position and also an idealist one. The challenge of interpretive
criticism is to tease these strands apart. The more fully this is accomplished, the better contemporary theory will be able to maintain the
multidimensional view. We arrive in this manner to the issue of contemporary relevance.

Theory Today

In pursuing the interpretive disputes about Parsons' functionalism and
idealism we have obviously abutted issues of contemporary theoretical
concern, for in trying to understand how Parsons actually formulated
such issues we must draw upon and articulate our own conceptual
understanding of what these issues entail. This understanding, in
turn, can be rooted nowhere other than within the disputes over
social theory as it is practiced today. What makes these discussions
"interpretive," then, is not their lack of contemporary theoretical
relevance, but the fact that relevance is pursued in reference to some
canonical text. If one brackets interpretive disputes, one can treat
the theoretical relevance of a text more directly, as, in a sense, a
theoretical contemporary in its own right.

What does "Prolegomena" have to teach us today? While I could
compose a rather long list of relevant topics, I will concentrate on
two areas: the morality of human action, and what this implies for
any sociological theory of institutional life on the one hand, and the
complex interrelationship of the rational and nonrational in social
action on the other.

In the opening paragraphs of "Prolegomena," Parsons suggests
that "modes of behavior and forms of relationship [do] not merely
exist, but are held by the individuals concerned as those which *ought*
to exist – there is a normative element involved" (p. 320, original
italics). There is a profound moralism at the heart of Parsons' theory.
His actors are imbued with a desire to be good, and they are understood as trying to conform with principles that express this moral
aspiration. Because moral principles are reference points for human
action, human beings want their institutions to bear an appropriate
relation to them. The fact that human beings make choices is essential here. It is because they have the ability to make choices that
normative standards of evaluation become essential. In an intellectual
world in which social theorists increasingly place their emphasis on

the banal instrumentality of action (e.g., Coleman 1990) or on the equally mundane practicality of prediscursive consciousness (e.g., Giddens 1984), I find this emphasis on the centrality of morality, and the respect for human dignity that this emphasis implies, extremely refreshing. It is also, in my opinion, a more accurate description of the empirical world.

Moral standards are essential – they are continuously referenced during the course of action. Because of this, the strength of actors' commitments to common norms – what I have called the question of horizontal integration – becomes central to the study of social conflict and integration. Indeed, alongside the more idealistic strand of Parsons' work stands an important discussion in "Prolegomena" in which he acknowledges that control by institutional norms is always imperfect. Because there is "always . . . divergence of value-attitudes" (p. 326), organizational and material sanctions and rewards – the secondary types of social control – are omnipresent. The result is what Parsons calls "an interlocking of interests" that can sustain patterned sanctions and rewards even when "moral attachment may dissolve away" (p. 327).

What follows from this acknowledgment is interesting, for Parsons does not assume that the disarticulation of moral and material sanctions simply allows power to be routinely maintained through coercion and manipulation. Insisting that "there would seem to be a limit to how far this process can go without breaking down the system" (p. 327), Parsons outlines this limit in a rather subtle way. One limitation on routine and unchallenged coercion is set by the fact that, even in a system in which the connection between systemic rewards and institutionalized values is virtually dissolved, personal esteem, if not social status, will still be allocated to individuals who act in accordance with strongly held values and norms. "It is not to be supposed," Parsons argues, "that the fact that it is to the personal advantage of the members of a community to conform to its institutional norms is proof that these norms depend primarily or exclusively on interest and sanctions for their effective enforcement" (p. 326). To the contrary, "the principal personal rewards, above all in social esteem, will tend to go to those who do conform with them" (p. 326).[3]

While what might be called the continuity of individual esteem allocation represents a permanent drag on the coercive maintenance of conformity, Parsons offers a more dynamic and systemic kind of limitation as well. Because, he suggests, action *does* have a moral dimension, it is unlikely that even coercive authority will be able to sustain an amoral and illegitimate order in a consistent way. Parsons does not offer here the obvious illustration. Because people who submit to coercion remain committed to moral values, when these values do not control the exercise of socially legitimate force such people will eventually rebel and try to institutionalize these values. What Parsons stresses is that those who wield coercive sanctions are themselves eventually subject to moral limits. "The strength of sanctions and the willingness to apply them," Parsons observes, "is to a large, though not exclusive, extent an expression of moral attitudes" (p. 327). This is particularly important because "the application of sanctions on a large scale depends upon organization" (p. 327). Parsons is doubtful that organizations can be successfully maintained without some relation to organized values.[4]

I turn now to the second theoretical issue that "Prolegomena" raises in what seem to be surprisingly contemporary terms – the relative rationality and nonrationality of action. In recent developments in the social sciences, there has been an increased tendency to depict social action as a "rational choice." Harnessed to network analysis, exchange theory seems well on its way to becoming the dominant paradigm in social psychology. Political theorists and class analysts emphasize the rationality of structural actors and groups. Social movements are depicted in a profit-maximizing way. Proto-economic models are applied even to intimate and private spheres like marriage.

What Parsons suggests early in "Prolegomena" is that rational choice is too often identified with the logical, "proto-scientific" character of the actor's reasoning process itself. He points out that this reasoning process, no matter how empirically sound, is only a means. Whether an action as such is rational can only be determined by comparing this reasoning process to the desired end. For only if the end is, in fact, rationally and "efficiently" achieved can the process by which an end is chosen, much less the action itself, be seen as rational. This evaluation cannot be made unless one can observe the end the actor has chosen. The problem, however, is that only some of the possible ends that actors choose are visible; there is a very large category of ends that is not. Parsons calls these transcendent ends, since they refer to the actor's desire to achieve an inner state of mind or a certain relationship to ultimate values.

If rational action is defined as the achievement of an end through the efficient choice of means, then an observer can label as rational only the application of rational means to empirical ends. Because

Types of ends		
Types of means	Empirical	Transcendent
Logical/practical	**1** **Rational action**	**2** *Economic consumption* *Political campaigns* *Organizational interaction*
Symbolic	**3** **Magic** *Conversation*	**4** **Religion** **Tradition**
	Secular rituals	

Figure 1   The ideal types of action
Note: Parsons' examples appear in bold face type; other examples appear in italics.

there is simply no certain method by which the achievement of an *un*observable end can be confirmed, the rationality of a wide range of what might be called "rationally reasoned" actions is impossible to evaluate.

Finally, not only are ends not all observable, but means are not all rational. Parsons points out that thought processes may not be logical or pragmatic. Offering a linguistic example, he demonstrates that reasoning may also be symbolic, arbitrary, and conventional. This is a fundamentally important point.

We end up with four ideal-types of action, which can be represented in Figure 1 as a cross-tabulation between types of ends and types of means.

Parsons' argument is that, far from being universally applicable, the concept of "rational action" applies only to cell 1. Parsons calls this kind of action intrinsically rational. In cell 4, Parsons places religious action, which involves transcendent ends and stereotyped, ritualized means. Here he also places the impact of tradition. In cell 3 Parsons places magic, the prototype of action that uses symbolic means to achieve practical ends.

This discussion demonstrates the relatively narrow relevance of rational choice theory and directs us to other important types of action. I would suggest, however, that in neither respect does Parsons go far enough. He has underestimated the symbolic, conventional penetration of practical reason, and the penetration of the symbolic by practical reason, in turn. The most important source of this under-estimation is that Parsons proposes a "type" rather than "analytical" approach. Yet, even if we maintain the ideal-typical approach, Parsons identifies only three prototypical categories of action when, even according to his own typology, there should be four. *Parsons fails to discuss cell 2*, actions in which logical and practical reasoning serves the achievement of transcendental ends. Even if the means of action are not conventionalized – "arbitrary" in the Saussurian or semiotic sense – the ends of action certainly may be. Therefore, the conventional or symbolic should not be limited to overtly "nonrational" phenomena like magic and religion, but be extended to the worlds of politics and economics. If consumer goods are symbolically rather than practically constituted (e.g., Zelizer 1985), if the goals pursued by politicians and organizations are not simply mundane but defined by myth, narrative, or semiotic code (e.g., DiMaggio and Powell 1983), then neither economic action nor political maneuvering can be considered simply as "rational action."

But even for the modes of action that Parsons identifies as signific-ant departures from rationality, his understanding – from our contemporary point of view – seems limited and rather stereotyped. Is not language, rather than magic, the prototype for action that combines conventional means with practical ends? Linguistically mediated action is not the yellow brick road to higher rationality that Habermas describes. It is, quite to the contrary, a guarantee that no human inter-action can escape an element of arbitrary form. Nor should Parsons limit cell 4 to religion and ritual with capital "R's." Actors who employ conventionalized means to achieve transcendental ends are not only voodoo chiefs, priests, or prophets. The most secular actors often exhibit the same kind of doubly conventionalized behavior. In his "religious sociology," the later Durkheim began to provide a theory to study rituals in their secular form (Alexander 1988c).

This discussion indicates that the ideal-typical approach that Parsons applies to the rationality question in this early essay is misleading. For example, Parsons' analysis gives the distinct impression that actions represented in cell 1 are quite common: logical means and empirical ends. Of course, Parsons does not simply leave this intrinsically rational means–ends combination alone. To the contrary, he insists that such action is typically bounded by a normative rule that sets moral limits on the means and ends which a rational actor can choose. This "add on" approach, however, seems mechanistic. It leaves intact easy assumptions about practical reasoning and empiricist notions about the observability of ends. Phenomology has allowed us, however, to understand that normative evaluation occurs from the *inside* of action, as typification. Semiotics and structuralism have allowed us to see that it is scarcely possible for the ends of an actor to fall outside of a conventionally established code. Action is not a means–ends black box surrounded by culture, personality, and structural position. Because it is a typifying movement, it is permeated, not just regulated by, symbolic codes. Because it continuously weighs costs and benefits in a strategic way, it is not just calculated in relation to objective conditions, but permeated *by* them. If action is always typifying and strategic, moreover, it is continuously inventive as well. It is through the ongoing processes of typification, invention, and strategization that personality, social structure, and culture become embedded and externalized in action (Alexander 1988a).

By showing that there is much more complexity to the relationship between ends and means than rational actor models allow, Parsons makes a general case in "Prolegomena" for this multidimensional position. When he stipulates that norms and conditions regulate means –ends rationality, he is groping for a model of action and its environments that can demonstrate this position in an empirical way.

Conclusion

While I have argued in this brief chapter for the interpretive and contemporary relevance of "Prolegomena," there is much in this early unpublished work that seems to have a thoroughly archaic form. The latter half of the essay digresses into discussions of law and concepts raised by Henry Maine. In Parsons' more mature work, moreover, he redressed some of "Prolegomena"'s most glaring deficiencies. He left the typological approach more thoroughly behind, and he employed linguistic analogies to great effect in his essays on the generalized media of exchange.

I believe, nonetheless, that the problems revealed in this early and still extremely interesting work remained central to Parson' thought. His idealist strain and conflation of culture with consensus stimulated a reaction that issued in the call for a conflict sociology. His difficulties in conceptualizing the process of action engendered reactions that emerged as the new micro-sociologies. His tendency to conceptualize culture as regulatory norms inspired the dissatisfaction that helped lead to more hermeneutical forms of cultural sociology. In reacting against the dominance of Parsons' functionalism, these new movements constituted the second phase of postwar sociology. However, as they moved from a challenging to a dominant and legitimate position, these movements became routinized and less influential. We are now beginning a third phase of postwar sociology. This new theoretical movement (Alexander 1988b) stresses synthesis and reintegration. It is this new climate that has facilitated the "discovery" and publication of Parsons' early work.

Notes

1	This chapter was published in 1990 as a commentary accompanying the first publication of a manuscript written by Talcott Parsons while an instructor at Harvard University, entitled "Prolegomena to a Theory of Social Institutions."

2	All page references in the text refer to Parsons 1990.

3	Although I think my account here is consistent with the somewhat less than systematic discussion in the text, I am exercising a fair amount of interpretive discretion. Parsons himself does not explicitly make the distinction between esteem as personal recognition for value-congruent behavior on the one hand, and subjective rewards for more institutional conformity – that is, status – on the other. Nor does he directly suggest that the continuity of esteem processes presents a brake on the routine coercive imposition of control. In making the former point, my analysis rests upon Jacob and Bershady's (1985) important essay.

4	This empirical observation, and the democratic moral aspirations that Parsons links to it, are echoed in a very precise manner by Dewey's pragmatist argument about the relationship between social control and voluntary, normatively related action:

> We must carefully avoid a meaning sometimes read into the term "control". It is sometimes assumed, explicitly or unconsciously, that an individual's tendencies are naturally purely individualistic or egoistic, and thus antisocial. Control then denotes the process by which he is brought to subordinate his natural impulses to public or common ends. Since, by conception, his own nature is quite alien to this process and opposes it rather than helps it, control has in this view a flavor of coercion or compulsion about it. Systems of government and theories of the state have been built upon this notion, and it has seriously affected education ideas and practices. But there is no ground for any such view. Individuals are certainly

interested, at times, in having their own way, and their own way may go contrary to the ways of others. *But they are also interested, and chiefly interested upon the whole, in entering into the activities of others and taking part in conjoint and cooperative doings. Otherwise, no such thing as a community would be possible.* . . . Control, in truth, means only an emphatic form of direction of powers, and covers the regulation gained by an individual through his own efforts quite as much as that brought about when others take the lead. (Dewey 1996 [1916], pp. 24–5; my italics)

References

Alexander, J. C.   1988a, Action and its environments. In J. C. Alexander, *Action and its Environments: Towards a New Synthesis*. New York: Columbia University Press, pp. 301–33.

——   1988b, The new theoretical movement. In N. J. Smelser (ed.), *Handbook of Sociology*, Los Angeles: Sage, pp. 77–102.

——   1988c, (ed.), *Durkheimian Sociology: Cultural Studies*. New York: Cambridge University Press.

——   1989, Sociology and discourse: on the centrality of the classics. In J. C. Alexander, *Structure and Meaning: Relinking Classical Sociology*, New York: Columbia University Press, pp. 8–67.

Camic, C.   1987, The making of a method: a historical reinterpretation of the early Parsons. *American Sociological Review*, 52, pp. 421–39.

——   1989, *Structure* after 50 years: the anatomy of a charter. *American Journal of Sociology*, 95, pp. 38–107.

Coleman, J.   1990, *Foundations of Social Theory*. Cambridge: Harvard University Press.

Dahrendorf, R.   1959, *Class and Class Conflict in Industrial Society*. Stanford: Stanford University Press.

Dewey, J.   1996 [1916], *Democracy and Education*. New York: Free Press.

DiMaggio, P. J., and Powell, W. W.   1983, The iron cage revisited: institutional isomorphism and collective rationality in organizational fields. *American Sociological Review*, 48, pp. 147–60.

Giddens, A.   1984, *The Constitution of Societies*. London: Macmillan.

Gould, M.   1989, Voluntarism versus utilitarianism: a critique of Camic's history of ideas. *Theory, Culture and Society*, 6, pp. 637–54.

Gouldner, A.   1970, *The Coming Crisis of Western Sociology*. New York: Avon.

Habermas, J.   1988, *Theory of Communicative Action*, vol. 2: *Critique of Functionalist Reason*. Boston: Beacon.

Jacobs, J. A., and Bershady, H. A.   1985, Moral evaluations in the social hierarchy: esteem as an independent dimension of social evaluations of inequality. *Status Inconsistency in Modern Societies: Proceedings of a Conference on "New Differentiations of Status Structures".* Verlag der Sozialwissenschaftlichen Kooperative. Duisberg: FRG.

Menzies, K.   1976, *Talcott Parsons and the Social Image of Man.* London: Routledge and Kegan Paul.

Parsons, T.   1990, Prolegomena to a theory of social institutions. *American Sociological Review*, 55 (no. 3), pp. 319–34.

Scott, J. F.   1963, The changing foundations of the Parsonian action scheme. *American Sociological Review*, 28, pp. 716–35.

Zelizer, V.   1985, *Pricing the Priceless Child.* New York: Basic Books.

Part III
After Neofunctionalism: Its Contribution to Theory Creation Today

8

The New Theoretical
Movement in Sociology

Sociological theory is at a turning point. The once youthful challengers
to functionalist theory are becoming middle aged. Their polemical les-
sons have been well learned; as established traditions, however, their
theoretical limitations have become increasingly apparent. Despair
about the crisis of sociology marked the birth of the postfunctionalist
epoch. Now, when this postfunctionalist phase is itself coming to an
end, one senses not a crisis but a crossroads, a turning point eagerly
anticipated.

Against the postwar domination of functionalism, two revolutions
were launched. On one side, there emerged radical and provocative
schools of microtheorizing, which emphasized the contingency of
social order and the centrality of individual negotiation. On the other
side, there developed vigorous schools of macro theorizing, which
emphasized the role of coercive structures in determining collective
and individual action. These movements transformed general theoretical debate and permeated empirical practice at the middle range. Even
as they have triumphed, however, the self-confidence and momentum
of these theoretical approaches has begun to wane.

They have become enervated because their one-sidedness has made
them impossible to sustain. This, at least, will be the central claim of
this chapter. I will demonstrate that one-sidedness has created debilitating contradictions within both the micro and macro traditions. It
has been in order to escape these difficulties, I will suggest, that a
younger generation of sociological theorists has set out an agenda of
an entirely different kind. Among this new generation of theorists
there remain fundamental disagreements. There is one foundational
principle, however, about which they agree. Neither micro nor macro
theory is satisfactory. Action and structure must now be intertwined.
Where in the mid-1970s the air was filled with demands for radical

and one-sided theoretical programs, ten years later one could only hear urgent calls for theorizing of an entirely different sort. Throughout the centers of Western sociology – in Britain and France, in Germany and the United States – synthetic rather than polemical theorizing now is the order of the day.

My ambition in this chapter is to provide an analytical reconstruction of this new and quite surprising shift in the progress of general theory. I must begin, however, by justifying the project of general theory itself. That theorizing at the general level – theorizing without reference to particular empirical problems or distinctive domains – is a significant, indeed, a crucial endeavor should, it seems to me, be beyond dispute. It has been general theorizing, for example, that articulated and sustained the developments I have just described. Crystallized by broad theoretical debates, moreover, these developments did not remain segregated in some abstract theoretical realm. To the contrary, they permeated every empirical subfield of sociology in turn. In American sociology, however, the significance and even the validity of general theory is subject to constant dispute. The reflection of a deeply ingrained empiricist bias, this questioning makes it more difficult to perceive broader developments and to argue about the direction of sociology in a rational and disciplined way. It seems clear that as a prelude to any substantive theoretical exercise, the project of general theory must be defended and the reasons for its unique relevance explained.

I will make this defense of general theory in the context of illuminating the special nature of a social science. I will argue that prediction and explanation are not the only goals of social science and that the more general modes of discourse that tend to characterize theoretical debates are just as significant. I will insist, moreover, that there are immanent in such discourse evaluative criteria other than empiricist ones. After making this case, I will try to articulate such truth criteria for the "presuppositional" level of discourse. Only at this point will I return to the substantive ambition that is at this chapter's central core. I will reconstruct the development of the micro and macro responses to the functionalist tradition and evaluate these discourses in terms of the validity criteria I have laid out. After identifying the theoretical projects which are emerging in response to the failures of these micro and macro traditions, I will sketch the outlines of what a new synthetic model of the interrelation between action and structure might be.

Sociology as Discourse and Explanation

In order to defend the project of general theory, it must be accepted that sociological arguments need not have an immediate explanatory payoff to be scientifically significant. Whether or not social scientists can accept this statement depends, first, on whether or not they regard their discipline as a nascent form of natural science and, second, on just what they conceive natural science to be. Those who oppose generalized argument not only identify sociology with natural science but view the latter as an anti-philosophical, observational, propositional, and purely explanatory activity. However, those who wish to legitimate generalized argument in sociology may also identify with natural science; in doing so, they point to the implications of the Kuhnian revolution and argue that nonempirical and philosophical commitments inform and often decisively influence natural scientific practice. It was this approach to the defense of generalized argument that I followed in my first book, *Positivism, Presuppositions, and Current Controversies* (Alexander 1982a).

This defense against the claims of a narrowly explanatory positivism has proved to be a limited one. There is no doubt, I think, that in response to such an argument a more sophisticated understanding of science has gradually emerged among social science practitioners. As a result, there has indeed developed a greater tolerance for general theorizing within some members of the empiricist camp[1]. By stressing the personal and subjective aspects of natural science, however, the postpositivist position has failed to account for its relative objectivity and its astonishing explanatory success. This failure has cast doubt on its defense of generalized argument in social science. That natural science has its own hermeneutic cannot be doubted. If, however, this subjectivity has not prevented the construction of powerful covering laws and an overall accumulation of factual knowledge, then it would seem that even a postpositivist social science can continue to be held to these empiricist criteria alone. Yet this conclusion is not warranted. Criteria other than explanatory success are deeply implicated in social scientific debate. As compared with natural science, arguments that do not have immediate reference to factual and explanatory concerns are omnipresent. One can only conclude that the strategy of identifying social science with an interpretive natural science is misleading. The defense of generalized argument in social science, then, cannot rest entirely on the Kuhnian redefinition of natural science.[2] It must also differentiate social from natural science in decisive ways. That both activities share an interpretive epistemology is the beginning, not the end, of the argument.

It is time, then, to recognize that the scientific hermeneutic can issue in very different kinds of scientific activity. Only in this way can the massive role of generalized thinking in social, as compared to natural, science truly be understood, much less accepted as a legitimate activity in its own right. Only insofar as its significance is recognized, moreover, can the truth criteria that are implicit in such generalized argument be formalized and subject to explicit rational debate. To abandon empiricism is not, after all, to embrace relativism in an irrationalist form.[3]

That science can be understood as a hermeneutic activity does not, I am suggesting, determine the particular topics to which scientific activity is allocated in any given scientific discipline. Yet, it is precisely the allocation of such activity that is responsible for the relative empirical or theoretical "feel" of a discipline. Even outspoken postpositivists have acknowledged that modern natural science can be distinguished from other kinds of human studies by its ability to exclude from its objects of study the subjective moorings on which it stands. For example, while Holton (1973) has painstakingly demonstrated that arbitrary, supraempirical "themata" deeply affect modern physics, he insists that it has never been his intention to argue that thematic discussions should be introduced "into the practice of science itself" (1973, pp. 330–31). He suggests, indeed, that "only when such questions were ruled out of place in a laboratory did science begin to grow rapidly." Even the forthrightly idealist philosopher Collingwood (1940, p. 33), who insisted that scientific practice rests upon metaphysical assumptions, allowed that "the scientists's business is not to propound them but only to presuppose them."

Why, despite the subjective aspects of their knowledge, are natural scientists able to make such exclusions? The answer to this question is important, for it will tell us why social scientists cannot. It is not because natural scientists are more committed to rational norms and procedures. Rather, the allocation of scientific activity depends upon what rational practitioners consider intellectually problematic. It is because natural scientists so often agree about the generalized commitments that inform their craft that more delimited empirical questions usually receive their explicit attention. This is precisely what allows normal science, in Kuhn's sense (1970), to proceed as an activity of empirical puzzle solving and specific problem solutions. Habermas is also particularly sensitive to the relationship between this empirical specificity and generalized agreement. Taking normal science to characterize natural science as such, Habermas (1971, p. 91) writes that the "genuine achievement of modern science does not consist primarily in producing truth [but in] a method of arriving at an uncompelled and permanent consensus."

Only if there is disagreement about the background assumptions that inform a science do supraempirical issues come explicitly into the play. Kuhn calls this a paradigm crisis. It is in such crises, he believes, that there is "recourse to philosophy and to debate over fundamentals." In normal periods of science, these nonempirical dimensions are camouflaged; for this reason, it appears that speculative hypotheses can be decided by reference either to sense data that are relatively accessible or to theories whose specificity makes their relevance to such data immediately apparent. This is not the case in social science, because in its social application science produces so much more disagreement. Because persistent and widespread disagreement exists, the background assumptions that remain implicit and relatively invisible in natural science here come vividly into play. The conditions that Kuhn defines for paradigm crisis in the natural sciences are routine in the social.[4]

By stressing the significance of disagreement in social as compared to natural science, one need not embrace relativism in a radical way. There remains the possibility for rational knowledge in the social sciences even if the empiricist conception of objectivity is abandoned. Nor does this recognition necessarily deny the possibility that covering laws can be constructed for social processes or even that relatively successful predictions can be pursued.[5] It is possible to gain cumulative knowledge about the world from within different and competing points of view (compare Wagner 1984). It is also quite possible to sustain relatively predictive covering laws from within general orientations that differ in substantial ways.

What I am suggesting, however, is that the conditions of social science make consistent agreement about the precise nature of empirical knowledge – let alone agreement about explanatory covering laws – highly unlikely. Because competition between fundamental perspectives is routine, the background assumptions of social science are routinely visible. Generalized discussion is about the sources and consequences of fundamental disagreement. Because background assumptions are so visible, then, generalized discussion becomes integral to social scientific debate, as integral as explanatory activity itself. In social science, therefore, arguments about validity cannot refer only to more empirical concerns. They cut across the full range of nonempirical commitments that sustain competing points of view.

Adherents to the positivist persuasion will respond to this argument by suggesting that, far from pervasive disagreement being the source of the difference between natural and social science, it is the result. They conclude (e.g., Wallace 1983) that if sociologists were only more faithful to the rigor and discipline of natural science, then the generalized and speculative quality of social science discussion would abate and disagreement eventually disappear. This argument is fundamentally misconceived. Far-reaching disagreement is inherent in social science, for cognitive and evaluative reasons.

Insofar as the objects of a science are located in the physical world outside of the human mind, its empirical referents can, in principle, more easily be verified through interpersonal communication. For social science, the objects of investigation are either mental states or conditions in which mental states are embedded. For this reason, the possibility for confusing mental states of the scientific observer with mental states of those observed is endemic. This is the social science version of the Heisenberg Uncertainty Principle.

Resistance to simple agreement on empirical referents also emerges from the distinctively evaluative nature of social science. In contrast to natural science, there is in social science a symbiotic relationship between description and evaluation. The very descriptions of the objects of investigation have ideological implications. Is society called "capitalist" or "industrial"? Has there been "proletarianization," "individuation," or "atomization"? Each characterization initiates what Giddens (1976) has called the double hermeneutic, an interpretation of reality that has the potential of entering social life and of circling back to affect the interpreter's definitions in turn. Moreover, insofar as it is difficult, for cognitive and evaluative reasons, to gain consensus about even the simple empirical referents of social science, about the abstractions from them that form the substance of social science theory there will be even less.

Finally, it is because there is endemic empirical and theoretical disagreement that social science is formed into traditions and schools (see chapter 2, above). These solidary groupings are not simply manifestations of scientific disagreement, moreover, but bases upon which such disagreements are promoted and sustained. Indeed, rather than accepting disagreement and the distorted communication that goes along with it as necessary evils, many social science theorists (e.g., Ritzer 1975) actually welcome interschool conflict as an indication of a healthy discipline.

For all of these reasons, discourse – not just explanation – becomes a major feature of the social science field. By discourse, I refer to modes of argument that are more consistently generalized and speculative than normal scientific discussion. The latter are directed in a more disciplined manner to specific pieces of empirical evidence, to inductive and deductive logics, to explanation through covering laws, and to the methods by which these laws can be verified or falsified. Discourse, by contrast, is ratiocinative. It focuses on the process of reasoning rather than the results of immediate experience, and it becomes significant where there is no plain and evident truth. Discourse seeks persuasion through argument rather than prediction. Its persuasiveness is based on such qualities as logical coherence, expansiveness of scope, interpretive insight, value relevance, rhetorical force, beauty, and texture of argument.

Foucault (1970) identified intellectual, scientific, and political practices as "discourses" in order to deny their merely empirical, inductive status. In this way, he insists that practical activities are historically constituted and shaped by metaphysical understandings that can define an entire epoch. Sociology, too, is a discursive field. Still, one finds here little of the homogeneity that Foucault attributes to such fields; in social science, there are discourses, not a discourse. These discourses are not, moreover, closely linked to the legitimation of power, as Foucault in his later work increasingly claimed. Social scientific discourses are aimed at truth, and they are constantly subjected to rational stipulations about how truth can be arrived at and what that truth might be.

Here I draw upon Habermas's (e.g., 1984) understanding of discourse as part of an effort that speakers make to achieve undistorted communication. If Habermas underestimates the irrational qualities of communication, let alone action, he certainly has provided a way to conceptualize its rational aspirations. His systematic attempts to identify modes of argument and criteria for arriving at persuasive justification show how rational commitments and the recognition of supraempirical arguments can be combined. Between the rationalizing discourse of Habermas and the arbitrary discourse of Foucault, this is where the actual field of social science discourse uneasily lies.

It is because of the centrality of discourse that theory in the social sciences is so multivalent and that compulsive efforts (e.g., Wallace

1983) to follow the logic of natural science are so misguided.[6] Followers of the positivist persuasion sense the tension between such a multivalent conception and their empiricist point of view. To resolve it they try to privilege "theory" over what they pejoratively call "metatheory" (J. Turner 1986); indeed, they often try to exclude theory altogether in favor of "explanation" narrowly conceived (Stinchcombe 1968). These distinctions, however, seem more like utopian efforts to escape from social science than efforts to understand it. Generalized discourse is central, and theory is inherently multivalent. If social science could actually pursue an entirely explanatory strategy, why would an avowed empiricist like Stinchcombe feel compelled to devote himself to the task of defending empiricism through discursive argument? The substance of Stinchcombe's (1968, 1978) arguments is ratiocinative; his goal is to persuade through compulsion of generalized logic.

Overdetermination by Theory and Underdetermination by Fact

The omnipresence of discourse, and the conditions that give rise to it, make for the overdetermination of social science by theory and its underdetermination by what is taken to be fact. There is no clear, indisputable reference for the elements that compose social science – definitions, concepts, models, or "facts." Because of this, there is not neat translatability between different levels of generality. Formulations at one level do not ramify in clear-cut ways for the other levels of scientific concern. For example, while precise empirical measurements of two variable correlations can sometimes be established, it is rarely possible for such a correlation to prove or disprove a proposition about this interrelationship that is stated in more general terms. The reason is that the existence of empirical and ideological dissensus allows social scientists to operationalize propositions in a variety of different ways.[7]

Consider, for example, two of the most conscientious efforts to move from data to more general theory. In an attempt to test his newly developed structural theory, Blau starts with a proposition he calls the size theorem – the notion that a purely ecological variable, group size, determines outgroup relations (Blau et al. 1982, p. 46). Drawing from a data set that establishes not only a group's size but its rate of intermarriage, he argues (p. 47) that the relationship he discovers between intermarriage rates and group size verifies the size theorem. Why? Because the data demonstrate that "group size and the proportion outmarried are inversely related." But outmarriage is a datum that does not, in fact, operationalize "outgroup relations." It is one type of outgroup relation among many others, and as Blau himself acknowledges at one point in his argument, it is a type into which factors other than group size enter. Outgroup relation, in other words, does not have a clear-cut referent. Because of this, the correlation between what is taken to be its indicator and group size cannot verify the general proposition about the relation between group size and outgroup relations. Blau's empirical data, then, are disarticulated from his theory, despite his effort to link them in a theoretically decisive way.

Similar problems emerge in Lieberson's (1980) ambitious study of black and white immigrants to the United States since 1880. Lieberson begins with the less formally stated proposition that the "heritage of slavery" is responsible for the different achievement levels of black and European immigrants. In order to operationalize this proposition, Lieberson takes two steps. First, he defines heritage in terms of "lack of opportunity" for former slaves rather than in cultural terms. Second, he identifies opportunity in terms of the data he has developed about varying rates of education and residential segregation. Both these operationalizations, however, are eminently contestable. Not only would other social scientists define the heritage of slavery in very different terms – for example, in cultural ones – but they might conceive of opportunities in ways other than education and residence. Because there is, therefore, no necessary relationship between the rates Lieberson has identified and differences in opportunities, there can be no certainty that his data demonstrate the more general proposition relating achievement and heritage. The measured correlation, of course, stands on its own as an empirical contribution. Still, the broader theoretical payoff is not there, for the correlation cannot test the theory at which it is aimed.

It is far easier to find examples of the contrasting problem, the overdetermination by theory of empirical "facts," for in virtually every broadly gauged theoretical study the sampling of empirical data is open to dispute. In *The Protestant Ethic and the Spirit of Capitalism*, for example, Weber's (1958/1904–5) equation of the spirit of capitalism with seventeenth and eighteenth century English entrepreneurs has been widely disputed. If the Italian capitalists of the early modern city states are conceived of as manifesting the capitalist spirit (e.g., Trevor-Roper 1965), then Weber's correlation between capitalists and Puritans is based on a restricted sample and fails to substantiate his theory. Insofar as this is true. Weber's empirical data was overselected by his theoretical reference to the Protestant ethic.

In Smelser's famous study, *Social Change in the Industrial Revolution* (1959), a similar distance between general theory and empirical indicator can be found. In his theory, Smelser argues that shifts in familial role divisions, not industrial upheavals per se, were responsible for the radical protest activities by English workers that developed in the 1820s. In his narrative historical account, Smelser describes fundamental shifts in family structure as having occurred in the sequence he had suggested. His more technical presentations of archival data (Smelser 1959, pp. 188–99), however, seem to indicate that these family disturbances did not develop until one or two decades after significant industrial disputes had begun. Smelser's theoretical concern with the family overdetermined the presentation of data in his narrative history, just as his technical, archival data underdetermined his general theory in turn.[8]

In Skocpol's (1979) more recent effort at documenting a historical and comparative theory, the same kind of overdetermination is exercised by a very different theory. Skocpol (p. 18) proposes to take an "impersonal and nonsubjective viewpoint" on revolutions, which gives causal significance only to "the institutionally determined situations and relations of groups." Her search is for the empirical data of revolution and the only a priori she acknowledges is her commitment to the comparative method (pp. 33–40). Skocpol acknowledges at various points, however, that local political culture and traditional rights do play a role (e.g., pp. 62, 138), and that political leadership and ideology must (however briefly) be essayed (pp. 161–73). In doing so, the theoretical overdetermination of her data becomes apparent. Her structural preoccupations have led her to leave out of her account of relevant data the entire intellectual and cultural context of revolution.[9] It is because these counter-theoretical data do not exist that Skocpol can proceed to interpret the subjective factors she does briefly mention in a determinately structuralist way.

Empirical undetermination of theory and theoretical overdetermination of data go hand in hand, and they are everywhere to be found. The result is that, from the most specific factual statements up to the most abstract generalizations, social science is essentially contestable. Every empirical conclusion is open to argumentation by reference to supraempirical considerations, and every general statement can be contested by references to unexplained "empirical facts."

In this way, every social scientific statement becomes subject to the demand for justification by reference to general principles.[10] Arguments against Blau's work need not be limited to the empirical demonstration that structural considerations are only one of several that determine outmarriage; one can, instead, demonstrate that the very stipulation of purely ecological causation rests upon presuppositions about action that are of an excessively instrumental kind. In considering Lieberson's work one can bracket the empirical question of the relation between education and objective opportunity in a similar way. Instead, one can suggest through discursive argument that Lieberson's exclusive focus on the heritage of slavery, and the way he operationalizes it in purely structural terms, reflects not only an a priori ideological agenda but a commitment to narrowly conflictual models of society. Smelser's work can be discursively criticized by questioning its logical adequacy or by criticizing the overemphasis on the internalization of family values in early functionalist models. Skocpol's argument can also be evaluated without any reference to empirical material on revolutions. One could demonstrate, for example, that she misconstrues "voluntaristic theories of revolution" – her polemical target throughout – as individualistic theories positing rational knowledge about the consequences of action.

To make such arguments is to engage in discourse, not explanation. As Seidman (1983) has emphasized, discourse does not imply the abandonment of claims to truth. Truth claims need not be limited to the criterion of testable empirical validity. Each kind of discourse has imbedded within it distinctive criteria of truth. These criteria go beyond empirical adequacy to claims about the nature and consequences of presuppositions, the stipulation and adequacy of models, the consequences of ideologies, the meta-implications of methods, and the connotations of definitions. Insofar as these claims become explicit, they can be seen as efforts to rationalize and systematize what is usually the merely intuited complexity of social analysis and social life. Current disputes between interpretive and causal methodologies, utilitarian and normative conceptions of action, equilibrium and conflict models of societies, radical and conservative theories of change – these are discursive, not, in the first instance, explanatory disputes. They reflect efforts by sociologists to articulate criteria for evaluating the "truth" of different nonempirical domains.

It is no wonder that the discipline's response to important works bears so little resemblance to the neat and confined responses that advocates of the "logic of science" suggest. Skocpol's *States and Social Revolutions*, for example, has been evaluated at every level of the sociological continuum. The book's presuppositions, ideology, model, method, definitions, concepts, and – yes, even its facts – have been clarified, disputed, and praised in turn. At stake are the truth criteria Skocpol has employed to justify her positions at each of these levels. Very little of the disciplinary response to this work has involved controlled testing of its hypotheses or the reanalysis of its data. Decisions about the validity of Skocpol's structural approach to revolution certainly will not be decided on these terms.[11]

In the following section I will suggest that a wide swath of recent sociological history can be interpreted in terms of the perspective I have just laid out. I will try to show that the truth value of these recent developments must be considered in primarily discursive terms.

Discursive Formations in the Postwar Era

Because it is discursive, sociology can progress in a narrowly empirical sense without any clear forward movement in more general theoretical terms. Discursive arguments and the rational criteria they imply are only subjectively compelling. They are accepted for reasons that are orthogonal to conventional empirical tests. This is simply another way of saying that social science flows inside of schools and traditions. The flow resembles the movement of a conversation more than the progress of a rational proof. It moves forth and back between limited and deeply entrenched ways of seeing. It looks more like a pendulum than a line.[12]

If we reflect on sociological theory since World War II we can see just such a pendulum pattern at work. The split between action theories and structural theories that has marked (very roughly) the years from the early 1960s did not develop in a historical vacuum. Every point on a pendulum responds to the motion that has come before.

Discourse about action versus structure emerged in reaction to Parsons' structural-functional work. Parsons had set out to end the "warring schools" once and for all. He had tried to bring idealism and materialism together in his systems theorizing, and voluntaristic action and structural determination together in his thinking about the individual. Yet, while in critical respects the most sophisticated

and far-reaching general theory yet conceived, Parsons' work failed
to achieve its goal. In part the problem was intellectual, for Parsons
did not actually pursue his synthesis in an even-handed way (Alexander 1983b). While acknowledging contingent action, he was in fact
more interested in socialized individuality; while formally incorporating material structures, he spent vastly more time theorizing normative control. There were social reasons for Parsons' failure as well.
Indeed, like the ideas that Weber called the switchmen of history, the
intellectual strains in Parsons' work provided the tracks along which
the ideal and material interests of entrenched theoretical schools and
traditions could run. Individualistic and structuralistic thinking are
deeply entrenched in the historical development of the social sciences;
it would take more than a sophisticated theoretical formulation –
even one that could maintain its synthesis in a more consistent way
– to knock them from their place.

Thus, even though Parsons' functionalist thinking opened up
new paths of theory and research in the postwar period, the pendulum was bound to swing back. Powerful theorizing emerged to open
up the black box of contingent order. Brilliant reformulations of
pragmatic, economic, and phenomenological thinking emerged. The
other new tendency, the macro one, opposed Parsons' idealization of
action. Returning to Marx and the instrumental stream of Weberian
thought, "structural" theory developed new and powerful versions of
macrosociology.

I do not wish to deny that these postfunctionalist movements often
took a decidedly empirical form or that contemporaries were often
convinced because of the new facts they revealed and the more powerful explanations they could provide. Symbolic interaction and ethnomethodology made breakthrough studies of deviance, collective
behavior, and social roles. The methodological polemics associated
with these studies, moreover, convinced many sociologists that more
individualistic and naturalistic approaches allowed greater access to
reality. The structural movement also made convincing empirical
claims for fields like stratification, modernization, and social change,
and for methodologies of a more concrete, historical, and comparative bent.

What I do wish to assert, however, is that the disciplinary success of
these postfunctionalist movements was not based primarily on such
empirical claims. In the first place, these claims were not in themselves simply empirical. They were embedded within, and thus were
in important ways an expression of, more generalized commitments

of a supraempirical kind. These powerful theoretical commitments, moreover, were not latent but manifest; as such, they themselves became principal foci in the postfunctionalist movement. It was, in other words, not just empirical studies in which postfunctionalist challengers engaged but in myriad highly generalized theoretical disputes. These disputes were omnipresent; they entered into the most ostensibly empirical work. The postfunctionalist movement, in sum, was rooted as much in discourse as in explanation; vis-à-vis Parsonian theory, and one another's as well, each position was justified through argument, not simply through the empirical procedures of verification or falsification.

In the following I will focus on what each of these perspectives presupposed about the nature of individual action and the origins of collective order. I will try to show what contemporaries found particularly attractive about these presuppositions, despite the fact that each tradition conceptualized action and order in a clearly one-sided and limiting way. Thus I will not just be examining discursive argument but engaging in it myself. I will try to demonstrate what these one-sided limitations are, and I will suggest that in a more synthetic model they might in principle be overcome.

Presuppositions and Theoretical Dilemmas

By presuppositions (Alexander 1982a, 1987b), I refer to the most general assumptions sociologists make when they encounter reality. Every social theory and every empirical work take a priori positions that allow observers to organize in the most simple categorical terms the data that enter their minds via their senses. Only on this basis can the more conscious manipulations that constitute rational or scientific thought be made. Presuppositions are subjects of discourse, and they are sometimes even discursively justified. For the most part, however, they originate in processes that precede the exercise of reason itself.

Perhaps the most obvious thing that students of social life must presuppose in their encounters with social reality is the nature of action. In the modern era, when one thinks about action, one thinks about whether it is rational or not. I do not mean to imply here that common sense equation of rational with good and smart, and nonrational with bad and stupid. Rather, in modern social science, this dichotomy refers to whether people are selfish (rational) or idealistic (nonrational), whether they are normative and moral (nonrational) or instrumental and strategic (rational), whether they act in terms of maximizing efficiency (rationally) or are governed by emotions and unconscious desires (nonrationally). In terms of empirical orientations, of course, the descriptions I have just offered – of rational action and of nonrational action – differ from one another in specific and important ways. In terms of theoretical practice, however, these orientations have, in fact, formed two ideal types. In the history of social theory these ideal types of rational and nonrational have demarcated distinctive theoretical traditions and discursive argument of the most polemical kind.[13]

How can these traditions be defined in terms that supersede but do not violate the more finely graded distinctions upon which each is based, in such a way, for example, that moralistic theories and emotionalist theories may both be seen as part of the "nonrationalist" tradition? The answer is deceptively simple; it is to see the dichotomy as relating to the internal versus external reference of action (see Alexander 1982a, pp. 17–79). Rationalistic or instrumental approaches portray actors as taking their bearings from forces outside of themselves, whereas nonrational approaches suggest that action is motivated from within. It is possible, in principle, to presuppose that action is both rational and nonrational, but it is surprising how rarely in the history of social theory this interpenetration has actually been made.

Yet to answer the central question about action is not enough. A second major issue needs to be presupposed as well. I refer here to the famous "problem of order," although I will define it somewhat differently than has typically been the case. Sociologists are sociologists because they believe there are patterns to society, structures somehow separate from the actors who compose it. Yet, while all sociologists believe such patterns exists, they often disagree sharply about how such an order is actually produced. Once again, I will cast these disagreements in terms of dichotomous ideal types because it is just this agglomerated antipathy that has characterized the empirical and discursive history of social thought (see Ekeh 1974, Lewis and Smith 1980). This dichotomy refers to the opposition between individualistic and collectivist positions.

If thinkers presuppose a collectivist position, they see social patterns as existing prior to any specific individual act, as in a sense the product of history. Social order confronts newborn individuals as an established fact outside of them. If the confusion aroused by Durkheim's (1937/1895) early formulations of this position is to be avoided, and if the necessity for "correcting" Durkheim's errors by developing equally one-sided discursive justifications on the other side is to be avoided as well, certain codas to this definition of collectivism must immediately be made.[14] If they are writing about adults, collectivists may well acknowledge that social order exists as much inside the individual as without; this is, in fact, an important qualification to which we will return. Whether it is conceptualized as inside or outside an actor, however, the collectivist position does not view order as the product of purely this-instant, this-moment considerations. According to collectivist theory every individual actor is pushed in the direction of preexisting structure; whether this direction remains only a probability or a determined fate depends on refinements in the collectivist position I will take up below.

Individualistic theories often acknowledge that there do appear to be such extraindividual structures in society, and they certainly recognize that there are intelligible patterns. They insist, however, that these patterns are the result of individual negotiation. They believe not simply that structure is "carried" by individuals but that it is actually produced by the carriers in the course of their individual interactions. The assumption is that individuals can alter the fundaments of order at each successive moment in historical time. Individuals, in this view, do not carry order inside of them. Rather, they follow or rebel against social order – even the values that they hold within themselves – according to their individual desires.

Once again, whether it is possible to combine some elements of this contingent position with a more collectivist emphasis is a matter I will take up in the following discussion. What I wish to emphasize at this point is that the problems of action and order are not optional. Every theory must take some position on both. The logical permutations among these presuppositions form the fundamental traditions of sociology. As such, they form the most important axes around which social science discourse revolves.

Presuppositions are so central to discourse because they have implications that go well beyond the explanatory concerns I have just defined. The study of society revolves around the questions of freedom and order, and every theory is pulled between these poles. Modern men and women believe that individuals have free will and that, because of this capacity, individuals can be trusted to act in responsible ways. To one degree or another, this belief has been institutionalized in Western societies. Individuals have been set apart as privileged political and cultural units. Elaborate legal efforts have been made to protect them from the group, from the state, and from other coercive organs like an established church.

Sociological theorists, whether individualist or collectivist, are likely to be as committed to the autonomy of the individual as other citizens. Indeed, sociology emerged as a discipline as a result of this differentiation of the individual in society, for it was the independence of the individual and the growth of his or her powers to think freely about society that allowed society itself to be conceived of as an independent object of study. It is the independence of the individual that makes order problematic, and it is this problematizing of order that makes sociology possible. At the same time, sociologists acknowledge that the everyday life of an individual has a patterned quality. It is this tension between freedom and order that provides the intellectual and moral rationale for sociology. Sociologists explore the nature of social order, and discursively justify the positions they adopted in regard to this question, because they are deeply concerned about its implications for individual freedom.

Individualistic theories are attractive and powerful because they preserve individual freedom in an overt, explicit, and thorough-going way. Their a priori postulates assume the integrity of the rational or moral individual, taking for granted actors' abilities to act freely against their situations, which are defined either in material or cultural terms. It is because of this natural convergence between ideological and explanatory discourse that individualism has been such a powerful strand in modern thought.

Social theory emerged out of the long process of secularization and rebellion against the hierarchical institutions of traditional society. In the Renaissance, Machiavelli emphasized the autonomy of the rational prince to remake his world. English contract theorists, like Hobbes and Locke, broke free from traditional restraints by developing a discourse claiming that social order depended on individual bargaining and, ultimately, upon a social contract. The same path was followed by some of the principal thinkers of the French Enlightenment. Each of these individualistic traditions was a strongly rationalistic one. While emphasizing different kinds of individual needs – power, happiness, pleasure, security – each portrayed society as emanating from the choices of rational actors. The crucial conceptual bridge between these traditions and contemporary theorizing in the social sciences was utilitarianism, particularly classical economics, whose theory of the invisible regulation of markets provided an elegant empirical explanation of how individual decisions can be aggregated to form societies.[15] It is from quasi-economic discourse that the central justifications for rationalistic modes of individualistic theorizing are largely drawn today.

Individualistic theories have, of course, also assumed a nonrational form. In its inversion of the Enlightenment and its revulsion against utilitarianism, romanticism inspired theories about the passionate actor (see, e.g., Abrams 1971) from Wundt to Freud. In its hermeneutic version, which stretches from Hegel (Taylor 1975) to Husserl and existentialism (Spiegelberg 1971), this antirationalist tradition takes on a moral and often cognitive form.

The advantages that an individualistic position bestows, then, are very great. Still, it can be achieved only at great theoretical cost. These costs emerge because such individualistic theories begin from a wholly unrealistic perspective about voluntarism in society. By radically neglecting the power of social structure, individualistic theory in the end does freedom no real service. It encourages the illusion that individuals have no need for others or for society as a whole. It also ignores the great sustenance to freedom that social structures can provide. It is upon such costs that the discourse against individualistic theory focuses its aim.

By acknowledging that social controls exist, collectivist theory can subject them to explicit analysis. In this sense, collectivist thought represents a real gain over the individualistic position, in moral as well as theoretical terms. The question is whether this gain, in turn, has been achieved only at an unacceptable price. What does such collectivist theorizing lose? How is the collective force it postulates related to the individual will, to the possibility of preserving voluntarism and self-control? In order to answer this decisive question, it is necessary to make explicit a point that has only been implicit in my discourse thus far. Assumptions about order do not entail any particular assumptions about action. Because of this indeterminacy, there are very different kinds of collectivist theory.

Whether collective theory is worth the cost depends on whether it presupposes the possibility for moral or expressive, that is, for nonrational, action. Many collectivist theories assume that actions are motivated by narrow, technically efficient forms of rationality. If such an assumption is made, then collective structures must be portrayed as if they were external to individuals and entirely unresponsive to their will. Political or economic institutions, for example, are said to control the actors from without, whether they like it or not. They do so by arranging punitive sanctions and positive rewards for actors who are reduced – whatever the specific nature of their personal goals – to calculators of pleasure and pain. Because such actors are assumed to respond rationally to this external situation, motives are eliminated as a theoretical concern. Such theorizing assumes that the actor's response can be predicted from analysis of the external environment alone. Rational-collectivist theories, then, explain order only by sacrificing the subject. In effect, they dispense with the very notion of an autonomous self. In classical sociology, orthodox Marxism presents the most formidable example of this development, and the coercive implications that surround its discourse – as revealed, for example, in recurring references to the "dictatorship of the proletariat" and the "laws of history" – have generated intense critical response (e.g., Van den Berg 1988). The same tendency to justify a discourse without a subject permeates every neoclassical theory that has collective ambitions, and Weber's sociology as well, as the controversy over the status of "domination" in the Weberian corpus demonstrates.

If, by contrast, collectivist theory allows that action may be nonrational, it perceives actors as guided by ideals and emotion. This internal realm of subjectivity is initially structured, it is true, by encounters with external objects – with parents, teachers, siblings, and books. In the process of socialization, however, such extraindividual structures become internal to the self. Only if this phenomenon of internalization is accepted can subjectivity become a topic for collectivist theory. According to this view, individual interaction becomes a negotiation between two "social selves." The dangers that such theorizing encounters are quite the opposite from collectivist theories of a more rationalistic kind. It tends to engage in moralistic rhetoric and idealistic justifications. As such, it often underestimates the ever-present tension between even the socialized individual and his or her social environment. This tension, of course, is most obvious when the theorist must consider an environment that is material in form, a possibility that cannot be conceptualized when collectivist theory is formulated in a one-sidedly normative way.

In the discussion of recent theoretical discourse that follows, I will focus on how presuppositional commitments have shaped sociological debate since the early 1960s. They have exerted their influence, of course, even if no attempt has been made discursively to justify them. The central figures in these debates, however, have sought such discursive justification. This, indeed, is what made them influential theorists. Through their discourse these theorists developed claims about the scope and implications of their theories, claims that stipulated "truth

criteria" at a supraempirical level. In the present section I have laid
out my own conception of what such criteria should be. When I
apply these criteria to recent theoretical debate, I will often be arguing
in opposition to the truth claims of the principal participants in these
debates. This, of course, is the very stuff of which social science
discourse is made.

Reconsidering Micro and Macro Theory

It is perhaps because of the discipline's methodological and empirical
focus that the massive renewal of individualistic theorizing in sociology
has been seen as a revival of "microsociology."[16] For, strictly speaking, micro and macro are thoroughly relativistic terms, referring to
part/whole relationships at every level of social organization. In the
language of recent social science, however, they have been identified
with the distinction between taking individual interaction as an
empirical focus, on the one hand, and taking an entire social system
as one's empirical focus, on the other.

When Homans (1958, 1961) introduced exchange theory, he was
renewing the very utilitarian position that had constituted the basis
of Parsons' (1937) earliest and most powerful critique. Not only did
Homans reject the collective tradition in classical and contemporary
sociology, but the interpretive strand of individualistic theorizing as
well. He insisted that the elementary forms of social life were not
extraindividual elements such as symbol systems but individual actors
of an exclusively rationalist bent. He focused on what he called sub-
institutional behavior, the behavior of "actual individuals," which be
believed to be entirely independent of socially specified norms. The
procedures through which individuals make calculations occupied
Homans' attention. So did the balance of supply and demand in the
actor's external environment. In Homans' rationalistic perspective
the social forces impinging on actors could only be conceived in an
objectified and external way.

Exchange theory became enormously influential in reviving the
case for microsociology. Its simple and elegant model facilitated
predictions; its focus on individuals made it empirically operational.
It also caught hold of a fundamental insight that Parsons and, indeed,
collectivist theorists of every stripe had ignored: It is through individual actors making decisions about the costs of contingent exchange
that "objective social conditions" become articulated vis-à-vis the

everyday life of individuals, institutions, and groups.[17] The price for such insights was high, however, even for theorists inside the paradigm itself. For example, Homans (1961, pp. 40, 54–5) was never able to define the "value" of a commodity in anything but a circular way; he was compelled to argue that it stemmed from reinforcing an orientation that was already in place. His conception of distributive justice showed similar strains (1961 chapter 12); he was forced to refer to "irrational" solidarity in order to decide just what the definition of an equitable "rational" exchange might be.

The other major strands of microtheorizing have taken up the interpretive side. Blumer (1969) was the general theorist most responsible for the revival of Meadian theory, although the tradition that Blumer (1937) labeled *symbolic interactionism* took up pragmatism only in its radically contingent form.[18] Blumer insisted that meaning is determined by individual negotiation – indeed, by the reaction of others to the individual's act. The actor is not seen as bringing some previously defined collective order into play. It is immediate situational relevance, not internalization, that defines attitudes. Through "self-indication" actors make objects even out of their own selves. It is the temporally rooted "I" of the actor, not the more societally focused "me," that determines the pattern of social order described in Blumer's work.

Though powerful, Blumer's most influential writing was almost entirely discursive in form; even when it was programmatic, moreover, it focused more on promoting the methodology of direct observation than on elaborating theoretical concepts. It is Goffman who must be seen as the most important empirical theorist of the symbolic interactionist movement. To most contemporaries, Goffman's work appeared merely to point interactionist theory in a more problem-specific and dramaturgic direction. Certainly his early work tends to support this reading. In contrast to the clear collectivist strains that emerged in his later theorizing, Goffman (e.g., 1959) emphasized individuals' desires to manipulate the presentation of self in opposition to socially structured roles, and he tried (1963) to explain institutional behavior as emerging from face-to-face interaction.

Ethnomethodology, and phenomenological work more generally, presents a more complicated story. Garfinkel was a student not only of Schutz but also of Parsons, and his earliest work (e.g., 1963) accepts the centrality of internalization. What Garfinkel explored in this early writing was how actors make social norms their own; he explored, that is, their "ethno" methodology. Emphasizing the constructed character of action, he described how, through cognitive techniques like "ad hocing" (Garfinkel 1967), individuals conceived of contingent and unique events as representations, or "indexes," of socially structured rules. In the process, he showed, these rules were in actuality not simply specified but modified and changed.

As ethnomethodology became a major theoretical movement, it was forced to justify itself in general and discursive ways. In the process, its concepts became more one-sided. Presenting itself as committed to an alternative sociology, ethnomethodology emphasized "members' own practices" over and against structure. That constitutive techniques like indexicality were omnipresent, it was now argued, should be seen as evidence that order is completely emergent, and the endlessly resourceful practice of orderly activity came to be identified (Garfinkel et al. 1981) with social order itself. That this kind of individualistic reduction is somehow inherent in a phenomenological approach is belied, however, by other strains that emerged from the ethnomethodological school. Conversational analysis (Sacks et al. 1974), for example, viewed speech as subject to strong structural constraints even if it did not usually conceptualize these constraints in a systematic way.

It is certainly an ironic demonstration of the lack of linear accumulation in sociology that, concurrent with this resurgence of microtheorizing, there emerged a strong movement toward equally one-sided kinds of macro, collectivist work. This movement began when "conflict theorists" justified themselves by defining Parsonian work as "order theory." Like the new microsociologists, these theorists, too, denied the centrality of internalization and the link between action and culture that concept implies. Rather than emphasizing individual consciousness as the basis of collective order, however, conflict theorists severed the link between consciousness and structural processes altogether. Dahrendorf (1959) gave to administrative power positions the central ordering role. Rex (1961) emphasized the allocative economic processes that gave power to the ruling class.

While conflict arguments certainly provided the most powerful justifications for structural theorizing in its initial phase, it was the Marxism of Althusser and his students (Althusser and Balibar 1970, Godelier 1967) that formulated the most sophisticated and influential discourse in its later phase. Drawing from Spinoza and as well as from modern linguistic and anthropological theory, this so-called structural Marxism analyzed historical developments as particular variations, transformations, and incarnations of fundamental structural principles. Rather than starting with the empirical and phenomenal diversity of social actions and lifeworlds, as contemporary microtheorists advised, these Marxist structuralists gave ontological and methodological primacy to the "totality." Although individual actions may deviate from structural imperatives, the objective consequences of these actions are determined by structures that exist beyond the actors' control.

While just as deterministic, this structural Marxism was less directly economic than other variants. It emphasized the political mediation of productive forces rather than their direct control (e.g., Poulantzas 1972). This discourse about mediation and structural "overdetermination" set the stage for Marxist theorizing with a distinctively Weberian cast. Critical political economists like Offe (1984/1972) and O'Connor (1978) focused on the function of the state in capitalist accumulation and tried to derive social problems and crises from "inevitable" state intervention.

While the most important discursive justifications for the new structural theory have come from Europe, its influence in America has depended on a series of influential arguments at the middle range. Moore's (1966) major work on the class origins of state formations provided the major impetus for this work, though it was much more classically Marxist than the neo-Weberian structuralist work that followed in its wake. The most imposing single work that followed Moore's was Skocpol's (1979). Skocpol not only provided what appeared to be a powerful new covering law to explain revolutions but offered a widely persuasive polemic against subjective and voluntaristic theories of revolution (in the name of her structural theory). Wright's (1978) class analysis takes up the same antimicro theme, arguing that ambiguities in a group's class consciousness come from "contradictory class locations." Treiman (1977) similarly produced what he called a "structural theory of prestige" that converted cultural into organizational control and denied to subjective understandings of stratification any independent causal role. In still another influential work, Lieberson (1980) put his explanation for racial inequality in the terms of this same highly persuasive discourse. He identified "structures of opportunity" with material environment and justified this by dismissing the focus on subjective volition as conservative and idealist.

The New Theoretical Movement

The efforts to reformulate sociology as either an exclusively action- or structurally oriented discipline emerged in response to frustration

with the unfulfilled promises of functionalist work and to fundamental disagreement with these promises as well. In the 1960s these
challenges to functionalism created a sense of crisis in the discipline.
By the late 1970s the challengers had triumphed and sociology seemed
to settle down, once again, into a secure if more fragmented middle
age. Marxist discourse permeated sociological writing in England
and the continent. In America, a new Marxist section of the national
association was formed and quickly gained more members than most
of the long-established sections. New sections on political and historical and comparative sociology followed, and their largely structuralist
approaches earned them a similar response. Micro theory also gained
tremendous authority. When ethnomethodology first emerged, it was
met with discourse that questioned its fundamental legitimacy and
dismissed it as either bizarre or corrupt (e.g., Coleman 1968, Coser
1975, and Goldthorpe 1973). By the late 1970s, its discursive justifications were accepted by many leading theorists (e.g., Collins 1981,
Giddens 1976) and taken seriously by most others. Goffman's work
passed even more quickly from controversy to classical status.

Yet, even as these once bumptious challengers became the new
establishment, even as the "multiparadigmatic" character of sociology
passed from daring prophecy (e.g., Friedrichs 1970) to conventional
wisdom (e.g., Ritzer 1975), the vital and creative phase of these
theoretical movements had come to an end. In the 1980s a strikingly
different phase of theoretical argument began to take shape. Stimulated by the premature theoretical closure of the micro and macro
traditions, this phase was marked by an effort to link theorizing
about action and structure once again. Such efforts were made from
within each of the newly dominant theoretical traditions, from both
sides of the great micro–macro divide.

There are social and institutional as well as intellectual reasons for
this new development in theoretical work. One certain factor is the
changing political climate in the United States and Europe. Most
radical social movements have faded away, and in the eyes of many
critical intellectuals Marxism itself has been morally delegitimated.
The ideological thrust that in the United States fueled post-Parsonian
discourse in its micro and macro form and that justified Marxist
structuralism on the continent is spent. In America, once-fervent structuralists are now looking for ways to use cultural analysis, and former
ethnomethodological sectaries are looking for ways to integrate
constructivist with traditional macro theory. In Germany, England,
and France, the new post-Marxist generation has been influenced by

phenomenology and American microtheorizing. The migration of Parsonian ideas to Germany (Alexander 1984), rather than renewing what is now seen as an obsolete debate, has inspired new efforts at theoretical reintegration.

There has been the passage of intellectual time as well, a passage regulated by the exigencies of theoretical rather than social logic. One-sided theories are provocative, and at certain junctures they can be highly fruitful. Once the dust of theoretical battle has settled, however, the cognitive content of their theorizing is not easy to maintain. Revisionism is the surest sign of theoretical discontent.[19] Those who seek to maintain an established tradition are particularly sensitive to its weaknesses, for it is they who must face the demands for discursive justification that gradually accumulate in its wake. In response to such immanent strains, talented students and followers introduce ad hoc revisions in the original theory and develop new and often inconsistent modes of discourse. The problem is that unless the entire tradition is overturned, such revisions end up being residual categories. The discursive arguments generated by criticism and reposte do have an unintended consequence, however. They highlight the weaknesses in the original tradition. In so doing, they make more likely openings, or cross-cuttings, between what once were boulderized traditions.[20] It is by studying revisionism within the micro and macro traditions that the new theoretical movement in sociology can be revealed.

Striking developments have occurred, for example, in symbolic interactionism. Although Goffman began his career more or less within the radically contingent tradition of Blumer, in his later writings there emerged a dramatic shift toward more structural and cultural concerns. The creative strategies of actors were still Goffman's target, but he (e.g., Goffman 1974) now referred to them as means of instantiating cultural and stratificational structures in everyday life. Similarly, whereas Becker's (1963) early impact on deviance theory derived from his emphasis on contingency and group behavior, his more recent work takes a decidedly systemic view of creativity and its effects (Becker 1984). Indeed, a spate of efforts by symbolic interactionists to systematize the links between actors and social systems has appeared. Lewis and Smith (1980), for example, have challenged the fundamental discursive justifications of the tradition by arguing that Mead, allegedly the founder of the school, was actually an antinominalist who took a collective rather than individualist position. Stryker (1980, pp. 52–4, 57–76) has gone so far as to present interactionism as if it were basically a modification of social systems theory itself (see also Alexander and Colomy 1985, Handel 1979, Maines 1977, Strauss 1978).

Similar developments can be seen in the rational action model revived by Homans' exchange theory. Students felt pressure to demonstrate that this polemically micro approach could cope with the truth criteria generated by macro-sociology. As a result, they gradually shifted the focus of analysis from individual actions to the transformations of individual actions into collective effects and, by extension, to unintended rather than purposive activity. Thus Wippler and Lindenberg (1987) and Coleman (1987a) now reject the notion that the connection between individual actions and structural phenomena can be viewed as a causal relation between discrete empirical events. Because there is, instead, empirical simultaneity, the linkage between micro and macro has to be seen as an analytical one sustained by invisible processes in the larger system. This analytical linkage is achieved by the application of "transformation rules," like voting procedures, to individual actions.

Theorists have been led by this focus on transformation to consider individual actions not as objects for analysis in their own right but as initial conditions for the operation of structural mechanisms. In this way, structural explanations – about the rules of constitutions (e.g., Coleman 1987b), the dynamics of organizations and intergroup relations (Blau 1977), the system of prestige allocation (Goode 1979) – have begun to replace utility arguments within the rationalistic micro tradition. There has also emerged extensive theorizing about the unintended effects of individual actions (Boudon 1982, 1987) and even about the genesis of collective morality (Ekeh 1974, Kadushin 1978, and Lindenberg 1983).

Although Garfinkel, the founder of ethnomethodology, continues to advocate a radical micro program (Garfinkel et al. 1981), and although the revisionist movement beyond one-sided theorizing is less developed here than within the other micro traditions, it seems impossible to deny that a similar unease and a similar movement permeate phenomenological sociology. Cicourel, for example, certainly one of the key figures in the earlier phase, has pushed for a more interdependent and synthetic approach (Knorr-Cetina and Cicourel 1981). A phenomenologically based "social studies in science" movement, while arguing for a new, much more situationally specific approach to science, refers routinely to the framing effects of social structure (Knorr-Cetina and Mulkay 1983, Pinch and Collins 1984). Although

Smith (1984) and Molotch (Molotch and Boden 1985) have both insisted on the indispensable autonomy of constitutive practices, they have produced significant studies that demonstrate how these practices are structured by organizational context and the distribution of power. These new phenomenological efforts, it should be stressed, do not simply involve revised explanatory schemes. They are deeply involved with new modes of discursive justifications, efforts that seek to incorporate the truth criteria of more structuralist work (see, e.g., Schegloff 1987).

Similar revisionist efforts mark a new movement beyond the confines of the rational-collectivist, or structural position. There has always been an abundance of internal contradictions in such theorizing, contradictions that, if anything, have been more pronounced in the work of its leading theorists. Rex (1961, pp. 113–28), for example, argued that a truce situation would eventually develop between ruling and subject classes that would introduce a period of tranquility and the possibility for new and more integrative forms of socialization. Why this would evaporate in the face of new and "inevitable" class conflict was something Rex asserted but never successfully explained. Whenever Althusser tried to reassure his readers that vis-à-vis the relative autonomy of political and ideological systems there would always be economic determination "in the last instance" (Althusser and Balibar 1970), his usually precise theorizing became lost in a gauzy metaphysical haze. Skocpol's (1979, pp. 3–15) insistence that non-structuralist explanations were individualistic was never discursively justified; her demotion of revolutionary ideology to conjunctural strategy rather than sociological cause (Skocpol 1979, pp. 164–73) revealed the weaknesses in her argument even if it allowed its surface coherence to be maintained.

It is only recently, however, that these strains in theoretical logic have manifested themselves by overt revision and by efforts to incorporate manifestly different discursive modes. On the American side of the structuralist school, Moore began to write about the subjective rather than structural sources of working-class weakness (Moore 1978) and about the proletarians' sense of injustice rather than objective injustice itself. Because the shift in the tenor of Skocpol's arguments has been more rapid and theoretically self-conscious, it illustrates the new theoretical movement in an even more suggestive way. It was in an effort to explain the Iranian revolution that Skocpol (1982) first raised the possibility that religious causes were comparable to economic and political ones. In a recent effort to justify her position vis-à-vis the discursive claims of a cultural critic (Sewell 1985), she has given up significant discursive ground, despite her insistence (Skocpol 1985) that cultural explanations must have a realistic and protostructural cast.

Indeed, from the early 1980s there has been an extraordinary cultural turn in what was until recently the securely structuralist domain of social history. Sewell and Hunt, once devoted to Tilly's version of conflict sociology, are now opponents of historical sociology in its structural form. Their writings have become major sources for an alternative, much more cultural discourse (Hunt 1988, Sewell 1985) and their explanations of revolutionary changes in French society directly counter structural models and causal proposals (Hunt 1984, Sewell 1980).[21] Darnton (1984), once a leading American exponent of Annalist "material culture," now offers interpretive criteria for historical truth and cultural reconstructions of popular myth as history. The "new social history" grew out of its association with the once new structural sociology. To many younger historians, such history now seems old and its definition of "social" much too restricted.

It is from anthropology, not sociology, that historians increasingly draw.[22] In that neighboring field, culture and meaning have assumed an increasingly central place, as the far-reaching significance of Geertz (1973), Turner (1969), and Douglas (1966) attests. Behind this shift in anthropology, of course, there stands the broad renaissance of cultural studies more generally conceived (see, for example, Alexander and Seidman 1990). This development has been sustained by the renewed interest in hermeneutic philosophy, the flowering of semiotic and poststructuralist work, and the introduction of a new version of Durkheimian sociology that is much more symbolic than before (see, for example, Alexander 1988a, Wuthnow et al. 1984, Zelizer 1985).

Sociology has only begun to be significantly affected by this shift in its intellectual environment. The new direction in Skocpol's work is one of the most important indications that the shift is beginning to be felt. The appearance of some polemically antistructural works of historical sociology (Calhoun 1982, Prager 1986) gives promise of a deepening of this development. At this writing, indeed, a new section on cultural sociology has been formed in the American Sociological Association and major new works of macrocultural sociology are in progress (e.g., Archer 1988, Eisenstadt 1986, Wuthnow 1987). While these cultural developments in American macrosociology are not linked directly to the antimaterialist movement of Gouldner's later work, they complement it in a clear and revealing way. In the sustained attack on "objective Marxism" that Gouldner (1982) issued just before his death, he called for a renewed appreciation of the voluntaristic tradition in American sociology. Only this antistructural tradition, Gouldner believed, is capable of theorizing an autonomous civil society against state and economy.

The culturalist revolution that Meyer and Scott (1983) have begun to effect in the sociology of organizations makes an oddly similar point. In a polemic against instrumentalist theories that tightly link organizational structures to the demands of external technical requirements, they argue for the "decoupling" of administrative arrangements and actual production activities. Because organizations are infused with the same meanings as the society at large, their actions should be viewed more as ritualistic reproductions of these cultural ideals than as rational exercises in efficient intervention. From this cultural perspective, the modern Western state is hardly an iron cage crushing civil society; it must be viewed, rather, as a controlling representational system that elaborates broader themes of cultural rationality. In a collection devoted to this approach, which has come to be called "institutionalism," Zucker (1988, p. 24) calls formal organizations the "cultural engines of modern social systems," and DiMaggio (1988, p. 5) polemically contrasts institutional theorists with "utilitarian and conflict theorists, who have assumed that organizations and the people in them are more plastic, calculating, and manipulable than they usually are."

This uneven but persistent challenge to structuralist theorizing and explanation within American macrosociology has been more than matched by the critical discourse against structural Marxism in Europe. In "The Poverty of Theory," Thompson (1978) launched a heated polemic against Althusserianism in the name of a voluntaristic and culturally centered critical theory. Only upon this revised theoretical basis, Thompson argued, could moral responsibility for radical political behavior be sustained. This essay became a lightning rod for what has become a fundamental reversal in theoretical sensibility. For example, in his early and still most widely cited article, Michael Mann (1970) attacked Marxist and liberal versions of consensus theory as overly emphasizing ideology, and he called for a more social structural approach to the problem of working-class consent. In the writing that followed he continued to focus on organizational issues like labor markets (Mann and Blackburn 1979) and state financing (Mann 1979). His later work – a massive reconsideration of the origins and patterns of organized social power – marks a

arture from this perspective. Not only does power become
a pluralistic fashion, but ideological linkages play perhaps
ritical historical role. Discussing the effects of Christianity,
ple, Mann (1986, p. 507) acknowledges, "I have singled out
vork] as necessary for all that followed." For Perry Anderson
. 1406), Mann's reviewer in the *Times Literary Supplement*
and himself a former leader of the British structural movement, this
turn toward the cultural has not been decisive enough. For Anderson's
current taste, Mann still "veers close to the characteristic modern confusion that simply equates power and culture" and he recommends
that culture be considered in a still more "autonomous" way. In its
insistence that the autonomy of religious elites is a critical issue for
comparative civilization development, Hall's *Powers and Liberties*
(1985) presents yet another example of this cultural turn in recent
historical sociology. As Anderson criticized Mann for not going far
enough, so Hall and Mann, and, indeed, Anderson as well, have been
taken to task by S. N. Eisenstadt (1987) for conceiving of religious
and political institutions as "ontologically separate" entities. Eisenstadt
calls for a more analytic approach, which will demonstrate that
"cultural visions . . . are constitutive elements of the construction of
social order and institutional dynamics."[23]

Outside of England there have been similar upheavals in the structuralist edifice. In Eastern Europe (compare Sztompka 1974, and
Sztompka 1984, 1986, 1993), Scandinavia (Eyerman 1982, 1984),
France (Tourraine 1977), and Italy (Alberoni 1984), theorists once
sympathetic to Marxist arguments have shifted their concern away
from the contradictions that limit action to the social movements
that respond to them. Elster's (1985) rational choice Marxism can be
seen as a similar effort to avoid determinism, but his narrowly rationalistic understanding of action has been sharply criticized (e.g., Lash
and Urry 1984, Walzer 1986) for its inability to encompass the
moral strivings of critical social movements.

This revolution against Marxism has been brought to a head by
the poststructuralist movement that originated in France. While in
principle as critical of symbolic structuralism as of Marxist reduction,
the main impact of poststructural theorizing on the social sciences has
been to reduce the influence of Marxist directions in critical thought.
In Foucault's theory (e.g., 1970), discursive formations replace modes
of production. In Bourdieu's (e.g., 1986), cultural capital replaces
capital of a traditionally economic kind. In Lyotard's (1984), the
historical contribution of cultural narratives about rationality and

rebelliousness replaces explanations that assume rationality and relate rebellion to domination alone.[24]

There has, of course, been an equally important movement against Marxism from the German side, one which for the practice of sociology has had even more widely ramifying effects. I am speaking here of the drastic shift in Jurgen Habermas's theorizing away from Marxist concepts to what he calls "communicative theory." I will discuss Habermas's ideas in the broader context of shifts in general theory itself. With this discussion, my presentation of the new theoretical movement in sociology will come to an end.

General theorizing from a macro perspective has always had a special position in social science. It is this relatively abstract and often rather speculative mode that reaches into the nooks and crannies of the discipline, orienting sociology by providing it with, if not a reflection of itself, then a reflection of its aspirations. In recent years the work of the most widely discussed general theorists has evidenced a decisive shift away from a one-sidedly structural bent. Giddens's earliest work (1971) was continuous with the structuralist thrust of conflict theory and neo-Marxism, but in the later 1970s he fundamentally changed his course. Giddens became convinced of the need for a complementary theory of action. Building from the phenomenological insistence on the reflexive nature of human activity, he developed a theory of "structuration" (1985), the intention of which is to interweave contingency, material structure, and normative rules. Collins' development shows a similar trajectory. Although more interested in ethnomethodology from the beginning of his career than Giddens, in his early work Collins (1975) presented primarily a case for structuralistic conflict sociology. In recent years, by contrast, he has embraced radical microsociology, both phenomenological and Goffmanian. He has also moved toward the "late Durkheim." Collins now (e.g., 1981, 1988) argues that chains of interaction rituals mediate social structure and contingent action.

Habermas, too, began his career with a more typically macrostructuralist model of social dynamics (Habermas 1973, 1989 [1962]). Although there are clear references to moral claims and to different types of action in that early work, they remained residual to his heavily political-economic model of institutional life. In his more recent work, however, Habermas (1984) explicitly and systematically develops theories about the normative and microprocesses that underlie and sometimes oppose the macrostructures of social systems. He has used individual moral and cognitive development to anchor his description of world-historical phases of "social learning," descriptions of speech acts to develop arguments about political legitimacy, and the conception of an interpersonally generated life-world to justify his empirical explanation of social resistance and strain.

What is missing from these macrotheoretical arguments is a robust conception of culture. Habermas shies away from cultural systems because the notion introduces an element of arbitrariness and irrationality into every conceivable stage of historical life. Giddens and Collins cannot embrace it because, overly influenced by microsciology, they conceptualize the actor in a highly discrete, altogether too reflexive way.[25] In contrast to these efforts, my own work began with a commitment to the macrocultural stance. I argued (Alexander 1982b) that because Marx lacked Durkheim's insight into the structure of symbolic systems his radical theorizing had an inherently coercive cast. Weber's political sociology followed in this Marxist vein, I suggested (Alexander 1983a), because Weber's conception of modern society denied the possibility of integrative cultural wholes. To argue for the significance of culture in this way is to recognize the central importance of Parsons' theoretical contributions, particularly his differentiation between culture, personality, and society. In this earlier work, however, I tended also to follow Parsons in his neglect of order in an individual sense. Since that time I have turned much more directly to theorizing in the micro traditions (Alexander 1985a, 1988b, Alexander and Colomy 1985, Alexander and Giesen 1987). I have outlined a model that conceives of action as the contingent element of behavior that can be differentiated analytically from mere reproduction. This action can be conceived of as a "flow" within symbolic, social, and psychological environments. These environments interpenetrate within the concrete empirical actor, who is no longer identified with purely contingent action as he or she typically is in the traditions of micro theory.

The new theoretical movement in sociology is advancing on a number of fronts and under various names. It will continue to do so until the energy of this current movement of the disciplinary pendulum is used up. In my view, the key to making this motion intellectually progressive is a more direct recognition of the centrality of collectively structured meaning, or culture. There is a yawning gap between most of the newly synthetic thrusts in general theory, on the one hand, and the turn toward cultural theory that has characterized the new macrotheorizing in its more substantive forms, on the other. Only if general theorists are prepared to enter the thicket of "cultural studies" – with, of course, their sociological armaments well in hand – will this gap gradually be closed. This time around, however, theorizing about culture cannot be allowed to degenerate into a camouflage for idealism. Neither should it be given an aura of objectivity that preempts individual creativity and the rebellion against norms.[26] If these mistakes are avoided, the new movement in sociology will have a chance to develop a truly multidimensional theory. This will be a permanent contribution to social thought, even if it will not prevent the pendulum from eventually swinging back once again.

Notes

1 One can observe this effect, for example, in the work of Kreps (e.g., 1985, 1987). Committed to the practical goal of developing lawful explanations for disaster research, he feels compelled to engage in an ambitious program of general theorizing and to make explicit his commitments at the most nonempirical, presuppositional level.

2 Kuhn (1970) himself, of course, would have been the first to insist that his redefinition of natural science did not deny to it a relatively objective and cumulative character and that social science had rarely achieved anything approaching this condition.

3 One form of irrationalism is precisely the danger in the resolutely "antifoundationalist" position that has been staked out by Richard Rorty. In *Philosophy and the Mirror of Nature* (1979), Rorty provided a sharply critical review of the history of Western philosophy. He argued that because the centuries-long effort to establish epistemological foundations for objective evaluations has proved to be unsuccessful, the effort to engage in such generalized reasoning should be abandoned. From here it is but a short step to the call to abandon social scientific efforts to construct general theories, either of society or of theory as such. Thus, building on Rorty, philosophers (e.g., Rajchman 1985) have argued for the reduction of philosophy to literary theory, sociologists (see, e.g., Waldell and Turner 1986) for a turning away from general theory to moral reasoning. In an effort to create some middle ground between positivism and self-styled hermeneutics, my argument in this chapter takes direct issue with such views. It is one thing to abandon the search for epistemological access to the "real" in a direct, reflective, "mirroring" sense. It is quite another to give up on the search for consensual, universal, and impersonal criteria for evaluation, that is, on the project of rationality itself. To conflate these abandonments is to put powerful exemplifications of rationality on a par with vulgar empiricism, as Sica (1986, p. 155) does when he characterizes Habermas's theorizing as "pointless rigidification in favor of the scientism he prefers." While such

arguments draw inspiration from hermeneutics, an understanding truly rooted in the latter need not, in fact, abandon the effort to construct cognitive truth; it must simply give up the utopian hope that a single ahistorical standard of truth can ever be established. It is, then, the distorted self-understanding of social science that must be set aside, not the discipline of social science as such. My aim in the following is to demonstrate that this discipline – as practiced, not as conceptualized in the terminology of positivist reconstruction – is neither empiricist nor lacking in the efforts, often enormously clarifying, to establish universalistic standards for objective knowledge. I have elaborated this position further in Alexander 1995.

4   This is one reason so many of the early applications of Kuhnian ideas to sociology (e.g., Friedrichs 1970) seem in retrospect hyperbolic and overblown. They proclaimed revolutionary upheavals in a discipline that had always been in a more or less continual state of sharp disagreement and theoretical upheaval.

5   In this respect Wagner and Berger (1984) and Wagner (1984) are surely correct to stress the similarities between scientific progress in the hard and soft sciences. By sharply separating explanatory research programs from what they call "orienting strategies," however, they overlook the discursive and generalized quality of social science argument and, therefore, the relativism that is inherent to all "progress" in the social sciences.

6   It is not simply that Wallace (1983) – who provides the clearest recent illustration of this viewpoint – is wrong to force social science theory into the natural science mold. It is that he mistakes a logical reconstruction of how natural science "should" proceed for a map of how good science is actually made. This strategy of reconstruction began with the philosophical ambition of the Vienna logical positivists to eliminate speculative and nonempirical ideas from philosophical thought. Whatever its merits philosophically – and they are real if ultimately limited ones – this logic should not be conceived of as providing the grounds for the practice of science itself. Practicing scientists have never been able to understand their own work in these terms – or in Popperian ones, for that matter – and this inability has been one of the strongest motivations for the growth of postpositivist understandings of natural science. The present chapter proceeds in this spirit; it is an attempt to understand what social science theory actually is, not what some of its critics think it should aim to be. Any critical agenda for sociological theory must be couched within an understanding of its distinctive character. In terms of recent debate in moral and political philosophy (e.g., Williams 1985, Walzer 1987), this represents an internalist position, as compared to the more abstracted, externalist position taken by sociology's empiricist, "logic of science" critics.

7 For a powerful demonstration of the inevitability of empirical under-determination, which is tied to a historical indictment of the origins of contemporary quantitative traditions, see S. P. Turner (1987).

8 It demonstrates Smelser's conscientiousness as a historical researcher that he himself presented data that, as it were, went beyond his own theory (see Walby 1986). This is not usually the case, for the overdetermination of data by theory usually makes countervailing data invisible, not only to social scientists themselves but often to their critics.

9 Sewell (1985) has forcefully demonstrated this gap in Skocpol's data for the French case.

10 This can be seen as the specifically social scientific version of the thematization that, Habermas (1984) has argued, must lay beyond every effort at rational argument.

11 There are far-reaching implications of this discursive view of social science that I will not be able to take up here. One of the most important is that it helps to explains why the classics continue to be so central to the structure and arguments of social science. Discourses that are not purely factual must be adjudicated by reference to standards that are widely available throughout the discipline and that do not, as a rule, have to be articulated in a formal way. In order to meet this need disciplines make a select number of works "classical." The universe from which classical works can be chosen, however, depends on intellectual achievement. The further one moves away from natural science – the more discursive truth criteria become explicit topics of discussion – the more that decisive formulations of rational truth depend on intellectual qualities (personal genius, sensibility, etc.) that are not progressive in the empiricist sense. It is because he accepted the natural science model that Merton (1967) denied the centrality of the classics. From a discursive perspective on social science, however, his distinction between the history and systematics of sociology cannot be sustained. I have developed this discussion about the role of the classics elsewhere (Alexander 1987a), and have drawn freely from this in this section.

12 This metaphor of conversation has also been employed by Rorty: "If we see knowing not as having an essence, to be described by scientists or philosophers, but rather as a right, by current standards, to believe, then we are well on the way to seeing conversation as the ultimate context within which knowledge is to be understood" (1979, p. 389). It is characteristic of Rorty, however, that he uses this metaphor to deny the relevance of pursuing either empirical truth or general theory, advocating instead a kind of philosophical historiography: "Our focus shifts from the relation between human beings and the objects of their inquiry to the relation between alternative standards of justification, and from there to the actual changes in those standards which make up intellectual history" (1979, pp. 389–90).

If social science is a conversation, attention to alternative standards of justification is certainly in order. This does not necessitate, however, a diminution of interest in the empirical "objects" of social science or the adoption of a purely historical – rather than systematic and foundational – approach to considering what these standards imply. Rorty himself is ultimately ambiguous on this point, as he is on many others. In a subsequent essay (1984) he insists, against the opponents of rationalist reconstruction, that we "want to imagine conversations between ourselves . . . and the mighty dead [philosophers] in order to assure ourselves that there has been rational progress in the course of recorded history" (1984, p. 51). Vis-à-vis earlier philosophers, he here advocates "finding out how much truth they knew" and endorses "such enterprises in commensuration" even if they are historically anachronistic (p. 53). Perhaps there is not such a great gulf between postempiricism and foundational attempts to establish rational evaluations, after all. That is certainly my contention here.

13 The claim that rational and nonrational have, in fact, informed broadly distinctive traditions in the history of social thought has been advanced by a wide range of different writers, for example, Parsons (1937), Hughes (1958), and Habermas (1971).

14 It is just such an overreaction against the standard misreading of Durkheim's position that marks Giddens' position (e.g., Giddens 1976). This overreaction has led him to an overly individualistic position on the order question.

15 In his subtle essay on the origins of modern economic theory, Hirschman (1977) has shown that contract theories that emphasized market exchanges originated as part of a struggle against the arbitrary power of despots and kings. He also suggests, however, that in its early stages – for example, in the work of Montesquieu – such contract theories had a relatively social and often normative and emotional bent, for such self-interested exchanges were supposed to civilize passionate and often destructive human instincts. The initial rationale for this prototype of individualistic and rationalistic theory, then, was clearly cultural and collective. As market theory developed, however, it became more purely materialistic in orientation, and the notion that contractual exchanges had any relationship to subjective motive dropped out. This account provides a historical documentation for the theoretical criticaism I make below – namely, that the whole topic of volition and will is eliminated by rationalistic and individualistic theories.

16 For a historical perspective on shifts in theorizing the micro–macro link, as well as a more detailed and systematic account of the analytic issues involved, see Alexander and Giesen (1987). I have drawn from this essay for many of the arguments that follow.

17 In explaining the success of exchange theory one would not want to underestimate the power and bombastic eloquence of Homans' discursive

justifications on its behalf. He first articulated exchange theory (Homans 1958) in a purely discursive way, in his highly publicized presidential address to the American Sociological Association. In the major introduction to his collection of essays (Homans 1962), he developed new modes of biographical and ideological discourse to justify exchange theorizing. His remarkable dedication to developing discursive justifications for exchange theory continued to be revealed in his autobiography (Homans 1984), which, I have argued elsewhere (Alexander 1987c), creates a series of not entirely accurate frameworks through which the exchange perspective is presented as psychologically, morally, scientifically, and historically inevitable.

18 Lewis and Smith (1980) demonstrate this point in a powerful and systematic way in their brilliant reinterpretation of the history of pragmatic social theory in America. That upon its publication this book became extraordinarily controversial points, in my view, to the danger its argument posed to the discursive justifications of symbolic interactionism in its Blumerian mode.

19 Elsewhere I have applied this conception of revisionism to the classical and Parsonian traditions (Alexander 1982b, 1983a, 1983b) and to Kuhn's work (Alexander 1982c). I have elaborated revisionism in contemporary theoretical traditions in much more detail in Alexander (1987b). See also chapter 2, above.

20 Eisenstadt (Eisenstadt and Curelaru 1976) was one of the first sociologists to become sensitive to the possibility for such cross-cuttings. As a functionalist who was himself straining to develop new forms of theoretical discourse, he was quick to point out similar attempts that were emerging in other traditions. Because he was committed to an explanatory and basically empiricist conception of social science, however, he viewed these openings as part of the linear progress of sociology rather than as one phase in the pendulum movement of a discipline which is as discursive as it is explanatory.

21 Another revealing example of the confrontation between the new cultural history and the once-new social history can be found in the relationship between Edward Berenson's and Eugene Weber's accounts of the behavior of peasants in nineteenth century France. Weber, long one of the major proponents of social history despite his moderate political stance, published a major work (1976) arguing that the backward and conservative mentality of French peasants had been transformed in the latter part of the nineteenth century as the result of technological and economic developments. Berenson, politically more liberal and more closely aligned with recent intellectual movements, reviewed Weber's book and criticized it for its materialism (Berenson 1979). Berenson's own work (1984) on the origins of the revolution of 1848 emphasizes, by contrast, the peasants' critical role and how their consciousness was transformed by their participation in the radical Christian movements

that enveloped much of the French countryside in the early nineteenth century.

22 This new preoccupation with anthropological theory is reflected in an entire issue the *American Historical Review* devoted to "the state of history" published by Rabb and Rotberg (1982). A major section is devoted to the relationship between anthropology – which is defined in distinctively cultural terms – and history (see the articles by Bernard S. Cohen, John N. Adams, Natalie Z. Davis, and Carlo Ginsberg, pp. 227–91). At the center of this relationship has been Clifford Geertz, whose work has had an enormous impact in America on both European and American history. Sewell spent five years at the Institute for Advanced Study, where Geertz is a dominant figure. Darnton, a member of the Princeton University history department, jointly taught seminars with Geertz for several years. A leading young historian of American history, Sean Wilentz, acknowledges the central role of Geertz in the Davis Center seminars (also at Princeton) from which he (Wilentz 1985) drew his collection of historical essays about ritual and power. Geertz, of course, was trained by Parsons, and though his work has become significantly more culturalist since then, his contemporary prominence provides yet another indication that social science discourse has turned back to the synthetic concerns that Parsons so forcefully expressed.

23 Eisenstadt presents this analytical approach as prototypically Weberian, but Thompson, Hall, Mann, and Anderson have at least as much a claim to this mantle as he. Weber's own corpus, after all, is a complex jumble of institutional, ideational, and genuinely reductionistic works (Alexander 1983a). In light of this legacy, it would be more accurate to see Eisenstadt's insistence on an analytic approach to cultural "institutionalization" as distinctively Parsonian, and the massive project of comparative civilizational history upon which he has been engaged (see, for example, Eisenstadt 1986) as a form of neofunctionalism. This circling back to Parsons's earlier synthetic work, in terms of ambitions and sometimes also in terms of actual concepts, is a significant and visible characteristic of the new theoretical movement I am describing here (see note 25). Mann (1986), for example, makes careful reference to Parsons' antireductionist approach to organizational capacity. When Meyer (1987) extends his institutional theory to civilizational history and criticizes comparative research for "a kind of reductionism in which we treat the forces and relationships within the Western situation as somehow natural or universal, ignoring their sociocultural constitution," the echos of Eisenstadt's and Parsons's analytic approach to culture are very clear.

24 This poststructuralist thinking has already begun to spread deeply into British sociology, as the recent writings by Thompson (1984, 1986) and Lash (1985) indicate.

25 As Archer (1985b) has observed. Giddens's exaggerated separation of individuals from their environments is the other side of his frequent over-emphasis on the coercive materiality of social structure.

26 These, of course, are the very errors that Parsons made in his effort to synthesize the warring schools of sociology two generations ago. Nonetheless, it is the same type of effort – to synthesize action and structure, culture and material force – in which the younger generation of theorists is currently engaged. It should not be surprising, then, that one of the guises that this new theoretical movement has taken is a broad revision and revival of Parsonian theory, which I have called neofunctionalism (see, for instance, the essays collected in Alexander 1985b, and Alexander and Colomy 1988). In her work advocating a renewed focus on culture in macrosociology, Archer (1985a) can also be seen as returning to Parsons' approach in a less orthodox way. Culture can be reinstated, she argues, only by avoiding the conflation of cultural patterning with social equilibrium. This argument is elaborated in her book *Culture and Agency* (1988), which represents a major effort to insert culture back into general sociological theory.

Even in the more orthodox strands of this revival the impact of the new movement can be seen. Although Luhmann (1979) has raised the radically macroconcept of "systems" to a new and overbearing height, it should not be forgotten that he explains the very existence of systems by referring to fundamental microprocesses, which he identifies as the individual's existential need to reduce complexity. In his more recent work on autopoietic systems (Luhmann 1987), moreover, he makes the dialectic of micro and macro into the very essence of modern societies. This emphasis has had a major influence on Munch's important efforts (1981) to reshape Parsons' systematic theory. While he generally criticizes the radical micro traditions and in this way follows Parsons' collective emphasis, he has moved to incorporate contingency into his revised four-dimensional models in a way that Parsons never contemplated.

References

Abrams, M. H. 1971, *Natural Supernaturalism*. New York: Norton.

Alberoni, F. 1984, *Movement and Institution*. New York: Columbia University Press.

Alexander, J. C. 1982a, *Theoretical Logic in Sociology*, vol. 1: *Positivism, Presuppositions, and Current Controversies*. Berkeley: University of California Press.

—— 1982b, *The Antinomies of Classical Thought: Marx and Durkheim*. Berkeley: University of California Press.

—— 1982c, Kuhn's unsuccessful revisionism: a rejoinder to Selby. *Canadian Sociological Review*, 7, pp. 66–71.

Alexander, J. C.   1983a, *The Classical Attempt at Synthesis: Max Weber. Theoretical Logic in Sociology*, vol. 3. Berkeley: University of California Press.

—— 1983b, *The Modern Reconstruction of Classical Thought: Talcott Parsons. Theoretical Logic in Sociology*, vol. 4. Berkeley: University of California Press.

—— 1984, The Parsons revival in German sociology. In R. Collins (ed.), *Sociological Theory*, San Francisco: Jossey-Bass, pp. 394–412.

—— 1985a, The individualist dilemma in phenomenology and interaction. In S. N. Eisenstadt and D. Halle (eds), *Macrosociological Theory*, Beverly Hills, CA: Sage, pp. 25–57.

—— (ed.) 1985b, *Neofunctionalism*. Beverly Hills, CA: Sage.

—— 1987a, On the centrality of the classics. In A. Giddens and J. Turner (eds), *Social Theory Today*, London: Macmillan, pp. 11–57.

—— 1987b, *Twenty Lectures: Sociological Theory Since World War II*. New York: Columbia University Press.

—— 1987c, Science, sense, and sensibility. *Theory and Society*, 15, pp. 443–63.

—— (ed.) 1988a, *Durkheimian Sociology: Cultural Studies*. New York: Cambridge University Press.

—— 1988b, *Action and its Environments: Towards a New Synthesis*. New York: Columbia University Press.

Alexander, J. C., and Colomy, P.   1985, Towards neofunctionalism: Eisenstadt's change theory and symbolic interaction. *Sociological Theory*, 3, pp. 11–32.

—— (eds) 1988, *Differentiation Theory and Social Change: Historical and Comparative Approaches*. New York: Columbia University Press.

Alexander, J. C., and Giesen, B.   1987, From reduction to linkage: the long view of the micro–macro link. In S. C. Alexander et al. (eds), *The Micro-Macro Link*, Berkeley: University of California Press, pp. 1–42.

Alexander, J. C., and Seidman, S. (eds) 1990, *Culture and Society: Contemporary Debates*. New York: Cambridge University Press.

Althusser, L., and Balibar, E.   1970, *Reading Capital*. London: New Left Books.

Anderson, P.   1986, "Those in authority," a review of *The Origins of Social Power*, vol. I by Michael Mann. *Times Literary Supplement*, December 12, pp. 1405–6.

Archer, M.   1985a, The myth of cultural integration. *British Journal of Sociology*, 36, pp. 333–53.

—— 1985b, Structuration versus morphogenesis. In S. N. Eisenstadt and D. Halle (eds), *Macrosociological Theory*, Beverly Hills, CA: Sage, pp. 58–88.

—— 1988, *Culture and Agency*. London: Cambridge University Press.

Becker, H.   1963, *Outsiders: Studies in the Sociology of Deviance*. Glencoe, IL: Free Press.

Becker, H.   1984, *Art Worlds*. Berkeley: University of California Press.
Berenson, E.   1979, The modernization of rural France. *The Journal of European Economic History*, 8(1), pp. 209–15.
—— 1984, *Populist Religion and Left Wing Politics in France, 1830–1852*. Princeton, NJ: Princeton University Press.
Blau, P.   1977, *Inequality and Heterogeneity*. New York: Free Press.
Blau, P., Blum, T. C. and Schwartz, J. E.   1982, Heterogeneity and intermarriage. *American Sociological Review*, 47, pp. 45–62.
Blumer, H.   1937, Social psychology. In E. D. Schmidt (ed.), *Man and Society*, Englewood Cliffs, NJ: Prentice-Hall, pp. 144–98.
—— (ed.)   1969, The methodological position of symbolic interactionism. In H. Blumer, *Symbolic Interactionism*, Englewood Cliffs, NJ: Prentice-Hall, pp. 1–60.
Boudon, R.   1982, *The Unintended Consequences of Social Action*. New York: St. Martin's.
—— 1987, The individualistic tradition in sociology. In J. C. Alexander et al. (eds), *The Micro–Macro Link*, Berkeley: University of California Press, pp. 45–70.
Bourdieu, P.   1986, *Distinction*. Cambridge, MA: Harvard University Press.
Calhoun, C.   1982, *The Question of Class Struggle: The Social Foundations of Popular Radicalism*. Chicago: University of Chicago Press.
Coleman, J.   1968, Review symposium on Harold Garfinkel's studies in ethnomethodology. *American Sociological Review*, 33, pp. 126–300.
—— 1987a, Microfoundations and macrosocial behavior. In J. C. Alexander et al. (eds), *The Micro–Macro Link*, Berkeley: University of California Press, pp. 153–75.
—— 1987b, Toward a social theory of constitutions. Unpublished manuscript.
Collingwood, C.   1940, *Metaphysics*. Oxford: Clarendon.
Collins, R.   1975, *Conflict Sociology*. New York: Academic Press.
—— 1981, On the microfoundations of macrosociology. *American Journal of Sociology*, 86, pp. 984–1014.
—— 1988, The conflict tradition in Durkheimian sociology. In J. C. Alexander (ed.), *Durkheimian Sociology: Cultural Studies*, New York: Cambridge University Press, pp. 107–28.
Coser, L.   1975, Presidential address: Two methods in search of a substance. *American Sociological Review*, 40, pp. 691–700.
Dahrendorf, R.   1959, *Class and Class Conflict in Industrial Society*. Stanford, CA: Stanford University Press.
Darnton, R.   1984, *The Great Cat Massacre and Other Episodes in French Cultural History*. New York: Vintage.
Di Maggio, P.   1988, Interest and agency in institutional theory. In L. G. Zucker (ed.), *Institutional Patterns and Organizations: Culture and Environment*. Cambridge, MA: Ballinger, pp. 3–21.

Douglas, M. 1966, *Purity and Danger*. London: Penguin.

Durkheim, E. 1937 [1895], *The Rules of Sociological Method*. New York: Free Press.

Eisenstadt, S. N. 1986, Culture and social structure revisited. *International Sociology*, 1(3), pp. 297–20.

—— 1987, Macro-sociology and sociological theory: some new directions (review essay). *Contemporary Sociology*, 16(5), pp. 602–10.

Eisenstadt, S. N. and Curelaru, M. 1976, *The Forms of Sociology: Paradigms and Crises*. New York: John Wiley.

Ekeh, P. K. 1974, *Social Exchange Theory: The Two Traditions*. Cambridge, MA: Harvard University Press.

Elster, J. 1985, *Making Sense of Marx*. New York: Cambridge University Press.

Eyerman, R. 1982, Some recent studies of class consciousness. *Theory and Society*, 11, pp. 541–53.

—— 1984, Social movements and social theory. *Sociology*, 18, pp. 71–81.

Foucault, M. 1970, *The Order of Things*. London: Tavistock.

Friedrichs, R. 1970, *A Sociology of Sociology*. New York: Free Press.

Garfinkel, H. 1963, A conception of and experiments with trust as a condition of concerted stable actions. In O. J. Harvey (ed.), *Motivation and Social Interaction*. New York: Ronald Press, pp. 187–238.

—— 1967, *Studies in Ethnomethodology*. Englewood Cliffs, NJ: Prentice-Hall.

Garfinkel, H., Lynch, M., and Livingston, E. 1981, The work of discovering science construed with materials from the optically discovered pulsar. *Philosophy of Social Science*, 11, pp. 131–58.

Geertz, C. 1973, *The Interpretation of Culture*. New York: Basic Books.

Giddens, A. 1971, *Capitalism and Modern Social Theory*. New York: Cambridge University Press.

—— 1976, *New Rules of Sociological Method*. New York: Basic Books.

—— 1985, *The Constitution of Societies*. London: Macmillan.

Godelier, M. 1967, System, structure, and contradition in "Capital." In R. Miliband and J. Saville (eds), *The Socialist Register*, New York: Monthly Review Press, pp. 91–119.

Goffman, E. 1959, *The Presentation of Self in Everday Life*. Garden City, NY: Doubleday.

—— 1963, *Behavior in Public Places*. New York: Free Press.

—— 1974, *Frame Analysis*. New York: Harper & Row.

Goldthorpe, J. 1973, A revolution in sociology? *Sociology*, 7(3), pp. 449–62.

Goode, W. J. 1979, *The Celebration of Heros: Prestige as a Social Control System*. Berkeley: University of California Press.

Gouldner, A. 1982, *The Two Marxisms*. New York: Seabury.

Habermas, J. 1971, *Knowledge and Human Interests*. Boston: Beacon Press.

Habermas, J. 1973, *Theory and Practice*. Boston: Beacon Press.
—— 1984, *Reason and the Rationalization of Society. The Theory of Communicative Action*, vol. 1. Boston: Beacon.
—— 1989 [1962], *The Structural Transformation of the Public Sphere*. Cambridge, MA: MIT Press.
Hall, J. 1985, *Powers and Liberties*. Oxford: Blackwell Publishers.
Handel, J. 1979, Normative expectations and the emergence of meaning as solutions to problems: convergence of structural and interactionist views. *American Journal of Sociology*, 84, pp. 855–81.
Hirschman, A. 1977, *The Passions and the Interests*. Princeton, NJ: Princeton University Press.
Holton, G. 1973, *Thematic Origins of Scientific Thought: Kepler to Einstein*. Cambridge. MA: Harvard University Press.
Homans, G. 1958, Social behavior as exchange. *American Journal of Sociology*, 62, pp. 597–606.
—— 1961, *Social Behavior: Its Elementary Forms*. New York: Harcourt, Brace and World.
—— (ed.) 1962, Introduction. In G. Homans, *Sentiments and Activities*. New York: Free Press.
—— 1984, *Coming to My Senses*. New Brunswick, NJ: Transaction.
Hughes, H. S. 1958, *Consciousness and Society*. New York: Random House.
Hunt, L. 1984, *Politics, Culture, and Class in the French Revolution*. Berkeley: University of California Press.
—— 1988, The sacred and the French revolution. In J. C. Alexander (ed.), *Durkheimian Sociology: Cultural Studies*, New York: Cambridge University Press, pp. 25–43.
Kadushin, C. 1978, Cast thy Bread upon the waters . . . Graduate Center, City University of New York. Unpublished manuscript.
Knorr-Cetina, K., and Cicourel, A. (eds) 1981, *Advances in Social Theory and Methodology: Towards and Integration of Micro and Macro Sociology*. London: Routledge & Kegan Paul.
Knorr-Cetina, K., and Mulkay, M. (eds) 1983, *Science Observed: New Perspectives on the Social Study of Science*. Beverly Hills, CA: Sage.
Kreps, G. 1985, Disaster and the social order: definition and taxonomy. *Sociological Theory*, 3, pp. 49–64.
—— 1987, Classical themes, structural sociology, and disaster research. In R. R. Dynes and C. Pellanda (eds), *Sociology of Disasters*. Goprizia, Italy: Franco Angell.
Kuhn, T. 1970, *The Structure of Scientific Revolutions*. Chicago: University of Chicago Press.
Lash, S. 1985, Postmodernity and desire. *Theory and Society*, 14, pp. 1–34.
Lash, S., and Urry, J. 1984, The new Marxism of collective action: a critical analysis. *Sociology*, 18(1), pp. 33–50.

Lewis, J. D., and Smith, R. L.   1980, *American Sociology and Pragmatism: Mead, Chicago Sociology and Symbolic Interactionism.* Chicago: University of Chicago Press.

Lieberson, S.   1980, *A Piece of the Pie.* Berkeley: University of California Press.

Lindenberg, Z.   1983, The new political economy: its potential and limitations for the social sciences in general and sociology in particular. In W. Sedsur (ed.), *Oknonomische Erklarung sozialen Verhalt,* Duisberg, West Germany: Sozial wissen schaftlicke kooperative, pp. 7–66.

Luhmann, N.   1979, *Trust and Power.* New York: John Wiley.

——   1987, The evolutionary differentiation between society and interaction. In J. C. Alexander et al. (eds), *The Micro–Macro Link,* Berkeley: University of California Press, pp. 112–13.

Lyotard, J.-F.   1984, *The Postmodern Condition.* Minneapolis: University of Minnesota Press.

Maines, D.   1977, Social organization and social structure in symbolic interactionist thought. *Annual Review of Sociology,* 3, pp. 235–60.

Mann, M.   1970, The social cohesion of liberal democracy. *American Sociological Review,* 35, pp. 423–39.

——   1979, State and society, 1730–1815: an analysis of English state finances. In M. Zeitlin (ed.), *Political Power and Social Theory,* vol. 1, Greenwich, CT: JAI Press, pp. 165–208.

——   1986, *The Origins of Social Power,* vol. 1: *A History of Power From the Beginning to AD 1760.* London: Cambridge University Press.

Mann, M., and Blackburn, R. M.   1979, *The Working Class in the Labor Market.* London: Macmillan.

Merton, R. K. (ed.)   1967, On the history and systematics of sociology. In R. K. Merton, *Social Theory and Social Structure,* New York: Free Press, pp. 1–38.

Meyer, J. W.   1987, Conceptions of Christendom: notes on the distinctiveness of the West. Paper presented at the Annual Meetings of the American Sociological Association, Chicago, August.

Meyer, J. W., and Scott, J.   1983, *Organizational Environments: Ritual and Rationality.* Beverly Hills, CA: Sage.

Molotch, H., and Boden, D.   1985, Talking social structure: discourse, domination, and the Watergate hearings. *American Sociological Review,* 50, pp. 273–87.

Moore, B.   1966, *The Social Origins of Dictatorship and Democracy.* Boston: Beacon Press.

——   1978, *Injustice: The Social Bases of Obedience and Revolt.* Boston: Beacon Press.

Munch, R.   1981, Talcott Parsons and the Theory of Action, Parts I and II. *American Journal of Sociology,* 86–87, pp. 709–49, 771–826.

O'Connor, J.   1978, *The Fiscal Crisis of the State.* New York: St Martin's.

Offe, C. 1984 [1972], *Contradictions of the Welfare State.* Cambridge, MA: MIT Press.

Parsons, T. 1937, *The Structure of Social Action.* New York: Free Press.

Pinch, T. J., and Collins, H. M. 1984, Private science and public knowledge. *Social Studies in Science,* 14, pp. 521–46.

Poulantzas, N. 1972, *Political Power and Social Classes.* London: New Left Books.

Prager, J. 1986, *Building Democracy in Ireland: Political Order and Cultural Integration in a Newly Independent Nation.* New York: Cambridge University Press.

Rabb, T. K., and Rotberg, R. I. (eds) 1982, *The New History: The 1980's and Beyond.* Princeton, NJ: Princeton University Press.

Rajchman, J. 1985, Philosophy in America. In J. Rajchman and C. West (eds), *Post-Analytic Philosophy,* New York: Columbia University Press, pp. ix–xxvii.

Rex, J. 1961, *Key Problems in Sociological Theory.* London: Routledge & Kegan Paul.

Ritzer, G. 1975, *Sociology: A Multi-Paradigm Science.* Boston: Allen & Bacon.

Rorty, R. 1979, *Philosophy and the Mirror of Nature.* Princeton, NJ: Princeton University Press.

—— 1984, The historiography of philosophy: four genres. In R. Rorty, J. B. Schneewind, and Q. Skinner (eds), *Philosophy in History,* New York: Cambridge University Press, pp. 49–76.

Sacks, H., Schegloff, E. A., and Jefferson, G. 1974, A simplest systematics for the organization of turn-taking for conversation. *Language,* 50, pp. 696–735.

Schegloff, E. 1987, Between macro and micro: contexts and other connections. In J. C. Alexander et al. (eds), *The Micro–Macro Link,* Berkeley: University of California Press, pp. 207–35.

Seidman, S. 1983, Beyond presentism and historicism: understanding the history of social science. *Sociological Inquiry,* 53, pp. 79–94.

Sewell, W. 1980, *Work and Revolution in France.* New York: Cambridge University Press.

—— 1985, Ideologies and social revolutions: reflections on the French case. *Journal of Modern History,* 57, pp. 57–85.

Sica, A. 1986, Hermeneutics and axiology: the ethical content of interpretation. In M. L. Nardell and S. J. Turner (eds), *Sociological Theory in Transition,* Boston: Allen and Unwin, pp. 141–57.

Skocpol, T. 1979, *States and Social Revolutions.* New York: Cambridge University Press.

—— 1982, Rentier state and Shi'a Islam in the Iranian revolution. *Theory and Society,* 11, pp. 265–84.

Skocpol, T.　1985, Cultural idioms and political ideologies in the revolutionary reconstruction of state power: a rejoinder to Sewell. *Journal of Modern History*, 57, pp. 86–96.

Smelser, N.　1959, *Social Change in the Industrial Revolution*. Berkeley: University of California Press.

Smith, D.　1984, Textually mediated social organization. *International Social Science Journal*, 36, pp. 59–75.

Spiegelberg, H.　1971, *The Phenomenological Movement: A Historical Introduction*. The Hague: Martinus Nijhoff.

Stinchcombe, A.　1968, *Constructing Social Theories*. Baltimore, MD: Johns Hopkins University Press.

——　1978, *Theoretical Methods in Social History*. New York: Academic Press.

Strauss, A.　1978, *Negotiations: Contexts, Processes and Social Order*. San Francisco: Jossey-Bass.

Stryker, S.　1980, *Symbolic Interactionism: A Social Structural Version*. Menlo Park, CA: Cummings.

Sztompka, P.　1974, *System and Function*. New York: Academic Press.

——　1984, The global crisis and the reflexiveness of the social system. *International Journal of Comparative Sociology*, 25(1–2), pp. 45–58.

——　1986, The renaissance of historical orientation in sociology. *International Sociology*, 1, pp. 321–37.

——　1993, *The Sociology of Social Change*. Cambridge, MA: Blackwell Publishers.

Taylor, C.　1975, *Hegel*. New York: Oxford University Press.

Thompson, E. P.　1978, The poverty of theory of an orrery of errors. In E. P. Thompson (ed.), *The Poverty of Theory and Other Essays*. New York: Monthly Review Press, pp. 1–210.

Thompson, J. B.　1984, *Studies in the Theory of Ideology*. Berkeley: University of California Press.

——　(ed.)　1986, Editor's Introduction. In C. Leford, *The Political Forms of Modern Society: Bureaucracy, Democracy, Totalitarianism*, Cambridge, MA: MIT Press, pp. 1–27.

Tourraine, A.　1977, *The Self-Production of Society*. Chicago: University of Chicago Press.

Trevor-Roper, H. R.　1965, Religion, the Reformation and social change. *Historical Studies*, 4, pp. 18–45.

Treiman, D.　1977, *Occupational Prestige in Comparative Perspective*. New York: John Wiley.

Turner, J.　1986, Review: the theory of structuration. *American Journal of Sociology*, 91, pp. 969–77.

Turner, S. P.　1987, Underdetermination and the promise of statistical sociology. *Sociological Theory*, 5(2), pp. 172–84.

Turner, V.　1969, *The Ritual Process*. Chicago: Aldine.

Van den Berg, A. 1988, *The Immanent Utopia: From Marxism on the State to the State of Marxism*. Princeton, NJ: Princeton University Press.

Wagner, D. G. 1984, *The Growth of Sociological Theories*. Beverly Hills, CA: Sage.

Wagner, D. G., and Berger, J. 1984, Do sociological theories grow? *American Journal of Sociology*, 90, pp. 697–728.

Walby, S. 1986, *Patriarchy at Work*. London: Macmillan.

Waldell, M. L. and Turner, S. P. (eds) 1986, *Sociological Theory in Transition*. Boston: Allen & Unwin.

Wallace, W. 1983, *Principles of Scientific Sociology*. Chicago: Aldine.

Walzer, M. 1986, Review of Jan Elster, *Making Sense of Marx*. *New York Review of Books* 32, pp. 43–6.

—— 1987, *Interpretation and Social Criticism*. Cambridge, MA: Harvard University Press.

Weber, E. 1976, *Peasants into Frenchmen*. Stanford, CA: Stanford University Press.

Weber, M. 1958 [1904/5], *The Protestant Ethic and the Spirit of Capitalism*. New York: Scribner's.

Wilentz, S. (ed.) 1985, *The Rites of Power*. Philadelphia: University of Pennsylvania Press.

Williams, B. 1985, *Ethics and the Limits of Philosophy*. Cambridge, MA: Harvard University Press.

Wippler, R. and S. Lindenberg. 1987, Collective phenomena and rational choice. In J. C. Alexander et al. (eds), *The Micro–Macro Link*, Berkeley: University of California Press, pp. 135–52.

Wright, E. O. 1978, *Class, Crisis, and the State*. London: New Left Books.

Wuthnow, R. 1987, *Meaning and Moral Order: Explorations in Cultural Analysis*. Berkeley: University of California Press.

Wuthnow, R., Kurzweil, E., Hunter, J., and Bergesen, A. 1984, *Cultural Analysis*. Routledge & Kegan Paul.

Zelizer, V. 1985, *Pricing the Priceless Child*. New York: Basic Books.

Zucker, L. G. (ed.) 1988, Where do institutional patterns come from? Organizations as actors in social systems. In L. G. Zucker (ed.), *Institutional Patterns and Organization: Culture and Environment*, Cambridge, MA: Ballinger, pp. 23–49.

9

After Neofunctionalism:
Action, Culture, and Civil Society

In chapter 1 of this book, I described the transition from an orthodox functionalism to a reconstructed neofunctionalism, and I suggested that the latter had succeeded in establishing itself in the field of contemporary social theory. As the preceding chapters attest, there is now quite a bit of neofunctionalist work, in terms of both discourse and research program, and these have had a growing effect on a fairly wide range of specialities in the sociological field.

Yet, as I also suggested in chapter 1, there is a paradox here. For by virtue of this very success one of the principal rationales for the neofunctionalist movement has disappeared. Parsons is now a "classical" figure. This means that while his ideas may continue to form the basis of traditions, they have also become available for use in more broadly synthetic, eclectic, and opportunistic ways. Inspired by the scope and ambition of Parsons' originating theory, neofunctionalism has been intent on incorporating the ideas of competing traditions and in developing new and more synthetic theoretical modes. While "Parsons" is a crucial resource in this endeavor, his ideas are, in fact, no more important than some of the critical achievements of other classical theorists, nor can they override the genial insights of some contemporaries as well. Perhaps it is only now, after "Parsons" has been rehabilitated, that it has become possible to link his ideas constructively with those in other traditions. That in doing so one moves beyond reconstruction to theory-creation is precisely the point. In my own work, there are three interrelated areas in which this movement beyond neofunctionalism is now taking place.

Action

One of Parsons' major theoretical achievements was to break down the concrete sense of the actor. Instead of describing individuals as taking part in a "society" outside of themselves, Parsons took an analytical view, suggesting that actors and societies were much more, and much less, than the concrete image that meets the eye. They are, in fact, compositions of different levels, of patterned meanings (the cultural system), of psychological needs (the personality system), and of interactional and institutional exigencies (the social system). With this three-system model Parsons early set his focus on what has come to be known as the micro–macro link. Actors, he believed, were not individuals per se, but specifications of broad cultural patterns that entered into role relationships and identities through socialization. Similarly, organizations were very different from the antisubjective "iron cages" of Weberian lore; they were sites where socialized motives and cultural patterns intermingled to form situationally specific norms that allowed functionally necessary roles to be performed in a mutually satisfying way.

This "three-system model" marks, in my view, a permanent contribution to social thought. Parsons was right to break down the concrete actor in this way. This deconstruction provides access to the interpenetration of subjectivity and objectivity, self and society, culture and need. These insights, indeed, remain very much on the agenda of social science today. Contemporary feminism, for example, too often seeks to explain sexism either as the result of patriarchical power, on the one hand, or psychological deformation, on the other, with scarcely any reference to the role of cultural understandings of masculinity and femininity that surely stand in between (cf., the critique by Bloch 1993, and the work by Lara 1998). Macrosociology, whether historical or contemporary in its reference, too often treats political, economic, and even cultural structures simply as networks of power (e.g., Mann), organizations that are constituted neither by meaning nor by motivation but by physical proximity and resource availability (cf., the critique by Eisenstadt 1989). For its part, cultural studies too often either treat culture as a constraint that is somehow "outside" the consciousness of concrete actors or, following Foucault, identify structures of institutional power with structures of cultural knowledge and eliminate the actor as an independent force.[1]

Yet, it is now clear that this deconstruction could not create a fully satisfactory micro–macro link. While Parsons created a credible general model of cultural, social, and psychological interpenetration, he did not produce an account of action as such, that is, of concrete, living, breathing actors making their way through time and space. What Parsons produced was a compelling macrosociological theory of the microfoundations of behavior; in doing so, however, he ignored the order that emerges from interaction as such (Rawls 1987). Parsons produced his three-system model in the late 1940s and early 1950s, before the "micro" revolution in American sociological theory got underway. When it did emerge, in the later 1950s, he did not change his theory as a result.

Micro theorists emphasized that the socialized self was the point where theories of action must begin, not end. Blumer wrote, for example, that actors always take their selves as an object. Goffman pointed out that conformity with values is not only the result of socialization but also a presentational strategy: idealization gains actors trust and space to construct the line of action they need. Garfinkel similarly bracketed the question of whether and how internalized values come to exist; values become operative and important, he believed, because actors take them to be there and know how to exhibit them in practice. Homans, too, considered value as a constant, treating as variable only the conditions of exchange. It is the different resources that individuals bring into the bargaining situation that explain the emergent organization of social life.

Parsons would have none of this. He neither appreciated the deepness of such insights, nor recognized their potentially far-reaching implications. This resistance was particularly damaging because, after the micro revolution, general theories of society simply had to change. The new microtheorizing stimulated the major new developments in macrosociological theory. The later ideas of Collins and Giddens were deeply affected by ethnomethodology and Goffman. Habermas's ideas were transformed by speech act theory and by the incorporation of *Lebenswelt* philosophy. Touraine's understanding of the social movement quality of postindustrial society was stimulated by action theories, Bourdieu's by phenomenology, Coleman's and Elster's by rational choice. It is this kind of crossing over, in fact, that defines the new theoretical movement in sociology.

My own efforts to conceptualize the micro–macro link (e.g., in Alexander et al. 1987) are indebted to these recent developments in general theory. At the same time, I remain deeply dissatisfied with them. They have avoided the negative results of Parsons' deconstructive ambition, but they have not incorporated its accomplishments.[2] In focussing on action they have conceived of the actor only in a concrete way. The challenge for theorizing action in the present time is to go beyond this position: it is to understand the contingency of concrete, empirical interactions between actors who are themselves analytically conceived.

If one examines the articles and books that have articulated the new movement in general sociological theory since the early 1980s, one recognizes a strong tendency to identify actors (persons who act) with agency (human freedom, free will) and agents (whose who exercise free will). I propose to think of this as a confusion of "agency" and "actor."[3] This is a conflation that provided the starting point for the anti-Parsonian microsociologists whose work I have just praised. Considering the polemical stakes, however, one might argue that for these theorists in the second phase of postwar theory the conflation of agency with actors was a necessary and productive error; certainly, it was one that stimulated some of their greatest work. The problem is that this concrete approach has been taken into the third phase; it has been continued by macrosociological theorists who, far from being engaged in a polemic against macro and analytic theorizing, are seeking to establish the micro–macro link.

From neo-Marxism to rational action theory, from reconstructed conflict models to social movement and practice theories, the dangerous legacy of this fertile but fundamentally misguided conflation of actor and agency can be found. On the one side, agency is equated with the heroic masterful actor, whether in an individual (Homans) or a collective (Touraine) form. On the other side, facing this actor, one finds the image of society, the macro-order, as a self-reproducing, "user unfriendly" system, an order that partakes neither of actors nor agency.

This is exactly what is implied, for example, when Giddens (1979, p. 80) asserts that "actors draw upon structural elements." Actors, in other words, are not themselves social structures but agents. In the course of their action, such putatively nonstructural agents make reference to objects, to social structures, that are external to themselves. To be sure, Giddens overtly identifies the latter as "rules" rather than simply resources, that is, as structures that can be subjective and not only material in their ontological form. But Giddens treats rules themselves as objectified and depersonalized, presenting them, for example, merely as "techniques or generalizeable procedures" (1984, p. 21), rather than as projections of subjectively experienced meaning. No wonder that Giddens (1979, p. 80) equates agency with "strategic conduct," that is, with the exercise of free will unconstrained by psychological identity or patterns of meaning.

Most of the other influential general theorists today have a similar problem. Because they assume that both actor and society have only a "concrete" form, they can identify agency – the dimension of action that is independent of external or internal constraint – only with the whole person, with the acting individual as such. Collins, for example, equates the macro, or extraindividual, reference with material, impersonal resources like property, power, and physical space. He understands agency as generated by internal, emotional, and strategic responses to these environments, which are outside the actor as such. Habermas equates political and economic activities with systemsrational organizations that externally impinge upon subjective life-worldly activities, leaving agency to pragmatic speech acts that, despite his references to the developmental cultural logic of Parsons and the psychological logic of Piaget, have no relation to cultural action or psychological need as such.[4] Luhmann's "autopoetic" systems, whether selves or institutions, are either tropes that obscure meaningful action and culturally ordered collectivities, or they are extraordinary reifications that deny such processes altogether. Joas and Honneth (cf., Alexander and Lara 1996) locate creativity in a similar kind of "philosophical anthropology," linking them to inherent qualities of actors rather than to dimensions of culture and social structure that can be vital resources in the construction of the capacities and identities of actors themselves.

I object to these identifications of actor with agency because they are guilty of misplaced concreteness. True, the traditional hierarchy of society and social actors is avoided, along with the microcosm/macrocosm idea in which actors are fit snugly into the social whole. But, rather than replacing or reinterpreting the familiar dichotomy between actors and structures, and allowing the subjective/objective dichotomy to be mediated in a new way, these identifications of actors with agency actually reproduce the dichotomy in another form. Rather than formulating a hierarchy, actors and structures are conceived horizontally, placed side-by-side in a manner that ignores how they interpenetrate with each other and create new, specifically social forms. What results is a mixture rather than a solution, a compromise rather than a reformulation. The notion that structures control actors who simultaneously constitute structures in turn – the incantation first produced by Bourdieu and later taken up by Giddens – describes a serial relationship rather than an interlinkage. Actors and structures are conceived to be empirically rather than analytically distinct. The result is a kind of juggling, keeping the balls of action and structure in the air at the same time. There does not emerge a fundamentally different vision of the relationship of actors and societies.

A more complex position is needed that combines both analytic and concrete perspectives. Actors are not simply agents (those who possess free will), nor are structures necessarily contradictory to the conditions under which actors exercise self-control and autonomy, an accomplishment which is not at all the same as agency or free will. If we define action as the movement of a person through time and space, we can see that, whether antiinstitutional and independent or conformist and dependent, every action contains a dimension of free will, or agency. We can even go further and suggest that agency is what allows actors to move through time and space. But actors per se are much more, and much less, than "agents."

There are many ways to express this distinction. In my own work, I suggest that agency is the moment of freedom which occurs within three structured environments, and that two of these – culture and personality – exist ontologically only within the actor, conceived as a spatially and temporally located person. According to this model, actors certainly have knowledge, but it is an error to say – as Bourdieu and Giddens do, following Garfinkel – that actors are "knowledgeable agents" as such. This is an error because the knowledge that actors have does not come from their agency as such but from the cultural environment which surrounds it and transforms it into identity. That this subjective knowledge is the result of early interactions with others does not mean, moreover, that it can be viewed only as the result of an agent's "practical" experience, of "practice" in the pragmatic sense. Some knowledge does, of course, originate in idiosyncratic learning processes, and all of it certainly is applied, in the concrete context of time and place, in a manner that is specific to the actual individuals involved. Yet it is misleading to identify most of this knowledge as the actor's own. Rather, it is society's knowledge, despite the fact that any particular social reference may or may not be widely shared. Even when it is not widely shared, however, rather than being generalized from a series of particular experiences it has been learned from gestalts that such sequential encounters are seen to present.

Action, then, is the exercise of agency by persons. To both sides of this phrasing attention must be paid. On the one hand, action can occur only in relation to two highly structured internal environments. Action is coded by cultural systems and motivated by personalities. On the other hand, personalities and cultural codes do not exhaust the contents of a person's subjectivity. There remains the extremely significant dimension of agency. Philosophers may understand agency, or free will, as an existential category; for sociologists it can be conceived as process, one that involves invention, typification, and strategization. These processes give pragmatic shape to the exercise of free will. They engage the structured, internal environments of action and move them through time and space. It is not only agency as articulated by these three primordial processes, then, but the agentic articulations of these internal environments that comprise "the actor."

This position can tell us something important about "social structures" as well. If actors are not only agents in the traditional sense, then structures are not only – not essentially, not even primarily – constraining forces which confront actors from without. Culture and personality are themselves social structures, forces that confront agency from within and become part of action in a "voluntary" way. Structures can be described as existing outside of actors only if we focus on a third environment for agency, the social system. I refer here to the economic, political, solidaristic, and ecological relations and networks formed by persons in the course of their interactions in time and space. Yet, because they are formed from concrete, empirical interactions – because they are, in fact, only aggregates of earlier actions themselves – it is impossible to conceive even of these "social system" components as things which exist independently of the patterned internal environments of the human beings who activate them.[5] All of which is to say that the internal and external environments of action must be conceived in an analytical way, even as the contingency of empirical interactions can only be understood in its concrete form.

Culture

These reformulations of action theory lead to a much greater emphasis on action's cultural environment, which must be conceived as an organized structure internal to the actor in a concrete sense. Among the general theorists in the new theoretical movement, however, there is virtually no recognition of culture as a structure analytically separated from agency. In his structuration theory, Giddens speaks of rules and procedures but he never investigates the textured patterns of symbolic life. In his communicative theory of justice, Habermas acknowledges culture only as it has been "linguistified" into a universalistic morality whose presuppositions can be discussed in a rational and conscious way. In his microtranslations of macrosociology, Collins understands meaning primarily as sedimentation from the emotion of interaction rituals. In Bourdieu's theory of practice, he does see culture as a structure, but his reductionist equation of culture with institutional structure means that culture has the effect of denying agency rather than illuminating it (cf. Alexander 1995).

This failure on the part of general theorists to consider culture as a structure internal to action is not entirely surprising; it reflects, after all, the same kind of concrete and empiricist approach to action that I described above. However, even specialists in cultural sociology – those upon whom general theorists writing about culture might be expected to rely – tend to treat culture in much the same concrete way. From the Birmingham school to the efforts of cultural sociologists like Archer and Swidler, action is understood as a process that often, or even typically, positions itself over and against "culture," standing outside patterned symbolic codes.[6] Cultural theorists, in other words, often make the same kind of mistake as does general theory itself. Equating action with creative, reflexive, or rebellious agency, they identify culture with patterns that exist only outside of the actors themselves.

In this context it becomes very clear that there is more involved here than theoretical issues alone. This shearing of culture from agency also reflects an ideological sensibility, one that is widely shared by general theorists and cultural specialists alike. For their approach to agency is not only conflationary but celebratory and even heroic. According to one tradition (exchange theory), actors are rational, autonomous, self-sufficient, wily, and clever. According to another (ethnomethodology), they are knowledgeable, reflexive, self-monitoring, and competent. In the rhetoric of a third approach (symbolic interactionism), actors are endlessly creative, expressive, and meaning-making. These descriptive terms have a certain validity if they are taken as characterizations of the analytical properties of agency; the capacity for freedom, after all, is at the core of the democratic traditions of Western life. These qualities must be questioned, however, if they are taken to be descriptions of concrete actions, that is, of the properties of actors. Yet this is exactly what usually is implied.

If we do not conflate actors with agents, we are forced to recognize that actors are not nearly so heroic as these accounts suggest. They are often befuddled, passive, self-deceptive, thoughtless, and vicious. How can this be so, if agency itself can be described in a positive way? The answer is that agency expresses itself only through its cultural and psychological environments, and these latter forces structure agency in what are sometimes extraordinarily harmful ways. By

ignoring or underplaying the negative elements of action, then, strong
theories of agency sometimes seem less like dispassionate efforts to
describe action than efforts to mobilize moral evaluations about it.
Touraine's "action theory" is a case in point. Against deterministic and
structural theorizing, Touraine has rightly emphasized the importance of voluntaristic self-starting and free will in structuring macrosociological life. Yet, on the basis of this analytic emphasis, he argues
– empirically – for the positive, historically progressive role of social
movements in postindustrial society, an elision that ignores some of
the most typical and dangerous "action" movements in the twentieth
century (cf. Alexander 1996).

Rather than theoretical generalizations about reflexivity, contemporary approaches to action – in general theory and cultural theory
alike – seem more like reformulations of the moral and political
tradition of natural rights. Instead of theorizing the relation between
action and its internal environments, they have produced uplifting
and hopeful elaborations of the normative discourse that underpins
democracy itself. But we should become conscious of this discourse,
not reproduce it. The first step is to recognize that it is a discourse;
we must deconstruct it as an ideology regulating action rather than
rationalize it as an explanation of action. Then we will see that good-
ness cannot be inherently associated with action; it can be attributed
to action only because of the particular kinds of social, psychological,
and cultural environments withn which agency is expressed.

Insofar as we acknowledge the internal environments of concrete
action, then, we will understand that action must be seen as a constant process of exercising agency through, not against, culture. That
means that typification – the agentic process that reproduces social
narratives and codes – is a continuous dimension of every action, not
"instead of" but "alongside of" the dimensions of creativity and invention.[7] Agency is inherently related to culture, not a process that stands
outside it. Because agency is "free," action is never simply mimetic;
it never simply reproduces internalized symbolic environments.
Action involves a process of externalization, or re-presentation: agency
is inherently connected to representational and symbolic capacity.
Because actors have agency, they can exercise their representational
capacities, re-presenting their external environments through externalization. This does not contradict the structural status of culture,
any more than Lévi-Strauss's "bricoleur" negated the power of myth
or Durkheim's insistence on the "religious imagination" eliminated
ritual.

Yet, if Parsons' three-system division allows us to understand culture as a relatively autonomous structure that informs social action and organization, it does not describe culture as an internal environment of action when the latter is understood in a concrete sense. Parsons fails to connect culture with the concrete actor because, in his approach to meaning, he fails to recognize that cultural analysts must construct "values" from the actual discourse – the speech acts – of socially situated actors. Values as such do not inform, inspire, or regulate concrete action; they are analytic (re)constructions by analysts themselves, (re)constructions that are generated precisely by abstracting away from the actual forms of representation in which evaluations are made. This allows us to understand why Parsons provides a remarkably thin theory of the internal structuring of symbolic process, despite his strenuous insistence on culture's important role.

The problem occurs because Parsons ignored a second intellectual revolution that has fundamentally altered the social sciences in our time. Since the early 1970s there has been a sea change in ideas about culture's role in society, a shift that is sometimes called – certainly inadequately – the linguistic or the discursive "turn." In the context of American debates, this turn is reflected in the series of fundamental challenges that Clifford Geertz issued to Parsons (and Marx), when he insisted, for example, that literary tropes should take precedence over functional demands in explanations of ideology (Geertz 1964) and that thick descriptions of meaning must take precedence over inductions about values and methods devoted to causal explanation (Geertz 1973). In France and England, the linguistic turn was reflected in the growing impact of semiotics and structuralism, approaches that worked with ordinary speech and routine, publically available texts, reconstructing from them intricately ordered symbolic codes and narratives that seemed able to explain the detailed texture of meaningful social life. These movements stimulated, in turn, the creation of a new symbolic anthropology in the writings of people such as Victor Turner, Mary Douglas, and Geertz himself. Eventually there emerged the enormously influential poststructuralism of Michel Foucault, which so powerfully proclaimed the social power of highly structured fields of cultural discourse. In Germany, hermeneutic philosophy also revived, with its claims that the understanding of social action must refer to the actor's experience of meaning and that such meaningful action can and must, as Ricoeur (1971) once put it, be interpreted as a text.

Because Parsons formed his initial understanding of culture before these developments emerged, there is certainly a biographical explanation for his failure to recognize their importance. At the same time, it is possible to see that from the beginning of his intellectual maturity Parsons was not at all sympathetic to strongly culturalist claims. One sees this, for example, in his early response (Parsons 1937) to the religious turn that Durkheim made in *The Elementary Forms*. While hailing Durkheim for recognizing the symbolic, Parsons criticized his program of "religious sociology" as idealism. Rather than seeing it as referring to the internal structure of symbols or to the continuing intensity of symbolic experience, Parsons reduced Durkheim's "sacred" to Weber's "charisma," i.e., to an episodic response to social crisis and strain, and he described Durkheim's understanding of ritual in a similar way.[8]

Rather than following Durkheim's suggestions for a broad focus on symbolic patterns, Parsons chose to focus on "values," which he defined as the subset of symbols refracted by functional needs and institutionalized in specific roles. In fact, however, as I have suggested above, Parsons gained access to values not so much through the interpretive analysis of actors' meanings or discourses but by generalizing from patterns of actual behavior in the social world. This is precisely what Durkheim was trying to get away from in his later writings. Durkheim was intent on creating a very different kind of sociology, one that would never confuse the analysis of social functions with the patterned understandings of actors themselves. Rather than the weak cultural theory of values that Parsons recommended – which allowed him so neatly to differentiate sociology from anthropology – the late Durkheimian position implies a strong theory that argues against such a disciplinary separation and, in the process, against any radical disjunction between "traditional" and "modern" societies as well.

Such a strong program for cultural sociology – one inspired by the later Durkheim (Alexander 1990, Alexander et al. 1993, cf. Emirbayer 1996) – allows us to explore further one of the most important implications of the approach to action and its environments I have recommended above. It allows us to link action more closely to meaning as actors themselves experience it and to the cultural forms that, in structuring meaning, give it more independence from institutional pressures and system exigencies than Parsons' value theory ever could allow. Actors are, in fact, deeply and continuously engaged in what Garfinkel called "indexicality." Yet, in converting the contingent into the expected – by employing patterns of understanding that already exist – they are not merely publically affirming a conformity with the values that effectively regulate social relationships. They are not, that is, merely engaging in "idealization" as Goffman understood it.

Actors typify not only vis-à-vis structures of meaning that are institutionalized, i.e., organized, sanctioned, and rewarded by or on behalf of the social system. At several points (e.g., Parsons and Shils 1951), it is true, Parsons did speak of the "pattern" integration of culture as straining against systemic or functional integration, and of the possibility of "cultural strain" that results. Most of the time, however, he understood strains as emerging from within the social system rather than culture. While his "theorem of perfect institutionalization" was conceived as an ideal typical model rather than an actual description of a frictionless social life, the concept clearly indicates that Parsons gave priority to social system over culture, to the institutional mechanisms which select from cultural patterns, to culture primarily as a mechanism for institutional regulation and control. He paid precious little attention to the internal codes and narratives of culture itself. Culture must be understood as socially relevant not in spite of, but because of its broadly coded and narrative form. It produces a "surplus of meaning" (Ricoeur 1977) in every action and institution, a surplus that creates tension and distance with every institutionalized and concrete act.[9]

Civil Society

This new thinking about action and culture has certain implications for analyzing social systems and their parts. Rather than trying to trace these implications in a general way throughout the various institutional domains, I will concentrate here on the civil sphere, the world of "civil society" that has become perhaps the most widely discussed social phenomenon in recent years (e.g., Cohen and Arato 1992, Calhoun 1992).

If one looks at the microtheories of the second wave of postwar theorizing from a macrosociological point of view, one can see that these descriptions of the concrete forms of interaction suggest an informal social order, one that is not dominated by large-scale, coercive structures but constructed through various forms of communication and reciprocity. Rational choice theorists emphasized competition in a manner that suggested equilibrium could be reached despite inequalities of power. Blumer (cf. Sciulli 1988) suggested that actors succeed in constructing coherent lines of conduct linking self and other. Goffman described actors' herculean efforts to present themselves as behaving decorously, despite his frequent emphasis on their hidden motives for domination and success, and he described the various forms of deference and impersonal yet constraining forms of solidarity upon which behavior in public depends and produces in turn. Garfinkel put interpersonal trust at the center of understanding, explaining that actors must postulate the existence of consensual rules and shared values even without any hard evidence that they actually exist. This postulate, and the forms of interaction it induces, enhances the likelihood that such informal trusting mechanisms actually will emerge.

However, when the innovators of the third phase of postwar theorizing – the new theoretical movement in sociology – incorporated the insights of microtheory, they paid almost no attention to this vision of an informally regulated, "civil" society that underlay its work. They incorporated its descriptive models of how concrete actors make reference to one another and to themselves, and built upon these "mechanisms" to develop macrosociological theories that emphasized communication, typification, self-reference, exchange, and the necessity for continuious action through space and time. But they ignored the larger sense of society that such processes had implied, which pointed to the authenticity of the moral order and to its resiliency as a resource for informal modes of social control. In Bourdieu's work, for example, habitually regulated life is manipulated by class and field domination and converted into strategic interactions through which actors seek to maximize capitals of various kinds. Habermas uses speech act theory and *lebenswelt* models of shared experience and interaction largely to construct normative alternatives to contemporary societies, not to describe processes within them; within the contemporary world, indeed, Habermas insists on the pulverization of informal relationships and trust by the "colonizing" systems of politics and money.[10] Giddens describes a late modern world in which risk and danger are paramount, in which the self is continuously threatened with extinction, in which trust has almost completely broken down. Collins' world is one of competition and conflict, where emotion and morality are exchanged through rituals that tend to reinforce hierarchies of money, prestige, and social power.

What these intellectuals in the new theoretical movement have done is to synthesize microsociological models of interaction with the conflict-oriented structuralism that formed the other side of theorizing in the second period of postwar work. Because they draw their map of the macro order from the materialist threads of Weberian and neo-Marxist theory, they employ a cartography of large processes that fails to explore the worlds of self, motivated choice, trust, normativity, and informal mechanisms of social control. It was this failure that Alvin Gouldner sharply criticized toward the end of his life. In *The Coming Crisis*, his radical denunciation of micro and macro forms of American sociology, Gouldner (1970) had himself emphasized coercive institutional power and class manipulation. After struggling with the deterministic and authoritarian tendencies that emerged in macrosociology over the next decade, however, Gouldner evidently began to change his mind. In the afterword to *The Two Marxisms*, he (1980) praised the subjective and local emphases of traditionally American forms of microsociology, arguing that they pointed to an understanding of a civil society outside the market and the state that structural theories ignored, not only to their scientific disadvantage but to their moral peril. Gouldner (1979) even gave a passing nod to the moral and normative macrosociological emphasis of Parsons himself, in the eulogy after Parsons' death that barely preceded his own.

For it was, in fact, exactly this kind of emphasis that had informed Parsons' theory of the macro order. Precisely because of the analytic nature of his theorizing, Parsons never lost sight of the manner in which larger structural processes were embedded in subjective expectations and informal, cultural forms of social control. With his three-system model, Parsons could argue that normative references and the subjective, responsible self were "always there"; with his theory of institutionalization, he could point to the existence of values that generated trust and respect within organizations; with his emphasis on normative and voluntary order, he could highlight the consensual and reciprocal elements in contemporary social life. In the last 15 years of Parsons' career, these general orientations ideas took their most interesting macrosociological form. Building upon Weber's understanding of legally regulated, universalistic communites, Durkheim's vision of organic solidarity, T. H. Marshall's model of citizenship, and most importantly perhaps his own sense and sympathy for the voluntaristic bases of American democracy, Parsons began to theorize about an intermediate realm of subjectivity he called the societal community. The latter, arguably, represented the most important contribution to macrosociology that Parsons ever made. It adds a fourth "sphere" to the traditionally two or three part divisions of

other macro models, pointing to a world that possesses the subjectivity of the lifeworld but, at the same time, the abstraction of more highly
rationalized systemic spheres. At once a sphere of individual recognition and a world of integration, the societal community provides
the sense of "peoplehold" that Parsons insisted was an important
component of citizenship. On this basis, he identified "inclusion" as
the fundamental, secular tendency of the contemporary world.

Yet this concept of societal community emerged only in Parsons'
later period, when his sensitivity to strain and contradiction, and the
critical character of his liberalism, had all but disappeared; when the
endemic tendencies of his theorizing to exagerate stability and integration were at their most pronounced; and when his substantive sociological ideas were coming more and more to be expressed in formalistic
terms. These tendencies, particularly in the face of the radical conflicts over normativity and power that emerged during the period,
had the effect of virtually burying the significance of this Parsonsian
notion of societal community. For microtheorists, the voluntaristic
character of the larger society was an implication they never thought
to connect with an emphasis in Parsons' work, and Parsons himself
never suggested any links between his own concept of societal community and their more actor-centered views. For the macrotheorists
of that second phase, Parsons' emphasis on this sphere was rejected
out of hand. In light of these earlier dynamics, it is not surprising
that recognition of the vitality of an intermediate sphere of subjectivity and morality plays so little role in the synthetic theorizing that
followed in the third phase.

In the last decade, however, the need for just this kind of thinking
about an intermediate sphere has seemed particularly urgent. New
kinds of self-regulating social movements emerged in the struggle
against authoritarian regimes, fighting successful revolutions not for
socialism but for democracy, solidarity, and the independence of the
private world of individual rights. These political practices revived
the eighteenth century concept of civil society, first among the activists
themselves, later among political philosophers and social scientists.
Concerns with a sociological approach to publicness, trust, solidarity,
and responsibility began to assume center stage.

I am not the first theorist (see Cohen and Arato 1992 and Mayhew
1990) to observe that Parsons' earlier approach to societal community helps clarify this newly emerging concept of civil society, which
remains confused and even mysterious despite the enormous debate
that has mushroomed in the 1990s. With this concept, Parsons tried to

explain how a sphere of solidarity can, in fact, be differentiated from both market and state as well as from more specifically ideational and emotional spheres like religion, science, and the family. I have been fundamentally influenced by Parsons' general orientation to these problems in the work on civil society in which I am currently engaged (e.g., Alexander 1991, 1992c, 1996, 1997a, 1997b, Alexander and Smith 1993). At the same time, there are serious problems in Parsons' understanding of the societal community, problems that neofunctionalism has long pointed to but which it is now possible, and necessary, to explore in a more critical and systematic way. These problems begin with the weaknesses I have identified in Parsons' cultural theory. These are related, in turn, to Parsons' underemphasis on the strains between societal community and the other social spheres, and to his failure to understand the importance of the interactional level of civil society, much less its psychology, in their concrete forms.

The very possibility of institutionalizing a societal community depends upon the valuing of universalism. For Parsons, this means choosing the universalistic rather than particularist side of the pattern-variable dichotomy that regulates role relationships; this is the specifically "cultural" dimension at stake. Institutionalizing universalism in this way also implies that normative control of power and interest is established through patterns of legal control. These cultural choices and new modes of control are possible, Parsons believes, because there has emerged in most modern societies a very high degree of value generalization: the growing abstraction of Durkheim's collective conscience, the movement away from the detailed symbolic structuring of individual and group activities toward rules that create generalized guidelines for highly different kinds of concrete acts. In the legal order of the societal community this suggests an increasing role for procedural norms. Particular identities and the contents of various claims are not considered as such; rather, organizations and authorities are mandated to consider all actors and claims in exactly the same way, no matter what their particular point of view.

Parsons' confidence in the possibility of this kind of institutionalization of universal forms of life was reinforced by his insight into how the spread of mass education affected socialization.[11] Parsons described the "educational revolution" as a kind of practical Enlightenment. This understanding, however, had the unintended effect of legitimating Parsons' anti-"linguistic" view of meaning in the modern era, for it suggested that the mythical and arbitrary elements in the symbolic motivations of adults were in the process of disappearing. As Parsons' saw it, the pre-adult timing of primary socialization ensured that modern citizenship values would have an a priori status; at the same time, the increasing length of the educational period of socialization has put into place a developmental process that increasingly decenters cognition, emotion, and morality, allowing them to become more "rational." Such highly educated and reflexive actors, according to Parsons, form the universalistic basis for the contemporary expansion of tolerance and inclusion. Controlling aggressive psychological impulses and regulating conflictual interaction, the increasingly transparent norms of educated persons ensure that contemporary institutions will respond not in closed but in open ways. Exclusion will become a relic of early stages in social development. Ascription and particularism, with their antimodern implications, are becoming things of the past.

If, however, socially relevant patterns of culture cannot be considered merely, or even primarily, as "values" that are specified and selected according to specialized exigencies and systemic needs, then the culture of civil society simply cannot be abstracted and generalized in the way Parsons believed. Certainly one can say that more universalizing cultural references gradually have emerged, but this universalism is expressed as much, if not more, by new code and narrative configurations – what I have called the "discourse of civil society" – than by the omnipresence of abstract rules. The internal symbolic structure of these patterns, moreover, makes it impossible to conceive of universalism as if it meant simply the putting into place of norms of fairness or procedural legal rules. In fact, the discourse of civil society can never be institutionalized as such, and it is for this very reason that it provides such a reflexive, often liberating mirror for the restrictions and abuses of civil and noncivil society.[12]

It is not only the transcendental and free-floating nature of universalism that creates new tensions, however, but the binary nature of symbolic classification itself. Universalism is not a choice that can exclude particularism from social life; it is a coded definition of categories of motives, relations, and institutions which take their meaning only in relation to what are conceived to be their opposites, that is, in relation to categories of "excluded" and "particularistic." The sacralized symbolic categories that construct universalism, in other words, can be defined only by publically contrasting them with the profane motives, relations, and institutions that characterize other kinds of individuals, institutions, and groups. It is for this reason that the excluded "other" always stands side-by-side with those who are included in the civil sphere. Educationally generated reflexivity can never stand entirely outside these arbitrary elements in understanding; they are inherent in the very process of meaning-making itself.

If such a "strong" cultural theory can highlight the tensions in civil society that escaped Parsons' more abstracted and denatured approach to reason, a more concrete approach to subsystems, to interaction, and to psychological motivation allows our understanding to be deepened in similar ways. The most debilitating problem in Parsons' approach to the relation between institutional subsystems was his identification of empirical, concrete differentiation with the analytical separations of his conceptual ("AGIL") scheme. Parsons believed not only that interchange between subsystems was necessary because they had become gradually differentiated and separated from one another, but that in modern societies these interchanges would tend to be symmetrical, reciprocal, and mutually fulfilling. Just as the societal community would be facilitated by the emergence of more universalistic culture, it would be supported by industrialization and the market economy, by cross-cutting ethnic obligations, by political federalism, by religious denominationalism, and by gendered role divisions in family life.

This confidence in institutional reciprocity derives, at least in part, from Parsons' insistence on institutionalization in his approach to culture, for it suggests that universalism typically will play a regulating role. Yet, just as the discourse of civil society is at once utopian and destabilizing, promoting demands for inclusion even while identifying those who "should be" excluded, so do the boundary relations of civil society operate in a paradoxical way. Certainly civil society receives facilitating inputs from institutions outside of it, but it is subject to destructive intrusions at the same time. The divisive classes generated by economic life, the oligarchies generated by political and organizational power, the gender and age hierarchies of families, the demonology frequently legitimated by religious institutions, and the ethnic, regional, and racial dominations so often generated by the very construction of national civil states – such intrusions fragment and split civil society even while its very existence promises participation and restoration of the social whole (see Alexander 1997b).

A more concrete, empirical approach to action contributes further to this process of creating a new theory of civil society. It points, for example, to the importance of face-to-face interaction. Not only do such Goffmanian ideas as "civil inattention" and "face work" become crucial elements of the democratic social fabric, but phenomena such

as "turn-taking," highlighted in ethnomethodological studies of conversation, come to be seen in a more historical and macrosociological
light. Simmel's understanding of exchange and conflict as forms of
integration, Mead's understanding of how the generalized other allows
spontaneous cooperation, and Boudon's insistence that actors seem
always compelled to offer "good reasons" can now be understood as
important descriptions of the distinctively interactional level of a civil
order. Such a concrete approach to agency also points to the role that
social movements play in allowing the contours of civil society to be
constructed and reconstructed in response to the tensions generated
by the discursive strains, institutional conflicts, and the psychological
and interactional dynamics of everyday life.

I have argued here both for the fundamental importance of Parsons'
analytic approach to synthetic social theory and, at the same time,
for the urgent necessity of going beyond it. Two revolutions have transformed contemporary social theory since the 1960s, neither of which
penetrated Parsons' most basic understandings. Microsociological theories explored the concrete nature of action and interaction; culturalist
theories opened up the model of culture-as-language and allowed a
more concrete focus on the actual patterning of discourse in texts
and speech. The analytic emphasis of Parsons' three-system model
calls for critical revisions in these approaches, but they, in turn,
demand a fundamental rethinking of his. I have explored some of the
institutional ramifications of these new ways of thinking in my discussion of civil society, which also suggests that institutional subsystems
most be understood in a much less equilibrating way.

These brief discussions can perhaps be seen as a prolegomena for
a new form of synthetic social theory. Hegel believed that in order
to truly surpass something one must include it in some new form.
I am pointing to a new wave of theory creation that goes beyond
the important achievements of neofunctionalism. If it eventually
succeeds in doing so, a principal reason will be that it has come after
neofunctionalism, not before.

Notes

1 Pierre Bourdieu manages to accomplish all three of these reductionist
   moves at the same (cf. Alexander 1995).
2 In his own recent effort to rethink the micro–macro link – which
   he describes as "the articulation between institutional and figurational
   structures" – Mouzelis (1995, p. 7) makes a roughly similar complaint.
   Arguing that "we must relate what is happening in theoretical sociology

today to the Parsonian 'constitutive' contribution," he suggests that "one can maintain that most current tendencies fail to appropriate creatively what is positive and useful in Parsons' oeuvre."

3 I draw here upon Alexander 1992a and Alexander 1993, which themselves develop ideas from Alexander 1987.

4 It is in response not only to increasingly powerful criticisms from feminist, communitarian, and Hegelian philosophers, and to developments in the work of his own followers, like Benhabib and Honneth, but in response to his long encounter with the cultural writings of Parsons and Weber that Habermas has come to acknowledge, in his most recent writings, that actors entering into Kant's "moral" sphere – Habermas's rationalized lifeworld of the public – can do so only on the basis of needs and identities formed in the "ethical," particularist world Hegel called the *Sittlichkeit*. As he remarks in his response to a critical collection responding to the English publication of his early work on the public sphere, "I think that I have in the meantime also changed my own framework so that the permanent autonomy of cultural developments is taken more accurrently into account" (Habermas 1992b, p. 464). In articulating this new approach, Habermas makes precisely the cultural argument for an analytic understanding of action I am calling for here.

> The social integrative power of communicative action is first of all located in those particularized forms of life and lifeworlds that are intertwined with concrete traditions and interest constellations in the "ethical" sphere (*Sittlichkeit*), to use Hegel's terms. . . . A public sphere that functions politically requires more than the institutional guarantees of the constitutional state; it also needs the supportive spirit of cultural traditions and patterns of socialization, of the political culture, of a populace accustomed to freedom.
>
> (Ibid., pp. 444, 453)

This acknowledgment of the internal environments of publically oriented action would entail a far-reaching reconstruction of Habermas's discourse–ethics approach to the nature of collective order in democratic societies. It points to the necessity of going beyond abstracted universalism and procedural minimalism to some substantive understanding of how the universalism can be grounded in thick cultural traditions. I discuss this in my discussion of civil society below.

5 For an insightful statement of this position, specifically in regard to the relationship between network theory and cultural sociology, see Emirbayer and Goodwin (1994). See also the forceful earlier argument of Kane (1990).

6 For criticism of the Birmingham School from this point of view, see Sherwood et al. (1993); for a discussion of the work of Archer and Swidler, as well as Robert Wuthnow, from this point of view, see also Rambo and Chan (1990).

7 In his laudable effort to insert creativity into the core of action theory, Joas (1996) fails to conceptualize typification as a simultaneous dimension of action, one that unfolds alongside of invention and strategization.

8 Parsons' (1968) later critical response to Geertz's essay, "Religion as a Cultural System," is similarly revealing in this regard.

9 This is precisely Eisenstadt's point, of course, in his insistence on the centrality of strain and tension in axial age civilizations (cf. Alexander 1992b). It is because of this recognition of surplus meaning that Eisenstadt turns institutionalization theory on its head, suggesting that institutionalization actually produces tensions rather than resolving them. For a similar insistence on the manner in which cultural norms allow an experience of transcendence that facilitates antiinstitutional action, see Dubet (1994).

10 This problem is only partially mitigated in Habermas's (1996) most recent work on law. While notably conceptualizing law as, indeed, an institutionalized moral sphere partially independent of economy and state, this work still fails to grapple sufficiently with the non-formal, symbolic discourses of the civil sphere, the existence of which Habermas has gestured to in the writings I discussed in note 5.

11 See Turner's (1993) probing essay, which places Parsons' theory of the educational revolution into contemporary debates about social change.

12 In this regard, I would take issue with the anticultural thrust of David Sciulli's (1992) theory of societal constitution, which in other respects represents a high water mark of neofunctionalist work. Sciulli believes that the independent power of a civil sphere – which he links particularly to the institutional autonomy of the legal domain – is compromised if actors are described as linking social justice and equality to particular kinds of cultural ideals. Justice can only have a formal, procedural base. In my view, by contrast, institutional processes will always remain linked with, though not of course reducible to, particular kinds of symbolic codes and narratives. Thus, whereas Sciulli criticizes Parsons for dwelling in the 1950s on socialization, values, and family psychological dynamics, I would criticise him for not pursuing these interests thoroughly enough. This anticultural notion that fairness and inclusion can only proceed on procedural grounds results in part from Sciulli's encounter with Habermas, whose work on discourse ethics and legal proceduralism has provided the most sustained exemplar for such a position. It is a position that also negatively affects the theory of civil society offered by Cohen and Arato (cf. Alexander 1994).

References

Alexander, J. C. 1987, Action and its environments. In J. C. Alexander, et al. (eds), *The Micro–Macro Link*. Berkeley and Los Angeles: University of California Press, pp. 289–318.

—— 1990, Introduction: understanding the "Relative Autonomy of Culture." In J. C. Alexander and S. Seidman (eds), *Culture and Society: Contemporary Debates*. Cambridge: Cambridge University Press, pp. 15–39.

—— 1991, Bringing democracy back in: universalistic solidarity and the civil sphere. In C. Lemert (ed.), *Intellectuals and Politics: Social Theory in a Changing World*, Beverly Hills: Sage, pp. 157–76.

—— 1992a, Recent sociological theory between agency and social structure. *Revue suisse de sociologie*, 18 (1), pp. 7–11.

—— 1992b, The fragility of progress: an interpretation of the turn toward meaning in Eisenstadt's later work. *Acta Sociologica*, 35, pp. 85–94.

—— 1992c, Citizen and enemy as symbolic classification: on the polarizing discourse of civil society. In M. Fournier and M. Lamont (eds), *Where Culture Talks: Exclusion and the Making of Society*. Chicago: University of Chicago Press, pp. 289–308.

—— 1993, More notes on the problem of agency: a reply. *Revue suisse de sociologie*, 19, pp. 501–6.

—— 1994, The return of civil society. *Contemporary Sociology*, 27, pp. 797–803.

—— 1995, The reality of reduction: the failed synthesis of Pierre Bourdieu. In J. C. Alexander, *Fin-de-Siècle Social Theory*. London: Verso, pp. 128–217.

—— 1996, Collective action, culture and civil society: secularizing, updating, inverting, revising and displacing the classical model of social movements. In M. Diani and J. Clarke (eds), *Alain Touraine*, London: Falmer Press, pp. 205–34.

—— 1997a, The paradoxes of civil society. *International Sociology*, 12 (1), pp. 115–33.

—— 1997b, in J. C. Alexander (ed.), *Real Civil Societies: Dilemmas of Institutionalization*. London: Sage.

Alexander, J. C., Giesen, B., Munch, R., and Smelser, N. (eds) 1987, *The Micro–Macro Link*. Berkeley and Los Angeles: University of California Press.

Alexander, J. C., and Lara, M. P. 1996, Honneth's new critical theory of recognition. *New Left Review*, 220, pp. 126–36.

Alexander, J. C., and Smith, P. 1993, The discourse of American civil society: a new proposal for cultural studies. *Theory and Society*, 22, pp. 151–207.

Alexander, J. C., Sherwood, S. J., and Smith, P. 1993, Risking enchantment: theory and methodology in cultural analysis. *Culture*, 8 (1), pp. 10–14.

Bloch, R. 1993, A culturalist critique of trends in feminist theory. *Contention*, 2, pp. 79–106.

Calhoun, C. C. (ed.) 1992, *Habermas and the Public Sphere*. Cambridge, MA: Harvard University Press.

Cohen, J., and Arato, A. 1992, *Civil Society and Political Theory*. Boston: MIT Press.

Dubet, F. 1994, *Sociologie de l'expérience*. Paris: Seuil.

Eisenstadt, S. N. 1989, Macrosociology and sociological theory: some new dimensions. *Contemporary Sociology*, 16, pp. 602–9.

Emirbayer, M. 1996, Useful Durkheim. *Sociological Theory*, 14 (2), pp. 109–30.

Emirbayer, M., and Goodwin, J. 1994, Network analysis, culture, and the problem of agency. *American Journal of Sociology*, 99 (6), pp. 1411–54.

Geertz, C. 1964, Ideology as a cultural system. In D. Apter (ed.), *Ideology and Discontent*, New York: Free Press, pp. 47–76.

—— 1973, Thick Description, in C. Geertz, *The Interpretation of Culture*, New York: Basic Books, pp. 3–30.

Giddens, A. 1979, *Central Problems in Social Theory*. Berkeley and Los Angeles: University of California Press.

—— 1984, *The Constitution of Societies*. London: Polity.

Gouldner, A. J. 1970, *The Coming Crisis of Western Sociology*. New York: Equinox.

—— 1979, Talcott Parsons. *Theory and Society*, 8, pp. 299–301.

—— 1980, *The Two Marxisms*. New York: Seabury.

Habermas, J. 1992a, Further reflections on the public sphere. In C. Calhoun (ed.), *Habermas and the Public Sphere*, Cambridge, MA: MIT Press, pp. 421–61.

—— 1992b, Concluding remarks. In C. Calhoun (ed.), *Habermas and the Public Sphere*, Cambridge, MA: MIT Press, pp. 462–79.

—— 1996, *Between Facts and Norms: Contributions to a Discourse Theory of Law and Democracy*. Cambridge: Polity Press.

Joas H. 1996, *The Creativity of Action*. London: Polity.

Kane, A. 1990, Cultural analysis in historical sociology: the analytic and concrete forms of the autonomy of culture. *Sociological Theory*, 9 (1), pp. 53–69.

Lara, M. P. 1998, *Moral Textures: Feminist Narratives as an Illocutionary Force in the Public Sphere*. Cambridge: Polity Press.

Mayhew, L. 1990, The differentiation of the solidary public. In J. Alexander and P. Colomy (eds), *Differentiation Theory and Social Change*, New York: Columbia University Press, pp. 294–322.

Mouzelis, N. 1995, *Sociological Theory: What Went Wrong? Diagnoses and Remedies*. London: Routledge.

Parsons, T. 1937, *The Structure of Social Action*. New York: Free Press.

—— 1968, Commentary on "Religion as a Cultural System." In D. R. Cutler (ed.), *The Religious Situation: 1968*. Boston: Beacon Press, pp. 688–94.

Parsons, T., and Shils, E. A. 1951, Values, motives, and systems of action. In T. Parsons and E. A. Shils (eds), *Towards a General Theory of Action*, New York: Harper and Row, pp. 47–275.

Rambo, E. and Chan, E. 1990, Text, structure, and action in cultural analysis: a commentary on "Positive Objectivity" in Wuthnow and Archer. *Sociological Theory*, 19, pp. 635–48.

Rawls, A. 1987, The interaction order sui generis: Goffman's contribution to social theory. *Sociological Theory*, 5, pp. 136–49.

Ricoeur, P. 1971, The model of a text: meaningful action considered as a text. *Social Research*, 38 (3), pp. 529–62.

—— 1977, *The Rule of Metaphor*. Toronto: University of Toronto Press.

Sciulli, D. 1988, Reconsidering Blumer's corrective against the excesses of functionalism. *Symbolic Interactionism*, 11, pp. 69–84.

—— 1992, *Theory of Societal Constitutionalism*. Cambridge: Cambridge University Press.

Sherwood, S. J., Smith, P., and Alexander, J. C. 1993, The British are coming . . . again! The hidden agenda of "Cultural Studies." *Contemporary Sociology*, 22 (3), pp. 101–14.

Turner, B. S. 1993, Talcott Parsons, universalism and the educational revolution: democracy versus professionalism. *British Journal of Sociology*, 44 (1), pp. 1–24.

Name Index

Subject Index